A Capital Case in America

How Today's Justice System Handles Death Penalty Cases from Crime Scene to Ultimate Execution of Sentence

A Capital Case in America

How Today's Justice System Handles
Death Penalty Cases from Crime Scene
to Ultimate Execution of Sentence

David Crump
and
George Jacobs

Carolina Academic Press
Durham, North Carolina

ISBN 0-89089-729-8
LCCN 99-069661

Carolina Academic Press
700 Kent Street
Durham, North Carolina 27701
Telephone: (919) 489-7486
Fax: (919) 493-5668
email: cap@cap-press.com
www.cap-press.com

Printed in the United States of America.

Contents

List of Illustrations

Foreword: Before the Execution

The state has shaved the convict's head to provide a better electrical connection. It has stuffed cotton into his nose to stem the hemorrhaging that inevitably will occur. From another room, behind a one-way mirror, the executioner turns a switch, and the first 1800 volts pass through the condemned man's body. The shock is so powerful that it raises him from the chair like a puppet, in spite of the restraints that hold him down.

An instant later, the convict's heart stops. His blood heats to a temperature of more than two hundred degrees Fahrenheit. Within the confines of his brain, the blood literally, actually boils.

The killing force is decreased to 200 volts, then increased to 1200, then shut off; and the attending physician steps forward to examine the corpse. When he pronounces the convict dead, the body is taken out by another door. There is very little ceremony. The whole process lasts about five or six minutes.

That is what an execution is like.

Several states, such as Kentucky, Nebraska and Georgia, still use electrocution. In 1997 the Florida Supreme Court temporarily stayed all executions after bright blue flames shot out of the leather headpiece strapped on condemned killer Pedro Medina. It seemed likely that electrocution soon would be replaced.

Because of these disturbing spectacles, many states have changed their methods. From Colorado to New York, from Connecticut to Illinois, they have opted for lethal injections, which create less of an appearance of barbarity. Less horror. Less visible effects.

But even with the quieter, gurney-and-needle method, the death penalty remains an ugly prospect.

Why do we do it? Why, today, do we use a form of sentencing that so many people disagree with, that so many people have condemned, that so many people believe is brutal, totalitarian, discriminatory, unconstitutional and unfair?

That is what this book is about.

Today, capital punishment is a bigger issue than ever before. There are hundreds of condemned prisoners on Death Rows throughout the nation.

The scene of the convict restrained in the electric chair or strapped to the gurney has ceased to be a mental image. It has become a reality.

And so the question today has taken on a new urgency: Why *do* we use capital punishment?

The answer, I think, is that the process of execution is only part of the capital punishment issue.

Behind every execution, there is another story: the story of the crime and the trial that happened *before* the execution. And that story is the "why" that lies behind capital punishment.

But let me take a minute to introduce myself before I go any farther.

My name is David Crump. I was an assistant district attorney in Houston, Texas, for almost four years. In other words, a prosecutor.

And on two occasions, it was my job to ask a jury to return a verdict of death.

When I got out of law school, I wasn't exactly in favor of capital punishment. And I haven't really changed my mind; I'm still not "in favor" of it. But to be perfectly honest, I had no difficulty in deciding to ask the jury for the death penalty in these two cases. The circumstances of the crimes left me no other choice.

These cases bore absolutely no resemblance to what you might see on a "Perry Mason" TV show. They were horrible murders. I thought death was the only sensible verdict to ask the jury to return, however much I may dislike the execution process.

The death penalty covers only a few kinds of murder. In my state, "capital murder"—the kind of murder that is subject to the death penalty—includes only the most brutal and inexcusable homicides. It includes murder by a prison escapee, murder by a hired killer, murder during rape or robbery—that sort of case. It is stranger-on-stranger murder, committed in cold blood, for the killer's own gratification or gain.

In other states, the superficial details differ, but the principle is the same. California, for example, calls it "first degree" murder "with special circumstances." Georgia uses a list of "aggravating" circumstances. But the special circumstances in California and the aggravating circumstances in Georgia include murder for hire, murder during rape or robbery, and multiple murders, just as in the cases I tried. In other words, capital murder in my state is similar to first degree murder with special circumstances in California or murder with aggravating factors in Georgia. The terminology varies, but the principle remains the same.

Only a small percentage of murders qualify for the death penalty. In fact, this is the point of these laws. A sailor who kills another sailor in a saloon does not qualify. Neither does a wife who deliberately murders her husband as a way of getting a "Smith-and-Wesson divorce."

The death penalty is confined, by law, to only one or two percent of the worst, most horrifying, most blameworthy kinds of murders. As Texas prison spokesman Larry Fitzgerald puts it, "Everybody on death row has done something extraordinary to get there."

For instance, one fellow I prosecuted had committed a whole series of execution-style robbery murders. He made one of his victims lie on the floor and then shot him in the back of the head. After he was arrested, he committed another murder by suffocating an inmate *inside* the county jail. And later, he told a roomful of television newsmen why he had done it: "for kicks." He added that he enjoyed it, and he "guessed" that he would kill again if given the chance. His story is in this book.

It was a death penalty case. And that was the sentence I asked the jury to return.

You may disagree. And if so, that's fine—because on an issue like the death penalty, everyone has an opinion that differs from everyone else's. Besides, this isn't just a book for death penalty supporters; it's for opponents too. It always surprises me, but I've had people tell me that their opposition to capital punishment was strengthened, rather than weakened, by reading about the cases in this book.

It depends on how you interpret the facts you read about. But in any event, capital punishment—and the crimes that lead to it—are a fact we all need to know about, so we can make an intelligent decision about them.

The fact is, there are, on the average, half a dozen convicted capital murderers sentenced to death every year in my home town. At the same time, there are other convicted capital murderers who are spared and sentenced to life imprisonment instead.

This book is the story of some of those capital cases.

It is a story that plays out over several decades and still is ongoing. A capital case never ends with the jury's verdict. There will be appeals, stays and petitions, usually in multiple loops, through both the state and federal courts, at the trial and appellate levels. Normally, there are repeated petitions to the Supreme Court. Also, an inmate can receive life in prison instead of death, and then, there is the possibility of parole in my state. Several other states, such as California, have created sentences of "life without possibility of parole," producing prisoners who will be inmates forever—called "L-WOPPs," for short.

The point is, stories about capital cases cannot be told without a book that spreads over more than two decades, as this one does.

When I decided to write this book, I was joined by my friend George Jacobs, who also was an assistant district attorney in Houston. We are both familiar with the capital murder cases that have been tried in Houston—too familiar, in fact. We lived with these cases day and night for years, because we prosecuted some of them on behalf of the people of Texas. We decided that the best way to tell what we know about capital punishment is simply to tell the stories of six cases in our city. The trials are randomly selected, in the sense that they all were held in one particular window of time. These cases could have happened anywhere — in New York, or Los Angeles, or Miami, or any of a thousand other American cities. They just happened to happen here.

"These kinds of murders aren't unique to our state," says Larry Fitzgerald, the Texas prison's Public Information Officer. Because the state leads the nation in the number of executions, it attracts media attention, and Fitzgerald points out that it is unusually open to the media. The Texas Department of Criminal Justice provides reporters with access, interviews, and information that other states don't. But Fitzgerald disagrees with the labeling of the state as the nation's execution capital. Instead, he says, "this is the victim's rights capital." As he puts it, "Texans believe in the death penalty, and they act consistently with their beliefs."

You will find evidence in this book to back up Larry Fitzgerald's views. You also will find evidence to support the arguments of death penalty opponents. And unfortunately, no matter where you live, you will see that these crimes are at issue everywhere in America.

I'm not going to equivocate. I personally have made the decision, on balance, that I support the death penalty. But I'm not so confident as to think I have all the answers, and the final decision is up to you, not me.

And so our purpose in telling you about these cases isn't just to entertain you. We want you, the reader, to confront these capital cases in the same way we had to, and to decide what ought to be done about them. Is the death of each of these men justified by his alleged crime?

Or, to look at it another way, can justice be done without capital punishment?

—David Crump

A Capital Case in America

How Today's Justice System Handles
Death Penalty Cases from Crime Scene
to Ultimate Execution of Sentence

PART ONE

From Offense to Trial: The Case of Kenneth Brock

THE KENNETH BROCK case was, in most respects, unremarkable. It certainly was not the type of crime to catch the attention of the national press. It was a killing during a robbery, and that is the most common kind of capital murder.

And yet the very senselessness and stupidity of the offense, alone, was enough to make this killing unique. Because what Kenneth Brock did was to execute a hostage by shooting him, at point blank range, in front of six police officers, who then became the State's principal witnesses in court.

The details are colorful. The defendant was captured after a chase with bloodhounds. A big, eloquent defense attorney urged the jurors to begin with a prayer for divine guidance. And the prosecutor quoted scripture in his final argument.

But although they are colorful, these aspects of the case don't make the Brock trial unusual. From Florida to Washington, from California to New York, death penalty prosecutions bring about a prayerful attitude in almost every juror, a sincere atmosphere of solemnity. The lawyers make arguments that might seem hollow anywhere else: simple, raw arguments that actually sound heartfelt when the hush that precedes deliberations descends on the courtroom. And this is true in sophisticated urban centers or in laid-back small towns. Whether it's north, south, east or west.

And as for the bizarre circumstances of Brock's crime: unfortunately they don't make the case unusual either. If you study the death penalty, you frequently find yourself saying, "My God. That's a terrible crime. It's the most inhuman (or most inexcusable or most pointless) murder ever." But soon after you say it, you'll come across another case that's just as inhuman and senseless, or more so.

In summary, Kenneth Brock's crime was bizarre, but sadly, not unusual. This is the story of the murder and of the trial that followed it.

‹

3

Chapter 1

The Offense and the Arrest

Sergeant P. M. Hogg was the first police officer on the scene. In fact, he "on-viewed" the robbery. In police jargon, that means he happened to see it as it came on view during routine patrol, not in response to a call.

The sergeant would later testify in court, "It didn't strike me as what it was, at the beginning." All he knew was that there was something suspicious going on. As he stopped his blue-and-white police car for a red light, he looked over toward the bright green-and-red neon sign hanging over the convenience store like a beacon in the darkness and rain. What he saw was the store manager walking stiffly out the door while another man, a smaller man, followed him like a shadow.

Sergeant Hogg turned his car sharply and drove into the parking lot in front of the store. Now the two men saw him. The smaller man moved quickly. He got behind the bigger man, the manager, and pulled him beyond the corner of the store. It was clear now to Sergeant Hogg what was happening, because now he saw the gun. The smaller man's hand reached around the heavy body of the store manager as he aimed at the police officer who was only a few feet from him. The hand rose and there was a flash, and Sergeant Hogg heard the reverberating "punch-*bang*!" sound of a .22 pistol being fired at him.

In the alley behind the store, the engine of the getaway car was running.

Sergeant Hogg pushed the button to his radio microphone. He gave the location of the store and requested backup to handle a robbery in progress.

The robber scuttled down the side of the store building toward the getaway car with his hostage in tow.

* * *

Inside the store, customer Ella Garver and her husband, Jim Wesley Garver, watched what was happening through the plate glass front of the store. When the two men rounded the corner out of view, they heard the report of the pistol. Still unable to believe that they had walked into a robbery, they stood frozen while the robber took the store manager away.

Jim Wesley Garver had brought his wife from work. She got off a little after one a.m. This convenience store was open at this hour. As they had walked in from the rainy, pitch-black darkness, they had seen the sandy-haired man standing strangely in front of the counter.

When the man had turned and pointed the gun at them and told them to lie on the floor, their first reaction, Jim Garver later said, was to think that the gun was a toy and that the man was joking. When he convinced them, Jim Garver told him, "Everything's cool, brother." The robber relented. He did not make them lie down. He even showed an odd kind of courtesy, the arbitrary courtesy that comes from violent power. "I don't want *your* money, brother," he reassured the Garvers as he emptied the cash register.

The store manager also reassured the Garvers. He was outwardly calm. Convenience stores like this chain were so often the targets of night-time robberies that the manager, Michael Sedita, knew to expect them. He had prepared himself for this. He kept firearms in the store, but being unable to reach them, he cooperated with the robber and was careful to do nothing to excite him.

"Come on," said the robber, as he pushed Michael Sedita in front of him, touching him lightly with the gun.

*　　*　　*

Outside the store, four young men sat in their car and watched with the same frozen disbelief as the Garvers.

They had been watching for some time. As they had driven up to the store, they had been surprised to see a sandy-haired man lean from behind the wheel of a white Dodge, bending across the woman who was in the passenger's seat, and fix them with a strange, wooden stare. The white car had gone around the store twice, with the sandy-haired man staring. For a moment, Phil Ochsler and Andy Hart, from where they sat in the front seat of Phil's father's car, thought they recognized him as a boy they went to high school with—but no, it wasn't him. Why, then, was he staring?

A moment later, the sandy-haired man walked around the corner of the store and went in. With his thick, matted hair and heavy beard, he was unmistakably the same man who had driven by. The woman was not with him. Nor was the car in sight.

The young men waited. They could not see inside the store.

It was not until the sandy-haired man walked out with the store manager, and the police car careened into the parking lot, and the robber shot at the officer that Phil Ochsler and Andy Hart were certain what was happening.

*　　*　　*

A few blocks north of the robbery, Officer G. W. Cormier sat in his blue-and-white in an Exxon station parking lot. M. J. Orlando, twenty-one years old and a rookie on the force, sat with him. Orlando was still in his probationary period. He had been in his new job less than six months. Cormier, himself only twenty-four, was breaking him in.

Cormier and Orlando sat talking to Officer W. E. Carmichael, who was riding solo in a separate police car.

While they sat there, Sergeant Hogg's call came over the radio, reporting the robbery and requesting backup.

From where they sat at the intersection of East Houston-Dyersdale Road and Tidwell Street, it was just a short drive to the little convenience store at East Houston-Dyersdale and Laura Koppe Boulevard. Cormier and Carmichael each knew Michael Sedita from stopping to check the store nightly. A second after they got the call, they were rolling.

As the three officers raced into the parking lot and slammed on their brakes, they saw Sergeant Hogg at the corner of the store. The sergeant cradled his shotgun, unable to get a shot at the robber—who was holding Michael Sedita between him and the officer.

Hogg knew Michael Sedita too. It was imperative to handle the situation quickly, and yet without frightening the robber. It was also imperative not to allow him to take Michael Sedita away from the scene.

The sergeant waved the other three officers away. "Go around to the rear," he directed. Quickly, the officers got back in their cars, drove around the block and parked the two vehicles where they blocked the robber's exit to the north down Surry Road, which ran behind the store. They dismounted and began to walk south toward the store with their pistols and shotguns in front of them.

Two more officers, J. D. Phillips and P. C. Jalomo, arrived from a side street. Together with Cormier, they hurried toward the rear of the store.

As they reached the alley, they saw a white Dodge Dart with its parking lights on and the motor running. Cormier was the first to realize that it was the getaway car. He spoke to the woman behind the wheel, ordering her out. Instead, as Cormier would later say in a sentence that displayed the terse understatement characteristic of police reports, "the car started pulling away at a high rate of speed." Cormier quickly fired two shots after it. Later, when the case reached court, the robber's lawyer would criticize the policeman for his marksmanship, suggesting that he could have done better had he thrown his gun at the vanishing automobile—for in the darkness and rain, shooting with a handgun, Cormier believed that he had missed the car completely.

The getaway driver had escaped.

But the robber himself was boxed in.

In the alley beside the store, the robber heard the squealing tires of the car leaving him. He heard the shots. He had been inching along the alley, burdened with a hostage who outweighed him by nearly a hundred pounds, having to position himself so that he did not expose himself to a clear shot from Sergeant Hogg, who remained at the head of the alley with his shotgun.

Cormier, Phillips and Jalomo reached the end of the alley. A hundred yards away, the distance of a football field, they could see Sergeant Hogg at the other end.

Between them and the sergeant, they saw the robber with his hostage. They were still in the alley. "Back up," said Michael Sedita. "He has the money. He told me he'd let me go."

"Back up," said the robber, threateningly. "Back up or I'll kill him." He had been left on foot and he was desperate.

"He is crazy," said Michael Sedita to the officers. "He'll kill me."

The officers stopped. Sergeant Hogg, who was proceeding cautiously down the alley toward the robber and his hostage, stopped too.

The robber ordered the policemen to put their guns down. "Or I'll kill him."

The three officers at the Surry Road side of the alley put their guns down on the street and backed away. They let the robber and his hostage past them.

The passageway was narrow. Cormier, Phillips and Jalomo were within ten feet of the robber at one point. They could hear his breathing, and they could hear the heavier breathing of the hostage, Michael Sedita. They could see the robber's eyes, white in the harsh light of a parking lot lamp, and they could see the moisture on his face. With a step or two, they could have reached out and touched him.

But they could do absolutely nothing to free Michael Sedita.

The robber was holding the storekeeper around the neck with his left arm. And his right hand held a pistol at the center of Michael Sedita's chest.

As he passed by the three helpless officers, the robber shifted his position laboriously, pushing Michael Sedita around in front of him in a slow and intricate ballet. As he inched ahead, the robber moved carefully, keeping the hostage always in the line of fire.

As he reached the end of the alley, the robber was obviously thinking about his next move.

There was an open stretch of pavement in front of him. Then there was Surry Road, and beyond that there was a thick wooded area. If he could get into that, the ground would swallow him up. But how would he do it? If he let go of the hostage, would he make it into the woods? And if he did, would he make it out the other side, or would the entire Houston police department be on the scene to surround him?

How would he escape?

The robber reached Surry Road and began pulling his hostage along it. He wanted to get away from the alley he had come from, away from the shopping center that it was part of, away from the light, away from the police officer's positions—as far away as he could.

When he had gone perhaps fifty feet down Surry Road, away from the alley, the robber paused. He looked at the officers. They were still standing where he had told them to stay. The robber looked quickly toward the woods.

And then he made his decision.

He raised his hand.

He pointed the gun, which he had been holding loosely, against Michael Sedita's chest.

Then, while the officers watched in disbelief, he pulled the trigger.

As Michael Sedita's body slumped against him, the robber slipped off balance for an instant. He looked at the officers again. Then he was running. He jumped over a weed encrusted ditch on the west side of Surry Road. By this time he was in high grass. A six-foot chain-link fence, with barbed wire on top, stood in his path, but he jumped it without hesitation. He was in a thick, wooded area, with undergrowth and weeds to cover him, seconds after his bullet exploded into Michael Sedita's chest.

The dying man fell, saying, "Oh, my God, I'm hit."

The rookie, Officer Orlando, had never seen anything like this. His stomach was in his mouth. As he would later say in court, "My heart was pounding as fast as it could and I was running as fast as I could." He got to the body of Michael Sedita and started giving him mouth-to-mouth resuscitation.

It took the officers some time to recover. In the confusion, Phillips fired six shots. Cormier fired twice, then ran to call an ambulance. Jalomo picked up his shotgun and fired twice. But the killer, assisted by the diversion he had created and by the element of surprise, had disappeared.

The officers stood for a moment, helpless, in the middle of Surry Road. When they would testify in court eight months later about the events of that moment, their voices would break and they would be close to tears. It is one thing to investigate a murder. It is quite another to watch one happen a few feet away when you are powerless to prevent it, especially if it is the murder of a man you have known and liked. And as the officers stood on Surry Road by the woods in a mood that was tinged with rage and even fear at the senselessness of it all, the most powerful thought in their minds was a meaningless question: *why?*

Why had it happened?

Why had the robber killed the hostage? Did he just have an itchy trigger finger? Was he crazy? Did he hate cops so much that he could not resist the temptation to do this perverse act in front of them? Was it a question of "manhood" for a punk who wanted to show how dangerous he was? Or was it a colder calculation, based on the knowledge that the officers could neither let him drag the hostage into the woods nor refrain from pursuing him if he left the hostage alive? Was it just a step the small sandy-haired man had taken to enhance his chances for escape?

But at the same time these questions revolved through their minds, the officers knew they would never know the answer. The only answer was that it was one more senseless killing that should not have happened. Michael Sedita was dying. The man who was hiding now in the woods had done it. And that was all anyone could say about it now. The officers fought the weakness in their limbs, fought the rising tide in their stomachs, and tried to do the best that they could at their job.

As backup units began to arrive in large numbers, Sergeant Hogg took steps to cordon off the wooded area into which the killer had fled. There were now perhaps twenty officers surrounding the woods.

Sergeant Hogg returned to the body of the hostage. Michael Sedita was dead. The officers called the Houston homicide division. Then they called the office of the Coroner, who in Houston is called the Medical Examiner.

Had it entered their minds to think ahead to the time the case would be tried in a Texas criminal district court, the officers could not, in their wildest dreams, have imagined the argument the killer's lawyer would make. For he would seek to exonerate the small sandy-haired man from the consequences of his crime by claiming that Michael Sedita's death had been caused by the conduct of the officers themselves.

* * *

M. C. Escobar was the investigator on duty at the Harris County morgue when the call came in. He arrived at Surry Road at 2:45 a.m., an hour after the murder.

A force of twenty police officers continued to surround the woods into which the killer had fled. Escobar went to work on the body a few feet from the woods.

First, he took photographs of the body from several angles. The police had already taken pictures of it, but Escobar conducted his own investigation. He knew that much of what he did would be duplicative of police efforts. It was simply his job to take nothing for granted. Escobar was part of a tradition of thoroughness and competence that made the Harris County Medical Examiner's Office one of the most respected Coroner's offices in the nation.

Putting away his camera, Escobar began to catalogue clothing and objects in the vicinity of the body. His efforts memorialized details that would be important to both the prosecution and the defense. His report indicated the killer's pathway, for example, by noting, "a handful of change in a bag was thrown in a ditch near where the body was found." The report also noted that Escobar found six .38 calibre bullets in the right front trouser pocket of the dead man—a fact of which the defense would make much at trial, because a strange quirk of jury psychology seems to make less culpable the murder of a man who knows the risk of death.

The next step for Escobar was to identify the body. Sometimes, this task can be stubbornly difficult or even impossible. Escobar well remembered the frustration of trying to give names to the mass murder victims of Elmer Wayne Henley (not to mention the strange case of the still unidentified human torso that had been found in the county fully a decade ago and now was affectionately called "Stumpy" by morgue workers). But the case at hand, with a dead man who had worked at a known location, would present no such difficulties. When it developed that the officers themselves could tell Escobar positively the identity of Michael Sedita, the experienced investigator was not surprised.

When he completed his investigation, Escobar placed the corpse on a stretcher. He covered it and gently loaded it into the ambulance. Knowing that the police officers, tough as they were, had been acquainted with the dead man and had seen him killed, Escobar was careful to treat the body with respect.

This attitude of respect was also completely in keeping with tradition. One of the remarkable things about the Harris County Medical Examiner's Office is its workers' sensitivity, in the face of their continuous acquaintance with death, to the feelings of the living for the bodies of the dead.

The officers watched, wordlessly, as Escobar drove away with the body of the man they had seen murdered.

* * *

For a time, the officers waited. They could not see into the wooded area. They could barely move through its thick undergrowth and they could search only slowly, with awareness of the danger they exposed themselves to. An occasional crackle of branches told them the killer was still inside their circle.

Shortly after 3 o'clock in the morning, the search reached its conclusion.

With barking and baying that sounded like explosions in the quiet morning air, a set of bloodhounds under the control of a deputy sheriff started into the woods. The dogs strained and pulled eagerly at their leashes.

The killer had been lying in the underbrush, waiting for an opening. A little movement had allowed him to survey the locations of the surrounding police officers. Perhaps he would have a chance. The woods would hide him well, because they were nearly impenetrable. But now he heard the dogs. Frightened, he began to move. When he reached a ditch and had to cross the road beyond it, he got down on his stomach and began to crawl.

A hundred feet down the road, an electrician named Joe Bill Walker sat in his pickup parked by the side of the road.

By happenstance, Joe Bill Walker would play a major role in this unusual case. His presence was itself the result of pure chance: He had been attracted to the scene by reports on a CB radio. He had a friend who was a wrecker driver, and his friend had been listening to the police band and had told him what was happening. Joe Bill Walker had come out here, to the wooded area near Surry Road, for the excitement it promised to bring. Now, as he sat waiting for something to happen, his eye caught something moving on the road.

The killer was as flat on his stomach as he could get. The dogs were behind him. But he could not see any police officers in his path ahead. He had almost made it. Almost—

The officers were still surrounding the wooded area, and now the hunted man was outside their cordon. The only thing that stood between him and freedom was this road. Joe Bill Walker, a man searching for adventure at 3 o'clock in the morning, just happened to be in the same place at the same time. It was almost unbelievable, a page right out of a dimestore mystery thriller: Walker, the amateur crime-fighter, was going to be instrumental in apprehending a desperado who had eluded a whole posse of lawmen with helicopters and dogs.

So it was that Joe Bill Walker, at 3 a.m. on a pitch-dark rainy night, had his moment in the sun.

"Here he is!" Walker shouted to the officers. "Here he is!" And he aimed his spotlight on the road.

The killer was startled as the bright light hit him. The shock made his heart race and he jumped reflexively. He ran across the road. There, there were some small houses, with shapes that looked like bushes, fences, places to hide—

But the dogs were almost on him. As he ran between two of the houses, they were barking explosively behind him, and there were police officers with their guns drawn. The killer had thrown his gun away, but the officers did not know that. He had a good chance of getting himself killed if he kept running. Or even if he tried to hide.

He decided to give himself up.

Officer W. R. Lilley was the man who made the arrest, simply because he was the closest officer to the killer when he gave himself up. Lilley was near his patrol car, ready to enter the passageway between the two houses where the killer had disappeared.

What happened next was as unexpected as any of the other events in this strange case. As Lilley prepared himself mentally for entry into a dark space that concealed a killer who, he assumed, was armed and dangerous, he saw the man surrendering to him; and then he was surprised to hear the killer blurt out an unsolicited confession to his crime.

"I observed the actor coming out from the west side of the house and cut across the yard coming toward me with both hands in the air, walking in a southeasterly direction," Lilley later wrote in his report, using the flat jargon characteristic of police documents.

"As he got within 10 feet of me he stated, 'I am the man you are looking for. I shot the store owner,'" Lilley reported.

"I shot the store owner," the man had said.

It was a crucial piece of evidence. It was an unequivocal admission of guilt. When the case got to court, there would be a defensive theory of the case, perhaps mistaken identity, or accidental discharge of the gun, or something else—and this confession would go a long way toward contradicting it. Lilley knew this, although he did not stop now to think about it.

Lilley did not have time to think, either, about the argument the killer's lawyer would make concerning the arrest, when the case reached court. What the lawyer would do would be to allege that the police had violated his client's constitutional rights. That argument would be part of an attempt to get evidence about the shooting thrown out of the case and hidden from the jury, so as to give the lawyer a better chance to get the killer acquitted. It would be one of the things that the defense lawyer would be required to do, as part of his job in defending this man. Lilley could not know, now, that in the process of making that argument, the lawyer would make multiple charges of misconduct against him and others in the handling of the arrest and investigation. Lilley could not know, now, that the lawyer would even argue that Lilley had violated the Supreme Court decision in *Miranda v. Arizona* by hearing the confession before warning the killer of his constitutional rights. It appeared to Lilley that he had acted properly. What could he have done? Should he have interrupted the blurted confession until he had had time to say, "You have the right to remain silent?"

Lilley did not think about that now, as the man walked toward him. He thought about safety, the arrested man's safety and his own, and he thought about getting the man securely into custody to prevent his escaping again. And he thought about identifying the killer, getting his name. And so he spoke to the arrested man, quickly had him frisked, and looked at his personal effects.

Now he had a close look at the man who had committed this senseless crime.

The man's name was Kenneth Brock.

During the coming days, the police would have time to learn a great deal more about Kenneth Brock. Now, Officer Lilley saw before him a normal-looking, 25-year-old caucasian man, apparently healthy and unremarkable except for a heavy reddish-brown beard and hair that were matted and dirty, as were his clothes. Lilley soon learned that Kenneth Brock already had an established "rap sheet;" his first arrest as an adult had followed just two years after he grew beyond the jurisdiction of the juvenile courts. At the present time, he was AWOL from the marine corps, and he had just recently gotten off probation for burglary.

In the days to come, the police would search Kenneth Brock's apartment and would find a variety of illegal drugs and a syringe of the type used to inject heroin. Using offense reports and line-ups, they would match his name to another robbery of a different store and to an attempted murder, in which he had stabbed a man in front of a number of witnesses, committed just nine days before the murder of Michael Sedita.

Of course, Officer Lilley did not know all these specific details about the man he arrested. He was concerned only with doing his immediate job, for now.

Lilley shouted to the other officers that he had the man in custody. Then, his report reflects, he handcuffed Kenneth Brock and placed him in his patrol car, whereupon Brock was "given legal warning" by Officer Cormier. Cormier read the rights, word by word, from a small blue card, called a "Miranda" card, a copy of which is issued to every Houston police officer to ensure compliance with the decisions of the Supreme Court.

It was the same Miranda warning that the Supreme Court had specified for states throughout the nation, from Maine to California. And so far, the investigation had followed a course that could have occurred anywhere.

Meanwhile, the body of Michael Sedita was lying in the Houston morgue.*

---

* The following names in this chapter were changed, without alteration of the incidents in which the persons were involved: Ella Garver, Jim Wesley Garver, Phil Ochsler, Andy Hart, Joe Bill Walker, Cynthia Morales.

The Kenneth Brock Murder Case. State's exhibit 25. This exhibit shows the defendant, Kenneth Brock, under arrest for capital murder. It is a blowup of a "mug shot" or booking photograph that was taken only a few hours after the offense.

The Kenneth Brock Murder Case. State's exhibit 13. This aerial photograph, taken from a police helicopter, shows the store in the left foreground (on corner), the alley at left center, and Surry Road and the woods in the background.

The Kenneth Brock Murder Case. State's exhibit 5. This photograph shows Surry Road, looking south from near the murder scene.

The Kenneth Brock Murder Case. State's exhibit 4. This photograph shows the alley, looking west toward the woods.

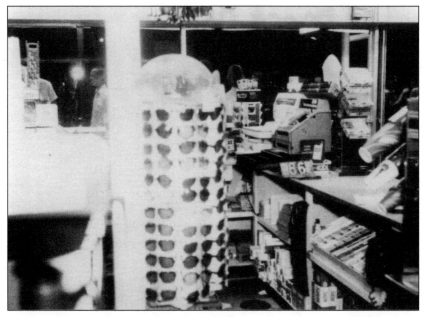

The Kenneth Brock Murder Case. Store interior. The defendant robbed the store manager before shooting him. Notice the open cash drawer.

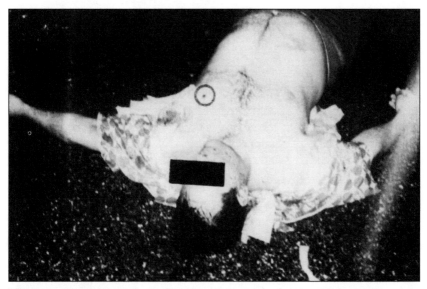

The Kenneth Brock Murder Case. Police photograph of victim. Michael Sedita was a college graduate who had a promising career before him. The bullet entry wound is circled; the projectile passed through his aorta.

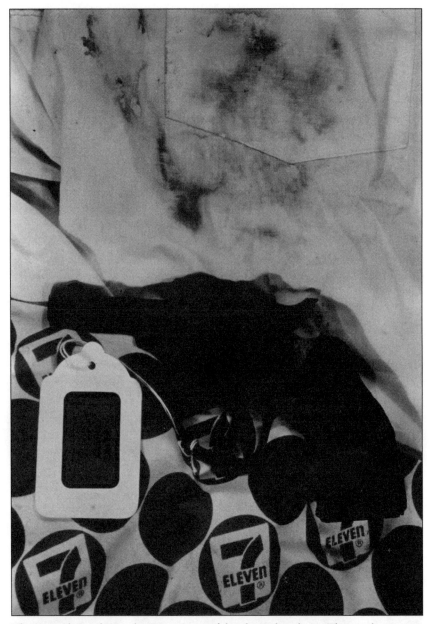

The Kenneth Brock Murder Case. Some of the physical evidence. The murder weapon was a .22 pistol. It was referred to during the trial as a "Saturday Night Special," and it was received into evidence as State's exhibit 21. The victim's smock, which was also introduced into evidence, bears the convenience store logo. His white shirt has a hole in the center of the pocket where the fatal bullet entered.

Chapter 2

The Defendant, the Victim, and the Investigation

At the county morgue, the remains of Michael Sedita lay face up, eyes closed, in a room kept at low temperature to retard decomposition. At eleven o'clock in the morning, ten hours after the murder, Doctors Sheldon Green and Ethel Erickson began the autopsy.

Nothing about the Houston morgue is the way one would think it ought to be. It is an oddly tidy place, with an antiseptic white background and small touches of color. Against this clean background, there are rows of battered bodies in different stages of mutilation or decomposition, waiting for the attention of the pathologist. Autopsied bodies, however, seldom have a mutilated appearance when released to a funeral home, at least not attributable to autopsy—because the medical examiner's office takes care to preserve the feelings of relatives to the extent that it is possible.

Perhaps the most surprising thing about the Houston morgue is the persons—and personalities—of the pathology staff. Dr. Ethel Erickson is a friendly, reassuring, even maternal woman, very feminine, with a ready smile and sense of humor. Of the two, Dr. Green looks more like a scientist should, with his wispy gray goatee and balding head—until, that is, one spots the colorfully informal Western string tie with the turquoise holder that is his trademark. Neither of the doctors, when one comes right down to it, has quite the expected appearance for this unusual line of work.

But be that as it may, their skill as pathologists is clear. When either of them is called to testify, it can take several minutes before he or she finishes listing such credentials as multiple advanced degrees, internships, residencies, medical school professorships, and experience in the field of "forensic pathology"—which is the macabre science of determining cause of death. If asked, "And how many autopsies would you estimate you have performed, doctor?" they would give estimates that ran into the thousands. The doctors' integrity makes them impregnable witnesses, and their skill enables them to refute the old maxim, "dead men tell no tales," when they talk about their work.

And now, under the tutelage of Doctors Green and Erickson, the body of Michael Sedita was about to speak volumes about his killer.

The doctors circled the body and recorded their findings into a goose-necked microphone that hung over the operating table. Before the incision, they made a careful examination of the body—weighing, measuring, examining it all over. They recorded each finding in flat, technical language: "The body was that of a well-developed, obese, 31 year-old white man, measuring 71 inches in length and weighing 241 pounds." They catalogued carefully the symptoms of death: "There was fixed rigor mortis and well developed posterior dependent lividity." In other words, the body had stiffened and become discolored, particularly in the dead man's back, where gravity had pulled the blood after it ceased to flow.

But the most important external detail was the garishly colored gunshot wound in Michael Sedita's chest. "Over the left pectoral region," Dr. Green dictated, "situated 4 inches below the suprasternal notch and 4 1/2 inches to the left of the midline, there was a gunshot wound of entrance, measuring 1/4 inch in diameter and surrounded by charred and abraded skin margins measuring 3/8 inch in diameter. There was no powder stippling. The abdomen was protuberant but soft. . . ."

These findings were of crucial significance. The recording of the location of the wound would allow Dr. Green to turn to the jury ten months hence and point out where the bullet had entered, using his own anatomy as a model. The charring and abrasion were even more important: they indicated that the gun muzzle had been within inches of the skin when fired. The absence of "powder stippling," together with the charring, allowed the examiners to be yet more specific. This evidence indicated a contact wound, in which the gun had been directly against the victim's chest.

Thus the doctors' observations, independently and scientifically made, corroborated the eyewitness accounts of the police officers, whose reports the doctors had not seen.

Now the doctors were ready to make the "Y" shaped incision on the victim's torso that begins the internal examination of a complete autopsy. Through this series of cuts, they would be able to enter the thoracic and abdominal cavities. They began at two opposite points near one end of the torso and cut to the middle. From that point, they cut straight toward the other end of the torso to form the stem of the "Y".

Upon peeling back the skin, they immediately encountered the damage the bullet had done.

"The rib cage showed, anteriorly, at the level of the 3rd intercostal space, a gunshot wound of entrance," they reported. "The right pleural cavity had about 1 pint of liquid and clotted blood. The left pleural cavity had 1 quart of liquid and clotted blood. . . . A .22 calibre, lead, copper-coat-ed bullet was recovered from the body of the 5th thoracic vertebra, slightly to the right of the midline."

The bullet was "moderately" deformed through its collision with Michael Sedita's backbone. Dr. Green marked it with his initial and the autopsy number so that he would be able to identify it in court. Meanwhile, it would be sent to the ballistics laboratory.

The doctors removed the heart. Routinely, they recorded that it "weighed 440 grams" and that its myocardium was "dark red and beefy." It had been healthy before the murder. But the damage from the bullet was most apparent here: The doctors dictated that at the "origin" of the aorta (*i.e.*, at its junction with the heart), "there was a gunshot wound of entrance with its largest diameter. . .measuring 2 centimeters in length, and with irregular, shaggy edges."

In lay terms, these entries meant that the bullet had torn a hole nearly an inch wide through the major connecting artery, right at the side of Michael Sedita's heart.

Now the autopsy was nearly complete. It had been done with care and skill.

If, at trial, the defendant claimed that the killing was accidental, a hundred separate details would be available to test this theory. Was it consistent with a bullet trajectory that was "horizontal, from left to right," as the autopsy had shown? With the path of the bullet inside the chest? If there was a claim of self defense, was it consistent with the placing of the gun, with its nearness to the body? The details went on and on.

The doctors removed and examined Michael Sedita's other internal organs, and then got ready to put him back together again.

* * *

Who was Michael Sedita?

The autopsy showed a great deal about the way he had died. But what had his life been like?

As the investigation progressed, it became clear that the most noteworthy thing about Michael Sedita's life was its normal, everyday *averageness*. He was the son of Mr. and Mrs. Joseph Sedita. He grew up in a middle-class area of north Houston known as The Heights, an area filled with small but comfortable old homes built during a time when every house was individually designed. Michael Sedita lived nearly all his life on a short, tree-lined street in The Heights called Bay Oaks. At the time of his death, still unmarried, he lived with his mother in that same house in The Heights where he had lived as boy.

He had lived there during high school. He had worked part-time, then, as a machinist's helper. And he worked part-time, as a youth, in a chain of convenience stores operated by the Southland Corporation under the Seven-Eleven trademark.

After graduation from high school, he went to college at the University of Houston. He worked his way through. His studies included basic accounting, management, advertising and merchandising. Finally, he graduated from the University of Houston with an A.B. degree in marketing. He went to work as a bookkeeper for an agricultural products firm.

Then, a few years after graduating from college, he decided to go back to work for the convenience store division of the Southland Corporation.

It seemed a good choice. The Southland Corporation was a diversified company, into such fields as insurance, food processing and retailing. The convenience store division, particularly, had had a phenomenal growth while Michael Sedita had been growing up in Houston. The stores filled a definite and expanding market. They had good management, attractive advertising, and wide name recognition in the areas they served.

The management program Michael Sedita entered required him to begin by working in an actual store, managing it. After learning the business fully from the inside, he could be moved — to the North Houston District Office of the Southland Corporation, for instance. That is why Michael Sedita was assigned to Store No. 12616, which was located in a shopping center between East Houston Road and Surry Road, to begin his management career at the Southland Corporation.

Working the night shift there, he had met Officers Hogg, Carmichael, Cormier and the others who stopped in regularly. For them as for many people who kept night hours, this store was the best place for quite a distance to shop or get coffee. The officers remembered Michael Sedita as a chunky man who had trouble keeping his weight down, but a hardworking, solid, friendly and cheerful fellow.

On the night he died, Michael Sedita worked the night shift there at Store No. 12616. That was the night, as chance would have it, that Kenneth Brock walked in and pointed his gun at the store manager.

And now, instead of progressing toward the North Houston District Office of the Southland Corporation, Michael Sedita was lying in the Harris County morgue on the autopsy table. He was no longer a human being. Doctors Green and Erickson did not stop to reflect on his life. Instead, they systematically removed his organs, sectioned them, and threw them one by one into a garbage can with a plastic lining as they finished examining them. Finally, they replaced his scalp and closed his chest with coarse stitches.

And when the gutted hull of the cadaver that had once been Michael Sedita was presentable enough to be picked up by the funeral home his family had engaged, Doctors Green and Erickson moved on to their next autopsy.

* * *

During the time that the dead body of Michael Sedita was lying in the Harris Country morgue, Kenneth Brock was standing in front of a magistrate at the Houston Municipal Courts Building.

There, a municipal judge read him, once again, the same rights that Officer Cormier had read to him a few hours before at the scene of his arrest. "You have the right to remain silent. If you give up that right, anything you say can and will be used against you. . . ," the judge was saying. This procedure could have happened in California, or Kansas, or North Carolina. The judge's title would be different; it might be that of a magistrate or associate judge, and the details of this ceremony would differ according to state law. But the core purposes would be similar: to ensure that the Miranda warning has been properly delivered, to consider bail, and to verify that there is probable cause to hold the defendant.

By now, the words were familiar to Kenneth Brock; in fact, they had already been familiar to him. The incident on Surry Road was just a point of culmination for him, something his life had been building toward since childhood.

Kenneth Brock was now 25 years old. He was the eldest child of Albert Jessie Brock and his wife, Dorothy, and he spent his earliest years in the small town of Eggnonfield, Florida. While Kenneth was still a child, his mother had divorced his father, who was an alcoholic and did little to support the family.

Soon his mother remarried. But Kenneth Brock's stepfather was not easy to live with, either, and the second marriage also ended in divorce. Kenneth Brock's mother went to work in Texas as a maid, cleaning out model homes. Meanwhile, as a result of his family situation, young Kenneth repeatedly had trouble staying in school.

It was while he was still in school, apparently, that his dependence upon drugs began.

Kenneth Brock had six younger sisters, who had a real affection for him, and it was natural for them to look up to him. But he was unskilled, uneducated, and unintelligent, and he had difficulty holding a job. He fell in with companions whose conversations were about burglaries, drugs and crime. He tried to compensate for his inadequacies by becoming a regular user of drugs—first alcohol, then barbiturates and other pills, and then, apparently, heroin.

While he still was in high school, Kenneth Brock was arrested for two burglaries. He was 19 years old, an adult in the eyes of the law, even though he was still trying to finish school. The prosecutor who was assigned to the burglary cases recognized them as ordinary economic offenses, probably drug-related, of the type that occurs dozens of times daily in a city like Houston. And in a plea-bargain that was standard for an offense of that severity, Kenneth Brock, with the advice of his court-appointed counsel, pled guilty in exchange for a recommendation to the judge by the prosecutor that the sentence be suspended.

That was six years ago. Since then, Brock had worked only sporadically. He had taken to selling drugs and to robbery to support his own use of drugs. Finally, in what seemed to be a last effort to salvage something worthwhile of his life, he enlisted in the Marine Corps and went to boot camp in North Carolina. But there, it quickly became evident that for Kenneth Brock, joining the Marines was a mistake, and so he deserted.

From that point on, his life went ever more steadily downhill. He lived in Houston with a girl named Cynthia Morales. She drove and he robbed. The murder of Michael Sedita was part of a series of crimes that included the other cases of attempted murder and robbery for which he was now wanted.

It was hard to say exactly how the events in his life had brought Kenneth Brock to the present. He had an intelligence in the low average range; that meant he was no genius, but it also meant there were many normal persons in the population with I.Q.'s far lower than his. And he was perfectly sane, with no debilitating psychoses. But heredity and environment had generated in him an aggressive, drug-dependent and impulsive personality. He was not a person who considered the future or its consequences before he decided to do anything.

And when he was surrounded by police officers after he robbed Store No. 12616, it probably seemed to Kenneth Brock that he had very little future to consider in any event.

Now, in the Municipal Courts Building, Kenneth Brock stood before the bench as the municipal judge finished explaining to him the charges he would face for the death of Michael Sedita. "Do you have any questions about these charges, or about the rights I have explained to you?" the judge asked him.

"No," said Kenneth Brock.

And with that, the defendant was taken to the city jail and held without bond.

*　*　*

Meanwhile, the police investigation moved into its follow-up phase.

At the jail, Officer Orlando inventoried articles taken from the arrested man's person. Orlando found that Kenneth Brock was virtually a walking cash register. In his pockets, Brock was carrying a large number of quarters, dimes and nickels. There was even loose change in his boot. The arrested man also was carrying 3 ten-dollar bills, 8 fives, and 37 ones. There was, finally, a live .22 bullet identical to that removed from Michael Sedita's body, which Orlando found in Brock's pocket.

The murder weapon was conspicuously absent. Officer Cormier asked Brock where it was. "I dropped it in the ditch," said Brock. He had simply thrown the pistol away before he jumped the fence into the woods.

Under several inches of water, amid a clump of high weeds that had to be cleared away, the officers found the pistol—right where the killer had told Cormier it would be.

Once the physical evidence had been found and inventoried, the officers submitted it to experts for testing.

The shirt that Michael Sedita had been wearing went to the Houston Police Department chemistry laboratory with a request that a nitrite test be conducted. Since the firing of a gun expels nitrite salts in a cone from the muzzle, the spreading pattern of the particles on the shirt would allow an estimate of the distance the gun had been from Michael Sedita's chest when the trigger was pulled. After testing the shirt, Chemist J. A. Zotter concluded that the pattern showed a loose contact wound.

Next door to the chemistry laboratory, firearms expert G. E. Martinez used the recovered gun to fire a bullet similar to the one that killed Michael Sedita into a special target filled with packing material. Then he examined the two bullets under a comparison microscope. If the grooves produced by the barrel were the same on both bullets, Martinez would be able to identify this pistol as the murder weapon. If they were perceptibly different he would be able to say that it was not the gun that had killed Michael Sedita. In the end, the cheap manufacture of the "Saturday Night Special" Kenneth Brock had used defeated the analysis, because it lacked the stabilizing grooves of more accurate, expensive pistols. Martinez was forced to conclude that it produced "insufficient definite and consistent characteristics to effect an identification."

Kenneth Brock's lawyer would make much of this failure at the trial, when the case finally reached court.

Other officers followed out another important lead: the license number of the getaway car. Within hours of the murder, they were calling the owner of the car. The call ultimately prompted the getaway car driver to surrender. Her name was Cynthia Morales, and the car belonged to her father.

At her father's urging, Cynthia Morales gave homicide detectives a written statement saying that she had been in the car with Kenneth Brock on the night of the murder. She said that they had been drinking—"a few beers." But Cynthia Morales maintained that during the robbery she had been "half asleep" and therefore she "did not know where Kenneth Brock had parked the car or what he intended to do."

She said she thought Kenneth Brock had gone into the store because he "needed some cigarettes."

The grand jurors saw the case differently, and they indicted Cynthia Morales for the robbery.

When the case reached court, no one was surprised to see that Kenneth Brock's lawyer had subpoenaed Cynthia Morales as a defense witness; but the defense attorney rested his case without ever calling her to testify in front of the jury. Her story was hard to believe.

* * *

Everyone who could see the State's evidence at this point was certain that Kenneth Brock had murdered Michael Sedita in cold blood. The evidence was overwhelming. After all, not every case has six police officers who can testify that they saw the defendant pull the trigger.

But before anyone in the criminal justice system regarded the outcome as foreordained, it had to be remembered that Kenneth Brock would have a defense lawyer. It would be that lawyer's job to see that the state's evidence was not the only picture the jury saw.

Brock couldn't afford a lawyer, of course. Most people charged with death penalty crimes can't. Even if they might have enough to pay a lawyer for a lesser charge, they face trials that usually don't result in guilty pleas and that often last for several months. A lawyer's fee for this kind of crime simply has to be more expensive; in some cases, the dollars run into five and even six figures. But no matter: Ever since *Gideon v. Wainwright*, nearly a half century ago, the Supreme Court has required the state to pay for a lawyer for anyone in Kenneth Brock's circumstances. Today, the taxpayer probably could expect a bill for fifty thousand to two hundred and fifty thousand dollars for defense counsel in a case like Brock's. For the required knowledge and responsibility, those are reasonable amounts.

Throughout America's history, there have been famous death penalty defense lawyers. Clarence Darrow's work in Chicago, for example. Melvin Belli in California, David Bruck in South Carolina, and Will Gray in Texas. Some of the big-name lawyers deserve their reputations; some may not. Kenneth Brock probably wouldn't get a big name as his appointed lawyer. But in most states, today, at least for trial counsel, judges make a real effort to appoint skilled defense attorneys. It's foolish not to, because death sentences require many reviews by appeal and habeas corpus, and claims of incompetency of counsel are frequent. Kenneth Brock could count on getting a lawyer who would mount a vigorous defense.

Under the rules of procedure, Brock's lawyer would have to be given all written statements of witnesses. In these, Ella Garver had described the killer's hair as "blond," while Phil Ochsler had said it was "reddish brown." There were literally dozens of similar discrepancies. They were the type of small variations that are typical of honest witnesses, but it would not be the defense lawyer's job to excuse them on that ground. Instead, it would be his job to magnify them as much as possible—and if a hole in the state's case resulted and caused Kenneth Brock's acquittal, well, that was the defense lawyer's job too.

That is how, in the United States of America, we maintain a system in which truly innocent people are protected from conviction.

The defense might conceivably be one of mistaken identity. After all, the defendant was not arrested in the tight circle of surrounding officers. The lighting had been poor. The witnesses' stories conflicted in the details. The defense theory might be that Kenneth Brock was just passing through when he was arrested, totally unexpectedly. The defense was not, of course, bound by the state's evidence, and details that would substantiate such a theory might be found.

This mistaken identity defense would not be highly credible, but then it did not have to be credible to be successful. All the defense had to do was to create a reasonable doubt in the minds of jurors to entitle Kenneth Brock to an acquittal. And the effectiveness of the defense might be enhanced by any number of unforeseeable occurrences. The jurors might turn out to be people who had an abiding animosity toward police officers, the judge might cripple the state's case by excluding crucial evidence, the defendant might cry in front of the jury and make a good witness. All of these things were quite possible, and they had certainly resulted in acquittals in "strong" cases before.

And actually, there was at least one defensive theory that would be much better than mistaken identity.

An experienced criminal lawyer could predict the best defense just from hearing the outlines of the state's case. To convict Kenneth Brock of capital murder, the state would have to prove that he killed Michael Sedita *intentionally*. If the discharge of the gun was an accident, the defendant could not be convicted of that offense.

So the best defense story might have the defendant tell the jury, "I didn't mean to shoot the store manager. The gun just went off. The police scared me, I was drunk out of my mind, there was a rock on the ground. I tripped over it, and that's why the gun discharged. Why would I shoot him? I had no reason to shoot him." The judge would instruct the jury that if they believed this accident defense, or even if it gave them a reasonable doubt, they must acquit Kenneth Brock of capital murder.

Prosecutors from Maine to California would recognize this defense as a familiar one. The defense of accident can be surprisingly effective, even when the state's witnesses swear that the killing was not an accident. It all depends on the unpredictable way in which the evidence happens to unfold.

It has to be remembered that the prosecution has the burden of proof, beyond a reasonable doubt. This is so, again, in every state, from Maine to California. Kenneth Brock's prosecutors would have to *disprove* the accident defense, *beyond a reasonable doubt*.

And there was another important factor in Kenneth Brock's case: the death penalty. Prosecutors everywhere will tell you that the death penalty increases the level of proof that a jury will demand. When the state charges a capital crime, it automatically increases its own burden of proof, because even though the words in the judge's instructions still are "beyond a reasonable doubt," real-life jurors tend to read the instruction as, "WAY beyond a reasonable doubt."

Ironically, the defendant's drug involvement—which the police had discovered in their search of his apartment—might even be used to bolster such an accident defense. He might testify that he was drunk and drugged and not conscious of what he was doing. In fact, the ingenious thing about an accident defense would be that it would turn all the prosecution's most devastating evidence to defense advantage. A theory of accident would actually be made more credible by the senselessness and brutality of the killing.

The prosecution's answer to this defense was also easy to predict, but it would be much harder to present to a jury. The defendant had fired at Sergeant Hogg, announced his intention to kill the victim, and escaped before the officers could shoot. His statements, actions and demeanor contradicted the defense of accident. But to *prove* that to a jury, beyond a reasonable doubt, would require exhaustive and convincing prosecution. It would also require intense concentration by twelve jurors willing and able to avoid emotional distraction by the biggest wild card in the case—the death penalty.

The state's case, to put it in the vernacular, was "pat." It was almost *too* "pat." And the apparent strength of the evidence just might turn out to be an illusion. The crime was clear to the police, but the outcome was no more clearly predictable than the end to a mystery novel. What would the *jury* do? That was the real question.

Chapter 3

Preliminary Maneuvering:
The Lawyers, the Judge, and the Jury

Assistant District Attorney Rex Emerson was the assistant in charge at the "intake" division the morning Kenneth Brock was arrested. "Intake" was a small cubicle on the first floor of the Houston police station, staffed most hours of the day by prosecutors who had the job of accepting or rejecting charges brought by police officers or citizens.

Intake is interesting for a prosecutor — but only the first time. The majority of prosecutors do not regard it favorably. For one thing, it involves a lot of waiting. For another, it is necessary in some cases to tell a police officer "no" — to refuse to file charges. The reason for a refusal sometimes reflects directly upon the quality of the work the officer has done, and the result is then unpleasant. The truth is, any good district attorney's office sometimes has an adversary relationship with the police department, rather than with the defendant. Citizen complaints, which have been through police channels and have already been refused, are even more unpleasant, because in most of the cases there is insufficient evidence for a lawful arrest; and the assistant in charge has to tell the citizen, with his beaten face flaring, that the criminal justice system will do nothing about it.

There are some compensations. Police officers who come into the office are usually in an expansive mood because they have just cleared a case and put an arrested person in jail, and the stories they have to tell are fascinating. And sometimes a lone state's attorney will get a challenging and esoteric question from officers: "Can I arrest this dude for flying his old Cessna while he was pilled up out of his mind?" (The answer: Yes, you can.)

More frequently, however, intake is just a job that has to be done.

As Emerson sat at intake, homicide detectives came in to file charges on Kenneth Brock. They were more somber than expansive this time.

Emerson talked to them for a few minutes and read the reports they presented. It was not just a murder, he realized, it was a capital murder, a death penalty case — and one of the first he had seen. Mentally he considered the types of killings that were capital: killing a police officer on duty, killing during an escape from prison, killing during a rape, robbery, arson, burglary, or kidnapping. . . .

This was a killing during a robbery. That meant it was a capital murder.

After studying the facts and getting a second opinion from another prosecutor, Emerson was satisfied that a charge of capital murder was justified. And so he drafted a capital murder indictment, charging that Kenneth Brock had "unlawfully and intentionally caused the death of Michael Sedita" while "in the course of committing the offense of aggravated robbery." Then he sent the papers he had drawn, together with the officers' reports, witnesses' statements and scientific evidence, to the grand jury division of the District Attorney's Office.

In some states, the indictment results from a preliminary hearing before a judge or magistrate. The defendant is "bound over" for trial after brief evidence from a few witnesses, enough to establish what the law calls "probable cause." This term means something less than proof; it means a reasonable basis for belief in the defendant's guilt. In other states, instead of a preliminary hearing, a grand jury composed of citizens evaluates the evidence. Sometimes the grand jury hears live witnesses, but sometimes, depending on state law, it doesn't. It considers written reports, and decides whether they show probable cause.

A few weeks later, a grand jury considered the case by reading the police report, witness statements, autopsy records and other evidence, and true-billed the papers Rex Emerson had drawn. Kenneth Brock was indicted for capital murder.

* * *

The indictment against Kenneth Brock went through the Harris County District Clerk's random filing procedure. There, it happened to be assigned to the 178th District Court.

That meant that it would be in the 178th District Court of Harris County that Kenneth Brock would be tried for capital murder.

The name of the trial court that hears capital cases varies from state to state. In California, it is called the "superior" court; in New York, it is the "supreme court, special term." In most states, it is a "district" court, presided over by the state's highest-ranking trial judges.

The courtroom of the "178th," as it is called for short, is big and imposing. It is two stories tall, and it is covered with traditional dark oak paneling. Its heaviness, however, is softened by the wear and tear of a thousand past trials. An uneven row of discolorations on the elegant wall behind the jury box shows where hundreds of jurors, while listening to evidence over many years, have leaned back too far in their swivel chairs. Incongruously, there are also cheap modern details, such as a black plastic sign that proclaims in white letters: "Throwing cigarettes on the floor is prohibited by order of the court." The floor gives evidence that this prohibition, like many orders of the court, is not enforceable.

An intricate panel, towering from floor to ceiling, adds an impression of solidity to the elevated bench that is the judge's position in the courtroom.

The judge of the 178th, Judge Dan Walton, was a big man with a square jaw, ever-present pipe, and a mane of curly gray hair that made him "look" like a judge. His powerful frame was a clue to the days when he had played college football as a consensus All-American end. Every criminal lawyer knew Judge Walton's judicial trademark: although he was, in the final analysis, a decisive man, he decided every question with painstaking care that was also painstakingly slow.

Judge Walton's mind did not run in channels that allowed preliminary matters to be decided quickly. On a typical Monday morning, when the day's docket might be overflowing with administrative matters, a chance visitor would see the judge sitting at the bench while a standing crowd of lawyers, witnesses and defendants silently waited for him to read every word of an inch-thick court file covering one of the dozens of cases on the morning's docket. "I've seen him studying even the edges of the papers," said one lawyer. Even if it was a simple matter of administration, such as appointing an attorney or even scheduling a hearing in the future, Judge Walton might start reading the papers, and if he did, every other case would have to wait while he read the arrest warrant, the bond, the indictment, the complaint, and every other paper in the individual file.

Because of this ponderous pace, Judge Walton had a significant backlog of serious felony cases. It numbered in the hundreds of rapes, robberies, burglaries, murders, thefts, and other assorted crimes.

But the very characteristics that made the judge so slow in dealing with his day-to-day docket made him the ideal judge to preside over a big case, a capital case. Prosecutors and defense attorneys agreed: if capital cases were to be assigned to a single judge in Harris County (as some administrators had proposed, to simplify docketing), no finer judge for the purpose could be selected than Judge Walton.

In addition to his painstaking care, Judge Walton was one of the brightest members of the Harris County judiciary. He had been a member of a prestigious firm in civil practice before entering public life. Both sides got a fair hearing before him. The defense had a full opportunity to present its version of the facts, and the prosecution was held rigidly to the rules of procedure and its burden of proof. And there was one other thing about Judge Walton that was important: His intelligence and meticulousness made him among the least likely of Houston's felony judges to be reversed by an appellate court.

When the random docket placed the case against Kenneth Brock in the 178th District Court, this assignment of the case to Judge Walton meant that the case would be slowly, deliberately, and carefully tried.

*   *   *

As Kenneth Brock came before the bench for arraignment, Judge Walton asked whether he had a lawyer. Brock didn't. A lawyer for this case would come cheap if he charged less than twenty thousand dollars, and of course Brock was indigent. Judge Walton read the file. Then he had the clerk prepare an affidavit of indigency for Kenneth Brock to sign, adding to the file. Finally he turned to the court coordinator, whose job was to expedite matters in the courtroom, and said, "Appoint Adrian Burk."

The most striking feature of the indictment, of course, was the gravity of the offense, and so the judge had wanted to appoint someone with experience, someone with old-fashioned toughness and nerve. The appointment of Adrian Burk meant that whatever else could be said at the end of the trial, there would be no one who would doubt that Kenneth Brock's counsel had given him the best kind of defense possible.

Adrian Burk was a close friend of Judge Walton's. Their backgrounds were even parallel: Burk had been an All-American football quarterback at Baylor University years ago.

As a trial lawyer, Burk was a master of the unexpected. Before a jury, he was voluble and expansive. He was also a convincing persuader. He could draw laughter from the most unexpected sources or turn the most insignificant matter into a serious inquiry, if it advanced his client's cause. Above all, he had some twenty years' experience in the use of credible arguments, both logical and emotional, in front of a jury.

Burk was a Baptist. He was devoted to his religion and taught in Sunday School. It was therefore not surprising that his manner before the jury was that of a fundamentalist preacher. His halo of gray hair, his big frame and flamboyant joviality, his dress that was conservative to the point of drabness, and his willingness to quote scripture and prayer before the jury would, unquestionably, mark his representation of Kenneth Brock as something out of the ordinary.

It was perhaps inevitable that the Big Baptist lawyer and the antisocial dropout murderer would form a closer relationship than is usual between lawyer and client. As time went by, Burk began to feel sympathy, friendship and finally love for this man whom the state was seeking to put to death. He brought Kenneth Brock supplies in the jail. Under his influence, Brock began reading the Bible.

It was Burk's aim, above all, to save Kenneth Brock's life.

Before trial, he would file a blizzard of motions. He would exploit them to discover the State's case and to pick and pull at it. This is the defense lawyer's job, honored in all fifty states.

Throughout the trial, he would use allegations that the prosecution was engaging in misconduct to try to blunt the damage of the state's case. This is today a standard defensive tactic in all fifty states, but Burk would employ it skillfully.

As the prosecutor struggled to get his evidence admitted, piece by piece, before the jury, Burk would struggle with equal zeal to exclude as much as he could.

He would fight over every part of the court's instructions to the jury. He would cross examine every witness vigorously. He would choose jurors that gave him the best chance at acquittal. Most of all, he would structure every part of the case, from jury selection to argument, so as to make his defense a coherent, comprehensible, and above all believable one.

* * *

The assignment of the case to Judge Walton and the appointment of Adrian Burk meant that there would be an able judge, and an able defender, to see that the Brock case was fairly tried from the defendant's standpoint.

Who would represent the point of view of the people of Texas?

The assignment went to Assistant District Attorney George Jacobs.

And since Jacobs is one of the authors of this book, perhaps this would be a good time for him to step forward and introduce himself.

"When I got the Kenneth Brock case to try," Jacobs says, "I had been at the District Attorney's Office for about five years. I had tried plenty of cases — all kinds of cases; everything from minor misdemeanors, traffic-court-type cases, all the way up to some pretty bad murders — but I'd never handled a capital case. I'd never even seen one.

"I figured that put me at a little bit of a disadvantage, in a way, with a lawyer like Adrian Burk. Adrian's been around for a long time.

"In fact, it made me nervous enough so that I can assure you, the *defendant* looked a lot more cool and collected than *I* usually felt whenever I walked into court — but, he was that way.

"I went to law school because I wanted to handle cases that were important. I wanted to have a chance to stand up for what I thought was justice in a particular situation. The law school I went to had its reputation mainly as a night law school, and it wasn't the fanciest school to go to, and I had to work to put myself through. I really had to want it. And I did.

"When I got out, I got lucky. I got a job with a judge, Judge Douglas, who is a judge on the Court of Criminal Appeals, which is the highest court in my state for criminal cases. The judges on that court each have a recent law graduate as a 'law clerk,' which means a research assistant and legal advisor. It was a one-year position, and he was a great man to work for, and I learned a lot.

"One thing I learned was that the ideas I had had about the criminal justice system weren't really the way it was.

"I saw that it was *hard* to prosecute someone who was really guilty, even if you had all the evidence, and make it stick. I was impressed with the fact that an assistant district attorney needs to be skillful at what he does, just like a criminal defense lawyer. That wasn't the impression I had before.

"When I got through with my year, I was really happy when I got a job with the District Attorney's Office in Harris County, which covers Houston."

During his five years, Jacobs settled down in Houston. He met and married his wife, Sharon, and moved to a house at the outskirts of the metropolitan area, where it fades into the Texas countryside, so that he could have plenty of room.

And he started out prosecuting misdemeanors.

The misdemeanor courts in Houston truly dispense bargain-basement justice, just as they do in most places. The cases were thefts of less than $200, simple assaults, and driving-while-intoxicated (called "driving under the influence" or "DUI" in some states, such as California). It was not unusual, at the time Jacobs started, for a team of three prosecutors to have to handle a docket of 100 to 150 cases a day. The next day, that meant, the same three would get another 100 to 150. There was obviously no way anyone could handle each case conscientiously; the workload put a premium on the ability to dismiss cases, even prosecutable ones, to concentrate on those cases in which the evidence and the need to prosecute was most clear.

"The method you learned right away was 'when in doubt, throw it out,'" Jacobs says. "There were a lot of cases where the people of this county didn't get justice — there might be a real bad assault, for instance, and it would be dismissed first thing out of the chute if the defense made noises that even sounded like self-defense. Not to mention the fact we plea-bargained everything cheap, just to move the docket. But looking back, I think it's a good thing for a prosecutor to go through. Since then, the first thing I think of if there's a substantial doubt in the case is to dismiss it."

After a year and a half of misdemeanor court, Jacobs "graduated" to prosecuting felonies — first burglary cases, then robberies, then murders. And now a capital murder.

"As far as prosecuting Kenneth Brock, I figured I did have some things going for me," Jacobs says. "I had a pretty good foundation in procedural rules from being with Judge Douglas, and I could usually stay calm in hot situations — usually — and in this case, I really had evidence I could believe in. I knew I couldn't out-orate Adrian Burk in front of the jury. So I was as meticulous as I could be in preparing my evidence. I made a notebook covering the testimony of every witness — that kind of thing. I didn't want to see this guy get acquitted just because I, individually, fouled up."

Jacobs would need every asset he had, and more, just to stay even with Adrian Burk in the Kenneth Brock case.

*   *   *

Now the stage was set for the kind of pre-trial skirmishing that marks the beginning of nearly every serious criminal case.

Burk would try to get Jacobs' evidence thrown out, and to get advantages in selecting the jury, and so forth. He would use the legal rules about admissibility of evidence, the Constitution, technical statutes, and any other legal principle he could that would serve his purpose, because that was his job—to attack the prosecution's case. The pre-trial stage offered an excellent opportunity.

Pre-trial is mainly the defense lawyer's show. The defense lawyer files legal papers, called "motions," in an attempt to get rulings from the judge giving the defense advantages at trial. For the most part, Jacobs could do nothing—other than try to prevent his case from getting hurt too badly by rulings on Burk's motions.

The filing of the motions was like throwing darts at a board. Some hit their mark and some did not. The best strategy was to throw plenty of darts, so Burk did. Sometimes, the strategy was apparent from the nature of the motion itself, but others had purposes that were far more subtle— to test the state's case, to put state witnesses on record in an unfavorable position, and the like.

For example, there was a "Motion for Discovery," in which Burk sought to inspect all the state's significant evidence (this motion was granted in part by the court, so it may be counted as a dart that hit the target). There was a "Motion to Produce Exculpatory and Mitigating Evidence," by which Burk sought to have the State and all its agencies search their files completely and turn over any information that might be useful to the defense (granted in full by the court). There was a "Motion with Reference to the Arraignment of the Accused," a "Motion for the Record of the Deceased," and a "Motion to Sequester Jurors." There were motions to have the prosecution produce criminal records of all witnesses (there were none, but Burk wanted to find out), and motions to stop the prosecution from going into all sorts of different types of evidence. Every motion had to be heard, and many of them added to Burk's store of useful information or gave him advantages at trial.

Pretrial procedure varies greatly from state to state, particularly the process called "discovery," which the defense lawyer uses to learn information from the prosecutor. In some states, such as Florida, discovery covers almost all kinds of evidence. The prosecutor cannot hide many of his hole cards. In other states, such as Texas, the discoverable information is more restricted. But in a capital case, a judge like Judge Walton would be expected to bend over backward to make the record show that the discovery process was fair to the defense.

And in every case, in every state, evidence showing possible innocence is automatically discoverable. Where there were discrepancies in witness statements, such as those describing the killer's hair as "blond" and "reddish brown," Adrian Burk was entitled to copies. In the end, Jacobs simply handed over his entire evidence file, a frequent custom in capital cases.

One of the most interesting motions Burk filed was called, simply enough, "Motion to Suppress Evidence." This kind of motion exists in every state.

By this motion, Burk sought to have all the defendant's confessions, admissions or statements of any kind hidden from the jury. That included the "I shot the store owner" remark, and it included the statement in which Kenneth Brock admitted where he had thrown the gun.

Burk knew the importance of these items of evidence, and if he could prevent it, he did not want the jury to hear them.

The Motion to Suppress contained standard claims. For instance, it alleged that the statements had been "forced" and "coerced" from the defendant in violation of the "Fifth, Sixth and Fourteenth Amendments to the United States Constitution." These allegations, of course, were euphemisms for a charge of police brutality. And the Motion to Suppress also contained another claim: it charged that Officer Lilley had violated the constitution in that the defendant "was not advised he had the right to seek legal counsel" or to "have legal counsel present at the time defendant made any statement to the police."

Here it was: the charge of wrongdoing by Officer Lilley. Presumably, the charge meant that Lilley should have stopped his arrest and interrupted the defendant's blurted admission until he could warn the defendant of his rights. It was an extravagant claim; but Burk, of course, was only doing his job. He had to make these allegations, because it was not up to him to see that Officer Lilley was treated fairly. His job, instead, was to get Brock acquitted, and the American system of justice depends on defense lawyers, like Burk, who pursue this goal single-mindedly.

Judge Walton held a lengthy hearing on the Motion to Suppress. Most of the important witnesses who would testify at the trial were called to the witness stand; the hearing turned into a little "trial before the real trial." Finally, Judge Walton rejected Burk's claims. Jacobs' evidence would not be thrown out; it could be heard by the jury. There had been no police brutality in this case. And the police had acted properly in warning Kenneth Brock of his rights.

Of course, Adrian Burk had still gained a great deal from the pre-trial phase of the proceedings. For one thing, some of his motions *had* hit the mark, and some of the evidence had been thrown out. For another thing, he gained a great deal from the Motion to Suppress itself, even though

Judge Walton had rejected it. How had he gained? In a very important way: It is always advantageous to a criminal lawyer to have the opposition's case spread out and revealed so that he can begin to pick it apart. As a result of the Motion to Suppress, Adrian Burk got a chance to cross examine most of the State's main witnesses at length during the hearing—to discover and challenge their stories. Now he knew, for instance, that if he were to present a defense of accident, the admission by Kenneth Brock— the "I shot the store owner" remark—would not be all that devastating, because there was no admission that the shooting had been intentional. Furthermore, during the hearing, Burk had collected bits and pieces of testimony from various witnesses that would help him argue to the jury that the killing was accidental. The hearing, in other words, helped Burk decide on the defense strategy he would use at trial, and it gave him ammunition to execute that strategy.

From Maine to California, defense lawyers approach their task in the same way.

And so, as the day of trial approached, Burk knew more and more about what he was up against and what he could use to combat it. His pretrial motions had occupied much of the months of November and December. They had been exhaustively thorough.

On January 6, the first working day of the new year, the final pre-trial process—the arduous process of selecting a jury—began. It was a little over seven months after the murder of Michael Sedita.

* * *

Jury selection did not actually get under way until the afternoon of the 6th.

Judge Walton was seated at the impressive wooden judge's bench in the 178th courtroom. At counsel table, Jacobs sat on one side, Burk and his client on the other. The judge had ordered that a supply of jurors be brought over and seated in the jury room. One by one, the "members of the venire" —as potential jurors are called—would be led into the courtroom by the bailiff and individually questioned first by Judge Walton, then by prosecutor Jacobs, then by defender Burk.

This is one of the ways in which Texas differs from most other death penalty states. The entire questioning of every juror is done individually. In most states, the jurors are examined in a group: They are asked group questions about their attitudes toward the death penalty and toward every other legal issue, and only those that give peculiar responses are examined, further, in private. It makes a difference: The process in Texas is meant to probe deeply. The lawyers work hard to put individual jurors on the spot and watch their reactions—often an unwise strategy in other states, where all the other jurors are watching, and the attorneys make every effort not to appear rude. The Texas approach, with individual examinations, also means a capital case takes much longer to try. The exhausting yet hard-fought process drags on like something out of a Charles Dickens novel, and it surprises capital prosecutors from other states who visit Texas.

Everyone knew it would take several weeks of hard work to select a jury for Kenneth Brock's case. It had now just begun. The bailiff had brought out a young man named Gerald Cline and seated him in the witness chair for examination.

". . . Mr. Cline," Judge Walton asked the first potential juror when he had been seated in the witness chair, "Do you have any conscientious scruples or conscientious objections against the imposition of death as a punishment for crime in a capital case?"

The juror, Mr. Cline, looked as though he had been asked to explain the general theory of relativity. He looked up at the judge quizzically. "Now what was that you were telling me?" he asked. "Say that again."

Judge Walton tried again. He knew that the question was tortuous in its wording, but something like this wording had to be used in questioning the juror—because these words were used by the Supreme Court in specifying how death penalty jurors were chosen.

"I say, do you have any conscientious scruples or conscientious objections against the imposition or infliction of death as a punishment for crime in a proper case?"

The lawyers looked at the juror intently and waited for his answer.

"I would say yes," said Mr. Cline. "It would depend on the case."

The judge, still not satisfied, tried to nail the answer down for the record. "Well, that's the reason I qualified the matter—'in a proper case,'" he told the potential juror. He explained that the decision was entirely up to the jurors what verdict they would render in the case. "I am simply trying at this time to ascertain whether you are conscientiously opposed to the law of the State that authorizes a jury to return a verdict that would result in imposition of the death penalty for a person found guilty of the offense of capital murder."

Now Mr. Cline understood. Promptly, he answered: "No, I'm not opposed to that."

Jury selection in a capital case is tedious. The potential jurors are questioned endlessly, one at a time, with the same questions repeated in little variation for each. But the tedium is that of an intricate contest, like the opening moves of a game of chess. Jurors are psychologically conditioned by this subtle opening process of adversary questioning; they can be influenced, persuaded or antagonized. More importantly, depending upon the way they answer the slow and deliberate questions put to them, they will be accepted or excused by lawyers who stake a good deal of the case upon a guess about their reactions to the evidence.

Examination of this first potential juror, Mr. Cline, was a typical example.

Gerald Cline was a truck driver for a gas company, unmarried and nineteen years of age. The lawyers knew this information from glancing at a form that Mr. Cline, and every other venire member, had had to fill out before arriving in the courtroom. From a glance at the form, and from seeing Cline's short hair and work clothes, the lawyers already knew a great deal about him that was useful.

For example, it was significant that he was a young person. It was also important that he was in a work position that did not require him to make difficult decisions. These factors favored the defense, because they indicated that he might be hesitant to make unpleasant decisions in a capital case. On the other hand, he was a working man who would not sympathize with a robber and who would do his duty if he saw it clearly, and that favored the prosecution. The lawyers knew that they would have to listen to Mr. Cline's answers carefully to know which of these tendencies to consider most likely.

From listening, the lawyers could see that this Mr. Cline was cautious. He might be suspicious of the prosecution's case if it left any stone unturned. But he was decisive once he understood, and he was unequivocal in saying that he was not opposed to the death penalty.

As Judge Walton finished qualifying the potential juror, Mr. Cline began to shape up as a man in the middle—a person who might be acceptable to both sides and who might be selected to serve on the jury. Jacobs started his questions slowly, recognizing Mr. Cline's potential importance.

The prosecutor was concerned, first of all, that Gerald Cline might be so cautious that he would not consider any evidence sufficient to prove a case beyond a reasonable doubt. So he started his questioning of this juror by explaining that the State had the burden of proof—but it was a proof beyond "reasonable" doubt, not beyond "all" doubt. "What it does *not* mean," Jacobs said to Cline, "and what is strictly *not* required, is that the State prove to you beyond all doubt, every single *iota* of a doubt, of a defendant's guilt, and I am sure you can see the reason for that, because it would be impossible."

Then Jacobs asked, "Can you agree with that and abide by it?"

"No, not really," said Gerald Cline.

"Why?" What's the problem there?"

The venireman was not able to articulate his objection immediately. He began, "Well . . . you should have all the evidence." Then he hesitated. "You know, like you say—" Then he hesitated again. "I can't really answer that without hearing the case . . . I would have to hear it, but—"

"You understand I'm not trying to pre-commit you to any verdict one way or another," Jacobs said, trying again. He explained, once more, that the burden of proof was "beyond a *reasonable* doubt." "Now it is impossible," he continued, "and the State cannot prove anything to you beyond *all* doubt. Do you agree with that? Or do you have a question about that?"

"I agree after you restated that," said Mr. Cline, now willing to commit himself. "You are saying up to a reasonable doubt, right? Okay. I agree with that, because you can't give a jury everything. That's impossible."

Strategically, Jacobs had reached his first objective with this venireman. It was essential to make sure that he would consider the witnesses in the light of reason, because the witnesses would not be Supermen—they would be ordinary human beings with ordinary memories and perceptions. Without this kind of questioning, there are some jurors who will reject overwhelming proof in the most surprising way, because of some minor conflict. At the same time, Jacobs had been careful to handle Mr. Cline with courtesy—in fact, with kid gloves. Examination of a potential juror, who, after all, will be deciding the case for or against the person who is doing the examining, is very different in this respect from the examination of witnesses.

Finally Jacobs said, "Your honor, we pass the juror."

Now it would be Adrian Burk's turn.

Burk, like Jacobs, started slowly. But when he got deeply into his examination, his own technique surfaced. It was a style different from Jacobs' style. It was neither better nor worse, neither more nor less effective—but it was distinctly different.

For one thing, Burk did not shrink from meaty subjects or from graphic terminology. He told Gerald Cline that the State of Texas "will ask you to vote to send this man" to his death, and "take his life."

That explanation got the juror's attention in a way that nothing else had yet.

With this elementary beginning, Burk asked, now, "Mr. Cline, do you know what a capital murder case is?"

"No, I don't."

Burk began to explain what a capital murder case was. "And do you understand how a person is put to death if he's adjudged guilty and the jury answers questions that cause him to be sentenced to death?"

"No, I don't really."

Burk was willing to tell him. Briefly but skillfully, he described how it was done. "That's our method of execution. I want you to understand all the ramifications of your verdict as a juror in this case," Burk said helpfully. "Are you with me?"

"Yes."

Burk went on, trying to engender in the juror a repulsion to the death penalty. "And do you believe it is just and fair punishment?" he asked finally.

"If proven guilty," said Mr. Cline.

The examination of Gerald Cline took the better part of an hour. Later, when the record was prepared, it occupied more than forty pages of type. But it had transformed Mr. Cline from a name on paper to a human being whose broad characteristics were now known to the attorneys. Ultimately, it was a picture the State could live with but the defense could not.

"What says the State?" Judge Walton asked.

"The State will accept Mr. Cline, your honor."

"What says the defense?"

Burk had a difficult decision to make. He could have the venireman removed from the jury by using one of his "peremptory challenges." He had fifteen challenges, but the state also had fifteen, and he did not want to squander them. Finally, Burk decided that although the juror's caution made him somewhat attractive, the odds were unacceptably high that he would vote in favor of the death penalty in this case.

"We will exercise our peremptory challenge, your honor," he said.

Gerald Cline was excused.

* * *

Jury selection droned on, and on, and on. Throughout this exhausting process, the lawyers struggled to stay at peak mental acuity.

They were assisted in this endeavor by occasional acrimony and occasional humor. For example:

". . . All right," Adrian Burk was saying to one juror after several days of jury selection had passed. "What do you do when you're not working?"

"Sleep, mostly."

"What else?"

"When I'm not doing that, I'm chasing women."

"When you're not sleeping or chasing women, do you have anything else that you do?"

"Well, I dance, play ball."

"Have you ever tried marijuana?"

"No,—I don't think so."

"Have you ever been around people that have tried it?"

"I don't know what marijuana is.". . .

"Do you know what 'conscientious scruples' means?"

"No, I do not."

This time it was Jacobs, not Burk, who used a peremptory challenge. Jacobs figured that a juror who bantered with the defense lawyer during a capital murder case, claimed not to know what marijuana was and answered questions about conscientious scruples without knowing what "conscientious scruples" meant, was not to be trusted to say whether the case had been proved beyond a reasonable doubt. Burk's ostensibly playful questioning of this venireman had in fact been strategic and skillful.

As the hours went by and stretched into days, and the days grew into weeks, each side's peremptory challenges were gradually exhausted. The attorneys were forced, to an ever increasing degree, to take chances in accepting jurors. The case inched into its third calendar week.

And then, suddenly, in the middle of the third week, there were twelve people who had been accepted by both sides.

The jury that would try Kenneth Brock had been selected.

There were six men and six women. They were a conglomerate mix of races, ages and occupations. A few were blue-collar workers and a few were housewives, and there were some white-collar workers among the twelve. Jury selection had educated all of them to have a keen sense of the concepts that they would have to use to decide the case. Jury selection had also removed those who said they could not, for one reason or another, be fair to the defendant, and it had removed those who said they could not, under any circumstances, sit as jurors in the trial of a capital case. What was left was a jury that was not perceptibly favorable either to one side or the other.*

---

* The following name in this chapter was changed, without alteration of the incident in which the person was involved: Gerald Cline.

Chapter 4

The Trial

On January 23, the twelve persons remaining from the process of elimination that is called jury selection stood, all in a group, and raised their hands. They swore the traditional oath required of all jurors in criminal cases: that they would "a true verdict render, according to the law and the evidence." The trial was about to begin.

"All right," said Judge Walton. "You may be seated, members of the jury. Mr. Jacobs, you may read the indictment."

Jacobs stood, faced the jury, and started to read. "In the name and by authority of the State of Texas, the Grand Jury of Harris County . . . do present that in the County of Harris and State of Texas, one Kenneth Albert Brock"—the jurors looked at the defendant—"did then and there unlawfully, and intentionally, cause the death of Michael Sedita. . . ."

Jacobs read on. The indictment was the all-important document that set forth the elements of the State's case, the facts that had to be proved. It was technically worded, dry and dull, but it was the first statement to the jury of the charge against Kenneth Brock in positive language. Jacobs read it slowly and distinctly.

". . . against the peace and dignity of the state," Jacobs said, reading the final words of the indictment. These archaic words were required, by law, to be at the end of every indictment in Texas. They were completely superfluous to the charge, and nobody knew what had prompted the Texas legislature in some long-forgotten session to require that they be there, but the indictment would be defective (and any conviction might be reversed) without them. Jacobs was careful to include them, even though they did sound a little out of place.

On the other side of the table, Kenneth Brock sat beside Adrian Burk. He did not have the matted beard, long hair or unkempt appearance of the time of his arrest. Instead, he wore spotlessly clean clothes, his face was clean-shaven, and his hair curled softly about his ears. At the beginning of his trial, for understandable reasons, he looked clean-cut and innocent.

Adrian Burk stood. Very firmly, he entered Kenneth Brock's plea to the indictment: "Not guilty!"

* * *

One of the first witnesses Jacobs called was Sergeant Hogg. He was unquestionably the State's most important witness. He had been the man in charge the night of the murder, and he was the only witness who had seen the entire event from start to finish.

That meant that Sergeant Hogg was also important for Adrian Burk, but in a different way: Burk needed to destroy or discredit the Sergeant's testimony.

And so some of the most vigorous lawyering of the entire trial came near the beginning, while this crucial witness testified.

"I grabbed my shotgun," Sergeant Hogg was saying, "and I proceeded to run around the corner, and when I reached the corner here, the defendant fired a shot at me."

Burk was on his feet, with a lengthy objection that concluded, ". . . the witness has testified to an extraneous offense for which the defendant does not stand indicted. It's prejudicial to the defense of the defendant and I object and ask that it be stricken from the record and that the jury be instructed to disregard it."

"That's overruled," said Judge Walton.

"I move for a mistrial, your honor."

"That's overruled."

"Please note our exception, your honor."

This would be the pattern that most of the trial would follow. Jacobs would struggle to get the facts before the jury in accordance with the rules of evidence, and Burk, who had no interest in having the jury receive evidence that incriminated his client, would struggle equally to have it excluded from the jury. He would cite to the judge as many legal theories as he could. And then he would make sure that his objections were fully reflected in the record, so that if an appeal was necessary he could hope that the Texas Court of Criminal Appeals would disagree with one of Judge Walton's rulings.

Burk even objected to evidence that did not directly incriminate his client. It had started with a diagram, marked as State's Exhibit 3, a diagram of the scene of the homicide. Jacobs wanted to show the diagram to the jury simply to facilitate the jury's understanding of the evidence; it would be easier if the jurors understood first where the convenience store was, where Surry Road was in relation to the woods, and so forth. But Burk, as might be expected, did not share the objective of simplifying the evidence for the jury; that would make it easier for the jurors to understand evidence that was incriminating. He objected when Sergeant Hogg tried to explain the diagram. "It has not been proved by this witness," he argued. "There is no testimony by him other than the fact that this looks like it, and we object because there is no showing by this witness that he is familiar with the distances indicated on it or the area as generally depicted by it. Further, there are statements on the exhibit that are prejudicial, and conclusions of law . . . and we object to the admission of State's Exhibit 3 into evidence."

Burk's objection covered all the bases. But Jacobs had covered all the bases, too. Before calling Sergeant Hogg, he had had three other witnesses testify. The first, Investigator Mark Argo, had testified about the way he had measured the distances on the diagram; the second, Deputy Sheriff Sherman Bradshaw, had taken aerial photographs from a helicopter so that the exact details of the crime scene could be compared with the diagram.

Judge Walton was ready to decide on Burk's objection. "That's overruled," he said. Jacobs' meticulous planning was beginning to pay off; the diagram was admitted into evidence.

"Note our exception," said Adrian Burk. He renewed his objection, so that the issue could be raised again—if necessary—on appeal.

With the jurors finally able to look at the scene diagram, Jacobs was now ready to move on to the meatiest part of the evidence. After objections from Burk to various questions, on the ground that they were about "extraneous offenses," were "repetitious," were improper "bolstering" of the State's own witnesses, were "hearsay," were "prejudicial," were "leading" the witness, suggested a "conclusion" to the witness, and several others, Jacobs moved Sergeant Hogg through the story of the killing. But Burk was a skilled and dedicated defender, and so every one of these objections had some arguable basis in the complicated law of evidence, and it took judgment to decide that they were inapplicable to the specific questions Jacobs was asking. The evidence moved slowly. Finally, Jacobs reached the point of the actual shooting.

"Had any officer attempted to approach Mr. Brock at that time, or had anybody fired, when he shot Mr. Sedita?"

"No, sir, they had not."

"Was anyone advancing toward him at this time?"

"No, sir, they were not."

"Did you yourself, or were you able to, observe any reason that would have caused the defendant, Kenneth Brock, to shoot Mr. Sedita?"

"No, sir, I did not."

"All right. Did you hear a shot fired?"

"Yes, sir, I did."

"Did you see a flash, or not?"

"No, sir."

"Exactly how far were the defendant and Mr. Sedita positioned from each other when the shot was fired?"

"They were sideways in the alley with the defendant behind Mr. Sedita."

This was the first time the jury had heard the details of the killing. They were listening carefully. Hogg was an excellent witness, with an attitude of quiet competence. But were the deliberateness and brutality of the offense really being conveyed to the jury? Jacobs, keenly aware that he had the burden of proof on all the issues, repeatedly underlined the details of that crucial instant. He started, again, with the taking of the hostage down the alley to Surry Road, and went through the story once more, in depth.

"So, then, if I understand you correctly, you had the defendant positioned between you, is that right?"

"Yes, sir, that's correct."

"All right. Did you make any statements, or say anything, to the defendant Kenneth Brock at this time?"

"No, sir, I did not."

"Did you hear other officers say anything to him?"

"I could hear muffled words, but I couldn't understand the words."

"All right. Now, after you had positioned him between you there on the road, tell the jury what happened next."

"We stopped there to avoid getting him into any kind of panic, and he walked on to approximately this position here, and a little farther down here to approximately here." The sergeant was indicating the movements on the diagram. "And there were words exchanged but I couldn't make them out. It was too far away from me then. And I heard a shot and saw Mr. Sedita fall."

"All right. Now, what had the other officers down at the other end of the road done, at that time, or what had you observed them do?"

"I observed them — they were at this point, when Mr. Sedita and the defendant were approaching them, and they had started backing up when the defendant shot Mr. Sedita."

Jacobs went on with the questioning, trying to make the jury see each part of the event with as much clarity as was humanly possible. For although the public image of the courtroom lawyer is that of a slashing cross-examiner, the fact is that direct examination of one's own witnesses sometimes is more difficult than cross examination — and, most of the time, more important. At one point, Jacobs had Sergeant Hogg physically demonstrate, using the actual pistol that had been recovered from the ditch, how Kenneth Brock had killed his victim. Jacobs used his own body to play the part of Michael Sedita. Like actors on a stage, the prosecutor and policeman played the crucial moment for the jury to see. Jacobs had the burden of proof, but he also had overwhelming evidence, and he wanted to get all of it that he could through to the jury.

Finally, when he was sure that everything in the sergeant's testimony was clear, Jacobs passed the witness.

Now it would be Adrian Burk's turn.

* * *

Burk's cross examination was apparently premised on the theory that the killing was precipitated not by any voluntary act by Kenneth Brock, but rather by the actions of Hogg and the other police officers.

"All right," he was saying. "Now, Mr. Hogg, what I'm getting at is that you gentlemen there obviously were intent on pressuring the suspect and prevailing on him to surrender, weren't you?"

"If at all possible, yes, sir."

"If at all possible, you wanted him to surrender?"

"Yes, sir."

"If at all possible, but what if it was not possible for him to surrender? Supposing his mind was too warped or crazy that he would not yield—"

Jacobs interrupted. "We object to the form of the question, your honor. Counsel is stating facts that are not in evidence."

"He's probably right, judge," said Burk. "I withdraw it."

Burk continued. "Mr. Hogg, do you think that you were putting too much pressure on whoever was in the alley with Mr. Sedita? Do you think you put too much pressure on him, whoever it was with Sedita, by pressuring him?"

"No, sir, I do not."

"Why?" Burk wanted to know. "You see, whoever this fellow was, he said, 'back up, back up.' He said that more than once, didn't he?"

"Yes, sir, he did."

"And as a matter of fact, the deceased told you to back up, this man was crazy, didn't he?"

"Yes, sir."

"The deceased, Mr. Sedita, told you, back up, this man was crazy?"

"Yes, sir."

"But still, Mr. Hogg, you all pressed on, didn't you?"

Hogg's answer was firm. "No, sir, we did not."

Now Burk saw the need to extricate himself gracefully, but his momentum carried him on. "I understand you were trying to do your duty as you saw it under the circumstances that you should do it, but—"

"No, sir, we did not press on. That's my answer to your question." Burk had pushed the matter too far, and it was now evident to everyone that the sergeant's first priority had been Michael Sedita's life.

But in spite of this gaffe, Burk had planted the seed of this idea that the police officers had produced the murder. It was a theme to which he would return, time and again, during the course of the trial.

And Burk scored a number of other points.

For one thing, he gave material assistance to his accident defense during the cross examination of Sergeant Hogg. He brought out a description of the scene as "full of chug holes and uneven terrain and a lot of things in it." This depiction of the road surface might help him make it more credible that his client could have tripped and pulled the trigger accidentally. Burk also emphasized the flimsiness of the gun: "Do you know anything about guns? Is that normal, for that to act like that?" He had Sergeant Hogg handle the weapon, demonstrating the light trigger pull and haphazard chamber action. When the sergeant replied, "Yes, sir, that's what's dangerous about those Saturday Night Specials," he had made his point—although he requested, and got, an instruction from Judge Walton that the jury was not to consider the derogatory "Saturday Night Special" characterization of the gun.

Burk also went over the details of the offense with Hogg, laying groundwork for the possibility that he could get later witnesses to contradict those details. He got Hogg to admit, at one point, that his testimony about the place he first observed the defendant was "wrong." He asked questions about whether anybody had threatened to shoot Kenneth Brock or whether Brock had "received any abusive treatment at the hands of any officers that night." He laid groundwork for his theory that intoxication had added to the accident: "Did his eyes look like they were a little blank, a little glazed over, fixed?" When Sergeant Hogg replied that they did not, Burk asked, "And you wouldn't say anything here that would deprive him of a fair trial, would you?" in a tone that all but said Hogg was a liar.

It was a vigorous cross examination.

*   *   *

The case would not have been complete without at least one serious charge of prosecution misconduct. Burk supplied it.

The charge arose over photographs that Jacobs began to introduce into evidence through Sergeant Hogg, photographs showing the scene of the murder. Burk complained that he had not had sufficient time before trial to see them. Further, Burk charged that Jacobs' failure to make them available for inspection, as he saw it, was a violation of the court's order on the defense motion for discovery.

"I would like to make this objection into the record, your honor," Burk began, "and point out to the court that heretofore, during preliminary matters that have been conducted outside the presence of the jury, the court has instructed the state's attorney, Mr. Jacobs, to make available to me on behalf of the defendant all of the photographs that the state intended to introduce into evidence here before the jury and before the court, and with that in mind, on the day of the court's ruling, I went to Mr. Jacob's office where I was shown approximately four photographs. . . ."

Jacobs interrupted. "Excuse me, your honor," he said as calmly as he could. "I don't know what Mr. Burk is going into, but since this happened outside the presence of the jury, I would ask that we approach the bench to see what his point is so that I can answer it at the bench."

It turned out that what Burk wanted was a dismissal of the entire murder case and the acquittal of Kenneth Brock on the ground that Jacobs had violated his client's right to discovery.

The judge had the jury taken from the courtroom. This was not going to be something that could be resolved by a whispered conference at the bench. In fact, it was becoming increasingly evident that it was going to take some time to unravel Burk's charge.

Before Burk could argue his motion, he had to produce evidence of the prosecution misconduct he was charging. The witness he called was, of course, himself. In the past, it may have been unusual for attorneys to testify in cases that they themselves were trying, but the practice has become increasingly common today—because allegations of prosecution misconduct have become a standard defensive technique.

Burk testified about the judge's order on his Motion for Discovery. The judge had ordered the prosecution to allow his inspection of all photographs related to the case. "At the close of trial proceedings on that day," he testified, "I went to Mr. Jacobs' office, whereupon he showed me, as I recall, four 8 x 10 photographs." The photographs that were now in issue had to been among those four.

When Burk had finished, the judge turned to Jacobs and said, "Any questions from the state?"

"Mr. Burk," Jacobs asked, "so that the record will reflect exactly what the situation is here, what time did you arrive in the courtroom this morning?"

Burk told him.

Then Jacobs got to the point. "And do you recall when you approached counsel table that I presented you with two packets of photographs and presented them to you for your examination and perusal, and I said to you, 'Mr. Burk, here are photographs we intend to offer in the trial of the case and pursuant to the court's order I am giving them to you at this time so that you may have an opportunity to examine them,' and I did present you with the photographs at that time, did I not?"

"Mr. Jacobs," Burk answered, "You handled me two packets of photographs with the statement that here are some additional photographs that I intend to introduce. I would correct you, sir: I do not recall and I do not intentionally dispute your word, Mr. Jacobs, if you said this . . . . That was the first time I had ever seen the exhibits."

Jacobs examined Burk further. The court's order covering the photographs had been entered in the afternoon, only two working days earlier, and Jacobs had furnished Burk the pictures he then had, immediately. The other pictures, which Jacobs had had to receive from the custody of the police, had been shown to Burk early this morning. In other words, it had taken Jacobs something between one and two actual working days to show Burk the pictures he did not have immediately available. Jacobs had not really violated the order of the court.

"All right," Jacobs went on. "Further, Mr. Burk, this morning before the jury was called in, you did return those pictures to me in the envelope that I had given to you, did you not?"

" I made certain, Mr. Jacobs, that the pictures you handed me were not mutilated, damaged, mishandled, marked or desecrated in any way . . . ," Burk replied in an ironic tone.

But that was not Jacobs' point at all. "And at the time you returned them to me, you made no request of me for additional time to examine them, did you, sir?"

"No, I did not, Mr. Jacobs."

In the end, Judge Walton overruled Burk's motions for dismissal of the charges, for a mistrial, and for exclusion of all pictures from evidence.

The jury was brought back in, approximately two hours after they had been removed at the start of the controversy over the pictures. The court reporter's notes, by this time, were so lengthy that the end of the pictures controversy appeared on page 3,417 of the transcript. The judge instructed the jury that the pictures at issue had been admitted into evidence.

As the trial progressed, Burk continued to use novel technical theories to exclude evidence. In one instance, he tried to get the testimony of a witness suppressed in its entirety because the witness had talked to the investigator, Mark Argo, in violation — as Burk saw it — of an order of the court. In another instance, he insisted on the right to see the original handwritten statement of a witness, and this demand led to a hearing at which seven witnesses were called outside the presence of the jury. The hearing only confirmed what had been apparent from the start — that the witness' statement had been typed from the handwritten form, then the handwritten original thrown away — and the judge overruled Burk's motion to dismiss the case on this ground, since the typed copy of the original was available to the defense throughout the witness' testimony.

* * *

"Would you state your name for the members of the jury, please?" Jacobs was saying to a new witness.

"Joe Bill Walker," said the witness.

The calling of Joe Bill Walker represented something of a minor triumph for the prosecution. He was the truck driver who had seen Brock crawling across the road, out of the woods, and had shined his spotlight on him. If Sergeant Hogg was, figuratively speaking, the Samuel Johnson of this story, Joe Bill Walker was its Boswell. But the officers on the scene had failed to get his name, not realizing how essential his testimony would be. It had taken Mark Argo days of work and plenty of ingenuity to locate him. The offense report that the officers had prepared had, mistakenly, identified the man in the truck as a wrecker driver, and through this slender lead, by contacting the officers and contacting, in turn, a number of wrecker drivers, he found one that was able to tell him the name of the man he was looking for.

Now, Joe Bill Walker sat on the witness stand and told the jury, "I got my spotlight and shined my spotlight on the road, and I seen this man" —he identified the defendant—"was crossing the road on his stomach."

The irony was not lost on the jury. Here was the amateur crime-fighter, lured to the scene because he heard a report on a CB radio that promised excitement, catching a desperate and dangerous criminal who had eluded a posse surrounding him with dogs and horses. It was a scene straight from the movies. And Walker, with his salt-of-the-earth mannerisms, did not let the jurors down, as he went on to describe Brock "easing along on his stomach like they do in the army."

It was important testimony. Without it, there would have been a hole in the state's story as Brock went from the woods into the residential area where he was arrested. Without it, Burk might have had a shot at a defense of mistaken identity. And the obvious attempt to escape the consequences of his crime that Walker's testimony so graphically showed would not assist Brock's defense of accident.

How would Burk deal with this testimony?

The approach Burk used was simplicity itself, but ingenious simplicity. Burk looked at Walker, with his faded blue jeans, his pearl-buttoned shirt, his boots and his short-sided haircut, and decided that an ounce of humor was worth a pound of exculpatory evidence. After establishing that Walker's truck was a half-ton pickup, he moved on to the heart of the matter:

"All right. I guess that you are one of those people that has got a KIKK sticker on the back?" (KIKK is a Houston radio station that caters to country tastes).

"Yes, sir," said Walker.

"And 'Drink Budweiser,' on the back, too?"

"No, Sir," said Walker happily, because although he didn't necessarily like Budweiser enough to put an ad for it on his bumper, he did like to talk about his truck.

"And a gun rack?"

Of course it had a gun rack. "Yes, sir," said Joe Bill Walker.

"And curtains?"

"No, sir, no curtains," said Walker, looking like he was thinking about putting them in, though.

"A Wallace for President sticker on the bumper?"

"No, sir."

"But that's the kind of truck you are talking about?"

"Yes, sir," said Walker, because Burk had, indeed, really hit on exactly the kind of truck it was. Walker was smiling because he liked to talk about his truck. The jurors were smiling, too, because they liked to listen to a man talk about his truck who so obviously enjoyed it.

Burk went on, following the assumption that a laughing jury is seldom hanging one.

After five or six more questions, Jacobs began to wonder whether Burk and Walker were ever going to stop talking pickup trucks. Finally, Burk began asking about Walker's stepmother's pickup truck — did it have a spotlight on it, too? — and this was too much for Jacobs, who objected that the question was "immaterial." But the judge, who was not going to stop Burk from defending his client in a death penalty case even if the defense was a little unorthodox, said: "Overruled."

Burk got some advice from Walker on the best place to buy a good spotlight for a truck ("You can buy them at Western Auto or K-Mart,") and then stopped talking pickup trucks. He talked with Walker a few minutes about whether he belonged to a union. Then he asked Walker whether he had "ever seen anybody who was drinking beer and popping pills who did or said things that they ordinarily would not do or say?" (yes, he had, Walker replied), and whether on those occasions Walker had "seen the glassy look in their eyes?" ("Yes, sir"). Then Burk got Walker to describe what the eyes of the man he saw crawling across the road that night were like. It was the intoxication theory again; since Sergeant Hogg had said Brock's eyes looked normal, if Burk could get Walker to contradict that, he would not only impeach Hogg's testimony but shore up his accident defense at the same time.

"He had a glassy-eyed look and they were also bloodshot," the witness answered. Burk had scored.

It was almost an anticlimax when, after Walker, Jacobs called Officers Jalomo, Phillips and Orlando to testify about the murder they had seen that night.

*   *   *

The state's evidence continued to build. Jacobs called the other officers, Ella and Jim Garver, Phil Ochsler, Andy Hart, and finally his technical witnesses: Martinez, the firearms expert; Zotter, the chemist; and, to end on a note of strength, Green, the medical examiner. Patiently, Jacobs brought out the details from each in the same way that he had from Sergeant Hogg.

But the more colorful testimony, in most instances, was elicited by Burk. His defensive theories began to gel, built on a foundation of folksy but at times brilliant cross examination. Basically, he had six themes that he developed throughout the case: (1) that the shooting was an accident; (2) that it had happened because the defendant was intoxicated to the point of being glassy-eyed; (3) that the investigation had been incomplete and incompetent; (4) that the police officers had beaten, abused and threatened Kenneth Brock; (5) that the police officers had pressured Kenneth Brock so intensely that they put him "in a box," "in a vise," or "in a bind" and thereby produced the killing themselves; and (6) that nobody could tell just what had happened that night, or even whether the man with the gun had been Kenneth Brock, because the lighting was too poor and there were too many discrepancies among the witnesses.

Finally, Jacobs got all his evidence in. He had been working carefully, slowly, without attracting attention. It all depended upon the jury. Would they respond to Burk's six themes, or to Jacob's one?

* * *

Jacobs rested his case.

Shortly after that, Burk rested too.

And with that, the jurors had heard all they were going to hear on the issue of Kenneth Brock's guilt or innocence.

There was one person, of course, who had been present the night of the homicide who was not called to the witness stand. That person was Kenneth Brock himself. The decision not to testify was Brock's own choice; it was a right he had under the fifth amendment to the constitution, the privilege against self-incrimination. The jurors would be instructed that they could not hold it against him. For in a very literal sense, Kenneth Brock owed nothing to the State of Texas in his trial—and he did not have to testify if he did not want to.

Chapter 5

The Arguments and the Verdict

"... but if you do not so believe, or if you have a reasonable doubt thereof, you will acquit the defendant and say by your verdict not guilty."

Judge Walton was reading his instructions to the jury. Texas law required the judge to give the jury a written copy of the instructions to take to the jury deliberation room. But first, the judge had to read them out loud with the jurors present in the courtroom. This repetition gave a special emphasis to the instructions, and so did the fact that the judge was the most influential person in the courtroom.

Judge Walton had earlier recessed the trial for a day to prepare the instructions he was now reading. He knew that it was common for convictions to be reversed on appeal in Texas if so much as one sentence in the jury instructions was improperly given. Adrian Burk had known that too, and he had filed written objections to every significant part of the instructions the judge was now reading. Those objections would be the basis for a major part of his appeal, if one was needed.

Now, as Judge Walton read the law that would control the case, the jurors were listening to every word. The judge explained the three possible verdicts carefully: first, capital murder; then, murder; then "not guilty."

The end of the instructions was the part with the greatest psychological impact. The judge had written the last paragraphs of the instructions to protect the rights of the defendant to a fair trial. "In all criminal cases," Judge Walton told the jurors firmly, "the burden of proof is on the state to prove the defendant's guilt *beyond a reasonable doubt*, and this burden remains on the state throughout the trial of the case.

"The defendant is presumed to be innocent until his guilt is established by legally admissible evidence, beyond a reasonable doubt; and in case you have a reasonable doubt as to the defendant's guilt, you will acquit the defendant and say by your verdict not guilty."

Jacobs listened to these words, which he had heard literally hundreds of times before, and he thought once again how difficult they made it sound for the state to make its required proof. No matter how horrible the crime was, no matter if it was committed in front of six policemen—those words applied to this case, just as they did to any case. The judge had told the jury no less than five different times throughout the instructions that the state had the burden of proof "beyond a reasonable doubt." The jurors had been hearing those words since the beginning of the case, and in fact this was a phrase the jurors had no doubt heard all their lives. Of course, the jury instructions contained plenty of elements that the prosecution wanted, too, but none had anything like the impact of these simple, eloquent words: "And if you have a reasonable doubt, you will acquit the defendant."

Was it possible? In the face of all the evidence, could the jury really acquit this defendant?

Jacobs knew the answer to that. Certainly, the jury could acquit the defendant. He knew better than to take anything for granted. Some jurors, he knew, hear the words "beyond a reasonable doubt" and expect a proof of near-magical perfection. Some jurors come into a case from the beginning with a cast of mind that makes no evidence convincing enough. The odds seemed against it in this case, but the chances of acquittal were real and sobering.

The judge finished reading the instructions.

It was time now for jury argument.

* * *

"I believe in our system of justice," Adrian Burk told the jurors as he started his argument.

Then, almost immediately, the big defense lawyer began to tell the jurors why they should acquit Kenneth Brock.

"This case, like a lot of other cases, kind of reminds me of an iceberg," he said. "An iceberg is out there in the water and you see some of it above the water and some of it you can't see, because it's underneath the surface of the water. And some things that transpired here in this trial can be discussed and others can't." Burk gave the jurors an example of what he meant: cash had supposedly been found in the pockets of the defendant, but "this may be one of the things that's under the water, I don't know. You didn't see any cash brought in here."

Burk was arguing the case exactly the right way. When all else fails, a defense lawyer can always make points by thinking of something the prosecution could have done but didn't and then arguing that the omission creates a reasonable doubt as to the defendant's guilt. Here, since the cash hadn't been brought in and put into evidence, it might not exist; and who could be sure, the inference went, that the entire prosecution case wasn't the same way? Of course, the argument was fatuous—there always has to be some item of evidence somewhere that the prosecution did not produce, otherwise the trial would never end—but neither Burk nor Jacobs was foolish enough to ignore it. In a criminal case, especially a capital one, anything can happen.

And Burk had plenty of other reasons why the jury should acquit Kenneth Brock, in case they didn't like his first one.

"I think and I submit to you that they are wrong in their identification," he told the jury. "They have no earthy idea whether that's the gun or not. . . . When they came in and told you that they identified him from what they saw out there in that alley, I think they are asking you to believe a fairy tale. I don't think they could."

In other words, the officers had arrested the wrong man and let the real killer get away. Reasonable doubt.

And even if Kenneth Brock had been on the scene of the crime, the killing had not been intentional, said Burk. It was an accident.

"If he intended to take a life, would he have done it in front of six police officers?" Burk asked the jury in an impassioned voice. That just didn't make sense; why would Kenneth Brock throw away his "ticket to freedom?" And now, Burk's words began to tumble faster and faster as he supported this theory of accidental homicide by jumping from one piece of evidence to another:

". . . Did they rush this man in a way that caused him to move suddenly, that caused Mr. Sedita to move? . . ."

". . . It occurred at night, a lot of it transpired down a dark alley. . ."

". . . The chemist told you that people that take those barbiturates and wash them down with beer and get loose—or 'stoned,' as one of the young men said—they get a glassy look in their eyes. . ."

Kenneth Brock had been jostled. He was intoxicated to the point of stumbling, moving on unfamiliar terrain, carrying a cheap flimsy weapon, frightened by police officers who were pressuring him beyond endurance, and he had been jostled and the gun had gone off. That was Burk's theory of the case. And as the big defense lawyer went on with the reasons for it, his argument became disjunctive, almost kaleidoscopic, to accommodate every bit of testimony he could remember: "The size of the two people. . . The light pull on the trigger. . . Maybe they rushed. . . Such an apprehension in this man's mind. . . that the gun discharged. . . ."

All the argument had to do to succeed was to create a reasonable doubt. When one listened to it, it seemed irresistibly persuasive.

And then, in his conclusion, the impassioned defense attorney pulled out all the stops.

" I have appreciated this opportunity to speak on behalf of Kenneth. I love him. *I love him.* You don't know him as I do, and I say that to you from the bottom of my heart."

There was not a trace of insincerity in Burk's voice. He was a man who lived his religion. He loved Kenneth Brock because he was another human being. But it was more than that: Adrian Burk knew Kenneth Brock, knew him better, by now, than many people know their friends. He loved him because he knew him. And he saw the machinery of justice, all of the police officers and prosecutors, arrayed against this one little defendant, trying to take everything he had: his freedom, even his life. He loved him because he was a man, a friend, an underdog. And he was committed at a visceral level to his defense. He wasn't just saying it; everyone could tell. Adrian Burk truly loved Kenneth Brock.

"You are going to be asked to return a verdict that could take this man's life from him," Burk went on. "I ask you to do one thing. . . that when you go back and you reach your verdict, that you speak for divine guidance and you ask His help in arriving at your verdict. And when you do that, I will be satisfied and grateful.

"Thank you."

With that, Adrian Burk ended his argument. He was emotionally drained. He sat down, heavily, and stared forward.

* * *

This argument had been exactly the type that was most likely to save Kenneth Brock from a capital murder conviction.

There was much in the argument that was questionable, even extravagant. It had rambled for the better part of an hour, and it was not likely to win any prizes in a debating society. But no one could fail to appreciate that a human being with protected legal rights was on trial after Burk's summation. And no one could avoid doubt on the crucial question of intentional-killing-versus-accident.

Jacobs stood up and held the sides of the podium, and he looked at the jury. Now it was his turn to speak.

"Mr. Burk has protected the rights of this defendant," he said. "I don't think there's any question about that. . . . And I think that's good. . . . Because I think we all know that nobody is going to be dragged into court and have any of their rights taken from them."

And then Jacobs started telling the jurors why the homicide was not an accident.

He argued the point the same way he had put in his evidence: by a painstaking and complete recitation of all the facts in the case. He reminded the jurors what Kenneth Brock had done. And when he had finished, the deliberateness of the killing stood out in bold relief.

Kenneth Brock had circled the store, looking. "I wonder how many times he drove around that store, planning his opportunity," Jacobs said. Brock had had his girl friend, Cynthia Morales, prepared for the escape. "He's got his getaway car out there. He's got somebody to drive it, and the motor is running and the lights are on and it's ready to go." Brock had pointed a gun at the people in the store and told them to lie down on the floor. That was "so nobody would think anything was wrong."

Kenneth Brock had planned the robbery, and he had planned to escape.

Brock had not even left the manager in the store when the robbery was completed. Instead, he had deliberately kidnapped the manager and calculatedly held him hostage. And then the killer had done something that spelled out his intent clearly. "Sergeant Hogg drove up in his car and got out, and he saw that it was a Houston policeman," Jacobs said. "And we knew right then that he was willing to do anything to get away, he would do anything to get away. Because he shot at Sergeant Hogg, a Houston policeman in full uniform coming toward him with a gun."

And what had Kenneth Brock done next, coldly and intentionally? Jacobs reminded the jurors that he had put Michael Sedita in a position where he was likely to be killed, by shoving him directly into the line of fire.

Deliberate act was piled on deliberate act as Jacobs recounted the evidence. The defendant had pulled the trigger with the gun squarely against Michael Sedita's chest, because the wound was a contact wound. It had gone through the victim's main heart artery. Kenneth Brock had held the pistol almost exactly perpendicular to Sedita's chest, because the trajectory through the thoracic cavity was nearly perfectly horizontal. The police officers had been taken by surprise by the killing, but Kenneth Brock had not, because he had crossed a ditch, scaled a six-foot chain-link fence, and disappeared in the woods before the officers could gather their wits to shoot. And the killer had nearly gotten away. Because it was by chance that a man in a truck had spotted him crawling on his stomach across the road.

Jacobs digressed a moment to express the indignation he felt such a deliberate crime should evoke. For Michael Sedita, he reminded the jurors, had been a human being. Sedita "had some rights too, and he never got a chance to have a trial."

Before murdering the storekeeper, Kenneth Brock had even announced his intentions for the whole world to hear. "He told them, 'Get out of my way or I'll kill him.' " Then, standing there where his getaway driver had left him, without any transportation, knowing that he could not escape— there were "helicopters, cars, officers all over the place"—Kenneth Brock knew what he had to do. And what he tried almost worked, Jacobs reminded the jury. "Because all the officers knew Mr. Sedita, and what do they do? They went running over to Mr. Sedita to help him, and that gave this man over here a few seconds, the time he needed to jump into those woods." Even when he was arrested, he was deliberate. "*I shot the store owner,*" he had blurted out.

"He killed him for the time he needed," Jacobs said. "And Mr. Burk talked about that—he stood there a minute, and why would he throw away his ticket to freedom? Well, he did it with this gun here." Jacobs even used Burk's own metaphor as he drove the point about Kenneth Brock home: His ticket to freedom? He used it; he cashed it in. "He cashed his ticket in!"

* * *

At 3:38 p.m., the jury retired to deliberate.

At 5:16 p.m., one hour and thirty-seven minutes later, the jury foreman sounded a buzzer and signaled that the deliberations had reached an end.

"Mr. Foreman," said the judge when the jurors had been assembled in the courtroom, "Have you reached a verdict?"

"We have, your honor," replied the foreman.

He handed the verdict sheet and instructions to the bailiff, who handed it to the judge.

* * *

The sound of a jury buzzer evokes a primal reaction in a trial lawyer. It makes his heart pound, his adrenalin pump, and his sweat glands work. Twelve people—twelve strangers—have life or death power over his case, a case that the trial lawyer has nurtured like his own child. They are about to exercise that power. The lawyer's reaction is involuntary, learned from the earliest leanings toward his profession, enhanced during years of law school training, and honed to a powerful edge by every triumph or defeat in a jury trial. Pavlov taught his dogs to expect food at the sound of a bell, and their reaction soon was unconscious and uncontrollable; the lawyer's reaction when a jury returns is just as deeply ingrained.

But for some reason, court personnel—the bailiff, the reporter, the judge—do not share the lawyer's urgency. Maybe it is because they are neutrals. They neither win nor lose. Come on, come on, Jacobs was thinking; and from where he sat, Adrian Burk felt the same mixture of excitement, doubt, suspense and dread. Do they send bailiffs to a special school to learn deliberateness in returning a jury verdict? Do judges study how to make the lawyers squirm by announcing it as slowly as possible?

But of course it wasn't so. The courtroom wasn't really moving in slow motion; it just seemed that way. The lawyers struggled to keep their composure. Their dignity. Their poker faces. Or at least, not to display too prominently the consuming self-doubt that is characteristic of the breed at this emotional moment of truth.

True to form, Judge Walton was slow and contemplative. True to form, he was slower—*much* slower—even than most judges. He inspected the verdict sheet carefully, holding it with both hands directly in front of his eyes. Everyone in the courtroom sat on the edge of his chair—except the jurors, who looked tired, frustrated, aged years by the process. Then, at last, the judge read the blank the foreman had signed. It said, "We, the jury, find the defendant, Kenneth Albert Brock, guilty of the offense of capital murder, as charged in the indictment."

* * *

Jacobs had won the case for the prosecution. That is, if anyone ever wins in a capital case. In this difficult moment, the prosecutor always thinks of the victim, and now, Jacobs remembered Michael Sedita, and the autopsy, and the poor man's exploded aorta. And he realized that he had won—nothing, really.

Besides, the verdict didn't end anything. The trial was just beginning. Next, there would be the penalty hearing—in which the jury would decide whether the death penalty should be imposed, or life imprisonment instead. And so even if it was possible to win a capital case, Jacobs had not won anything. Not yet. The lawyers would now begin a battle of words, for the hearts of the jury, using the limited tools of the law and the evidence, fighting with primitive energy on both sides—over Kenneth Brock's life or death.

Chapter 6

The Penalty Hearing

Adrian Burk's client had been convicted of capital murder.

That meant that Kenneth Brock was facing the death penalty.

The next step was the penalty hearing. The jurors would hear additional evidence, receive additional instructions from the judge, and hear jury arguments from the lawyers about the sentence. It was, in effect, a new and separate trial—a trial about whether Kenneth Brock should get the death penalty.

At the end of the penalty hearing, the jury would have to answer the questions required by the Texas capital murder statute. Was the killing deliberate or premeditated? Was there a probability that the killer, Kenneth Brock, would be so violent in the future as to be a continuing threat to society? Those were the life-or-death questions.

Today, the statute requires a third question. Taking into account all the evidence of "the offense, the defendant's character . . . and [his] personal moral culpability," the jury must decide "whether . . . there is a sufficient mitigating circumstance . . . to warrant that a sentence of life imprisonment rather than a death sentence be imposed."

In other words, the law now requires that the jury actually decide between life and death, at least when there is mitigating evidence. But in Brook's time, only the first two questions applied to him.

If the jurors answered "No" to either question, Kenneth Brock would be sentenced to life imprisonment. Adrian Burk would have saved him from the death penalty.

But if the jurors were satisfied beyond a reasonable doubt that the answer to both questions was "yes," Kenneth Brock would be sentenced to death.

The case was a long way from being over, in other words. The hardest part was just beginning.

For Adrian Burk, it meant tremendous pressure. He had felt pressure, of course, during the trial on guilt or innocence, but it was nothing like the pressure now that the penalty hearing was about to begin. He knew that Jacobs would argue that the death penalty was the only proper and just sentence in the case. With equal conviction, Burk believed that Kenneth Brock's life deserved saving, and he intended to save it. He started fighting toward that goal with all of his skills, all of his strength, and all of his love for this misfit, underdog friend of his who was on trial.

Burk knew that his best chance to prevent a sentence of death would be to stop the prosecutor from proving that Kenneth Brock would be prone to future violence. That was the most difficult question the jury would have to decide.

Jacobs was certainly ready to go forward with his proof on that issue. He had his witnesses present, sitting outside the courtroom. There was Jean Pace, whom Brock had robbed the day before the murder of Michael Sedita. There was Warren Nettles, whom Brock had stabbed and nearly killed, senselessly, nine days before killing Sedita. And there were others: a probation officer and a deputy district clerk, to testify about Kenneth Brock's criminal record.

Adrian Burk knew that if the jury heard this evidence, their reaction would be to find that Kenneth Brock was a violent man, if they were sensible. He knew, therefore, that he had to prevent the jury from hearing this evidence.

And so Burk called upon the tool that he had used so well during the guilt-innocence phase of trial: the rules of evidence, which could be used to exclude testimony from the jury.

One of the rules of evidence in Texas was a rule against "extraneous offenses." Previous offenses had to be kept hidden from the jury, this rule said, unless they were directly relevant to an issue the jury would have to answer. This "extraneous offense" rule was the obvious one for Burk to use to object to Jacobs' evidence. Of course, Jacobs would argue that the previous offenses were directly relevant to the defendant's propensity to violence and therefore admissible. Burk would simply have to persuade the judge otherwise.

Knowing what was coming, Burk acted quickly. Before the jury was even brought into the courtroom to hear the penalty evidence, Burk made a motion to the court to exclude Jacobs' evidence. No witness should be permitted to testify about "extraneous offenses," he argued. In fact, the prosecutor should be ordered not even to ask questions about them in the presence of the jury.

Judge Walton listened to Burk's motion and was frankly uncertain how to rule on it. If he let the jury hear Jacobs' evidence, Judge Walton knew he would be courting a reversal of the conviction if the Texas Court of Criminal Appeals disagreed with him; and a reversal would mean that the entire process, from jury selection on, would have to be done all over again. But if the judge excluded the evidence, he would be hiding from the jurors information that they needed to reach an intelligent decision on the crucial issue.

Finally, the judge decided to hear all the evidence by himself before making a ruling. He would conduct a dry run of the whole penalty hearing before he let the jury hear anything.

* * *

"Would you state your name for the court, please, ma'am?" Jacobs asked his first witness in this unusual hearing before Judge Walton.

"Jean Pace," said the witness.

Jean Pace had been a clerk at another convenience store—a different one from the one where Michael Sedita had worked. She told the judge how Kenneth Brock had robbed her, the day before Sedita's murder.

"I looked up and this guy was coming around the counter at me with a gun," she said. "He came around the counter and grabbed me and pulled the money out of the register."

Kenneth Brock had gotten away with forty-seven dollars that time.

When Jacobs had finished examining Jean Pace, Burk cross-examined her. He asked her how many times she had been robbed.

"Three times," was the witness' answer. Understandably, she said she no longer worked for the Southland store chain.

Brock had known exactly what he was doing and had been cold and deliberate. "He didn't say anything to anybody in the store and he had the gun to my neck," said Jean Pace.

The second witness was Warren Nettles.

"It happened real fast," Nettles said. "And unexpectedly. And he stabbed me in the right chest, and I shoved him, and he come back at me two or three other times. I don't remember if I had four or five stab wounds."

Nettles described how it had come to pass that Kenneth Brock had attempted to murder him. Brock had been "hanging around several people and trying to sell quaalude." Quaaludes were "downers;" they were pills similar to barbiturates. The assault was unprovoked, Nettles explained. Even Burk's cross examination brought out no reason for it. "He had been hounding me, more or less, and several other people in there," the witness said. "I even bought him a glass of wine to keep him off me. I had gone into the rest room and he followed me back there. I played him a game of pool just to satisfy him. He was too drunk to play, and I turned around from the pool table and had stepped over to the bar, and I just felt something behind me."

"All right," said Judge Walton to Jacobs. "In the interest of time, I will inquire of state's counsel, do you have any authority that you rely on in the proffer of this matter of extraneous offenses?"

From the way he asked the question, Jacobs sensed that the judge was going to exclude the evidence.

Jacobs told the judge his position: evidence of violence was directly relevant because violence was the issue that the capital murder statute required the jury to resolve.

Burk's answer to that was short. "And I would say to the court, your honor, that this man's rights would be violated if it was shown to the jury."

"Well," said Judge Walton, "the court is going to sustain the defense motion to suppress the matter of extraneous offenses."

This ruling cut the heart out of the prosecution's case. The jury would not know about Kenneth Brock's other crimes when they deliberated on his sentence. Once again, the life-or-death issue had been reduced to a game with abstract rules, like a game of chess, and Burk had won a significant point that might well be checkmate.

Burk, of course, was only doing his job—the difficult, unpopular and important job that society and the court had assigned to him. And he was doing it properly, and well. The rules of evidence are set up not only to search for the truth; also, they bend over backwards to be fair to a criminal defendant. That was part of the purpose of the rules. If they tilted in favor of the defendant, the tilt wasn't accidental. It was built in, by the law. To Jacobs, the result seemed unfair to the state, unfair to the people, unfair to the victim, and unfair to the jurors who would have to decide how much protection to give to Kenneth Brock's possible future victims; and now they would be partially blindfolded. What better, more relevant evidence could there be? But from Burk's perspective, it was a question of equal justice. The rules were written to ensure a fair trial to every criminal defendant, whether rich or poor—and yes, whether innocent or guilty. Hiding the truth? If so, that's what the rules required. They ought to be enforced equally, no matter what the consequences were. And *that*—that, of course, was exactly what Adrian Burk was appointed to do. He was properly doing his job.

* * *

Jacobs went ahead with the evidence he had left.

The court's ruling only applied to offenses for which Kenneth Brock had not been tried and convicted. In other words, Jacobs could still show the jury about any instance in which Brock had actually been convicted. There was only one conviction: Kenneth Brock had pled guilty in 1967 to the offense of burglary with intent to commit theft. Jacobs called the deputy district clerk to the witness stand and introduced the judgment and sentence into evidence before the jury. At Jacobs' request, the clerk told the jury what sentence the defendant had served: "He was given five years in the Texas Department of Criminal Justice. And it was suspended, and he was given five years probation."

This was not very persuasive evidence of Kenneth Brock's propensity toward violence.

And it became even less persuasive when Adrian Burk cross-examined the deputy clerk about the meaning of the sentence.

Burk made sure the jury knew that the "suspending" of the sentence meant that Kenneth Brock was not actually sent to prison. And he made sure the jury knew that the probation had not been revoked. That meant that Brock had served the probationary period without incident. The conviction had been seven years ago, and during that seven years, Brock (according to Burk) had been a good citizen. At the end of the probationary period, the probation and the conviction had been dismissed, as Texas law required when the probation was not revoked. Burk made sure the jury knew the case had been dismissed. He even pointed out that the dismissal meant that Kenneth Brock "got all his civil rights back" and "could vote."

By the time he had finished, Burk had accomplished something almost unbelievable. He had turned this burglary conviction into the equivalent of a good-conduct medal for his client.

Jacobs went on to the next part of his evidence. He would be allowed to present "character" witnesses against Kenneth Brock.

And his first character witness was none other than Jean Pace, the storekeeper whom Brock had robbed.

The irony of the situation was obvious to everyone but the jurors, and it had been carefully kept from them under the strangely careful conditions required by the rules of evidence. It came down to this: Jean Pace would be allowed to testify that Kenneth Brock had a bad reputation, but she would not be allowed to testify to the facts that gave cause to that reputation—the fact that he had robbed her, for instance. Before calling Jean Pace to the witness chair, Jacobs had carefully "prepped" her, and he had cautioned her not to say anything about the robbery. If she did, the judge would have to grant a mistrial, and the case would have to be started all over again, because the jury would know the truth about Kenneth Brock —but like a contaminated laboratory experiment, they would have been tainted by an external influence prohibited by the necessary sanitary conditions that ensured the result. The Rules of Evidence.

Even the question Jacobs had to ask Jean Pace was almost comical. Its ludicrous wording was required by the complicated law of Texas evidence. Jacobs had prepped the witness about the questions he would ask, too, because he knew that they frequently caused witnessed to stare in confusion.

"Jean," Jacobs asked, "will you tell the jury, based upon your one meeting with the defendant, Kenneth Brock, do you know his reputation in the community in which he lives for being a peaceful and law abiding citizen?"

Yes, answered the witness, she did indeed know that reputation.

"Is that reputation good, or is it bad?"

"Bad."

That was as far as Jacobs could go. He hoped that the jurors could read between the lines. Jacobs called three other character witnesses, each of whom had been a victim of, or a witness to, a violent offense by Kenneth Brock. Each time he was limited to the sterile "reputation" question he had asked Jean Pace.

Then he rested his case in the penalty hearing.

It was not exactly overwhelming proof. All the jury had heard from the state in the penalty phase of trial was four witnesses who testified vaguely that Kenneth Brock had a bad character, plus a deputy clerk who told about a suspended sentence for a non-violent crime seven years ago.

And now it was time for the defense to present its case on the penalty issue. And the defense lawyer was ready to bury the State's evidence.

* * *

Unlike the prosecutor, Adrian Burk had plenty of evidence that he would be allowed to have the jury hear. He started by calling the defendant's sister, a young woman named Linda Brock. She obviously was a nice person, who cared about her brother, and she made a good appearance before the jury.

Burk started by having Linda Brock give the jurors a picture of Kenneth Brock's home life. It was a picture designed to elicit sympathy from the hardest of hearts.

"My daddy was an alcoholic and my mother had to support seven children by herself," Linda Brock told the jury.

Kenneth Brock, said Linda, was the product of a broken home. His mother had divorced her father, and had remarried, and that had not worked out either. Little Kenneth had at first been "attentive" to his school work, but his father had mistreated him and even ordered him to leave home, and that had made it hard for him to stay in school.

That was when Kenneth Brock had been driven to alcohol and drugs.

Drugs, Linda said, were something that made little Kenneth into "a different person." It was not really his fault, either. "When he is smoking joints and he takes a pill, it takes over him and he doesn't know what he's doing."

Burk was making points, and he was not about to stop here. What he did next was nearly unbelievable from the perspective of the technical, sterile rules of evidence; but, in keeping with Burk's flamboyant style, it was skillful lawyering.

"I'm going to ask that the bailiff please bring in Mr. Brock's other five sisters," said the defense attorney. "The five Brock sisters, Nancy, Alma, Debra, Elizabeth, and Rhonda."

The prosecutor suddenly realized what Burk wanted to do was to line up the five girls, dressed in their Sunday best, to show the jury what a nice family Kenneth Brock had and how much they loved him.

Jacobs objected to this unusual procedure. In the first place, it was not evidence; and in the second place, it was not relevant to anything but sympathy, and the jury would be instructed that it was supposed to decide the case "without bias or sympathy." But Judge Walton, mindful of what was at stake, overruled the objection. He was not going to stand in the way of Kenneth Brock's defense, even if the prosecutor thought it took on the dimensions of a dog-and-pony show. In a death penalty case, who is to say what is relevant? Who is to say what is true and what is illusion?

When the five sisters, looking innocent and demure, had been exhibited to the jury, Burk turned to Linda Brock, who was still on the witness stand. "Do all these five girls work?" he asked her.

"All but the two youngest ones," replied Linda Brock.

Linda Brock set the tone for the entire defense in the penalty hearing. Burk also called as witnesses Kenneth Brock's mother, a lady with whom Kenneth Brock had lived as a youth ("Kenneth always puts his arms around me and kisses me"), and a friend of Brock's who described his appearance on the day of the murder ("He was messed up on tuinals. . . . His eyes were glassy and he was kind of stumbling around and he just wasn't himself. . . .").

Burk had done a good job. An excellent job. It was unorthodox, maybe; but then again, maybe not, because nearly every successful death penalty defense appears flamboyant, emotional, and undisciplined—and unorthodox. The defense must, absolutely must, tap into the human factor. Burk had touched all of the right buttons. At times, Jacobs had objected; at times, he had protested. A few times, he had blinked in disbelief at Burk's extravagance. His showmanship. But he had to admit, the whole picture was extraordinarily effective. Sympathetic—and human. And when he thought about it carefully, Jacobs had tremendous respect for the defense lawyer. If I were defending a man convicted of capital murder, he thought, I hope I'd have the inventiveness, the determination, and the guts to do the same kind of job for my client. And I wonder what the jury will do, now!

* * *

The courtroom filled rapidly after Burk rested his case. Now would come the explosive moment that the entire trial had been inching toward from the beginning.

The attorneys would pull out all the stops as they gave their jury arguments. In the words of the Texas capital murder statute, these would be arguments "for and against the sentence of death."

A few of the spectators knew what to expect, because they had seen capital cases before. They knew that the defense lawyer would not dwell on the evidence in the case very heavily; instead, he would spend most of his time denouncing the death penalty as capricious, unfair, discriminatory, brutal, totalitarian, irrevocable, final, and ungodly. In fact,the defense lawyer would refer to the act of "burning" or "frying" or "pulling the switch on" his client instead of just calling it the "death penalty." The prosecutor would counter all this by eulogizing the victim, invoking the rights of law-abiding citizens, characterizing the death penalty as a form of societal self-defense, and talking about "saving the life" of the defendant's "next victim."

These kinds of arguments were to be expected, because experience showed they were effective in capital cases.

Burk stepped before the jury. And he did not disappoint any of the spectators, as he stepped almost immediately into his role.

"You have got to approach this with a serious, prayerful manner," he told the jurors, "because you are going to be asked by the State of Texas to pull the electric switch on this man."

He even gave the jurors a step-by-step chronology of an execution. "What takes place when a man is condemned? . . . First he is given a shower. . . . [They] strap him in the electric chair, shave your head, and run twenty-five hundred volts or however many volts of electricity through your body until a doctor comes in there. And after your body has cooled off, he places a stethoscope and determines you are dead, and you are taken out another door."

Warming to his subject, Burk had a great deal more to say about the death penalty.

". . . It's unfair. And it's unfair from this standpoint: . . . you don't see any rich people getting the electric chair."

". . . Two thousand years ago, they were throwing Christians to the lions."

". . . Five hundred years ago, pickpockets were hanged in public, just drug out and hung from any sapling or tree that would hold them."

". . . There is a thin veneer that separates you and me and us and this man here and everybody in this world from being savages, and we call that thin veneer civilization and Christianity."

". . . I'm not concerned with your acting like a lynching mob, but I'm pointing out for you . . . if you give him the death penalty, there can be no appeal from the fact that he got the death sentence."

It was going to be a difficult summation for Jacobs to follow.

But the prosecutor, too, stepped into his expected role.

"I guess I should have brought the family of Michael Sedita in here and let them cry for you," said Jacobs. "But I knew that wasn't necessary. And he had friends and loved ones, too, but we don't get to see them. We don't get to hear about them. But they have to live with the fact that Michael Sedita had his life taken from him by this defendant over here without a trial, without a jury. Taken from him by this defendant over here without cause."

Jacobs was well aware that the main question the jury would have to answer was the one concerning the "probability" of the defendant's future violence. Was that probability such that it would make the defendant a "continuing threat to society?" A great deal of Jacobs' evidence on this issue had not been heard by the jury. It was excluded by the rules of evidence. But as Jacobs began to argue on the point, it became clear that there was also a great deal of evidence about violence that the jury had in fact heard.

And as his argument progressed, Jacobs built a convincing case based on that evidence.

First, there was the burglary offense. The defendant had broken into someone's house with intent to steal. It showed a contempt for the law and created a situation with high potential for violence. Kenneth Brock had been put on probation, given another chance, but he did not reform. That was clear, because it was after the burglary offense that the character witnesses had known him.

The character witnesses were a second indication. Not a single person had had anything good to say about Kenneth Brock. Every one of them knew him, and every one had said he was a violent person. One of them, Jean Pace, had met him in a convenience store, where she worked, on one occasion, and she said that he was not a "peaceful, law-abiding citizen." Jacobs walked right up to the line: he couldn't tell the jurors about the robbery, but he could talk about the character evidence — and he could hope, as he stayed within the rules, that the jury would figure it out. And the defendant's own sister had said that he was a regular user of drugs, and that they changed him into "a different person," a violent one. Given the pervasive availability of drugs, did that not make him a threat to society?

The killing of Michael Sedita had been deliberate, execution-style murder. It had started with the endangering of the lives of several innocent people. Kenneth Brock had pointed a gun at them and told them to lie on the floor. Then he had shot at, and tried to kill, a Houston police officer just because he was trying to stop a robbery and kidnapping. Finally, rather than surrender, Kenneth Brock had shredded Michael Sedita's aorta and left him to bleed to death in the middle of the road, for no other reason than to create a momentary diversion. What more did it take to show a man who was a "continuing threat to society?" What other kind of person would do that?

The answer to the penalty questions was yes, Jacobs said. The penalty hearing evidence, taken together with the evidence about the offense, justified the death penalty. "Vote it. Not only the testimony cries out for it, the facts cry out for it and that wasted life cries out for it. Let me leave you with one thought and then I will let you get on with your verdict. I don't read the Bible much, but when you get to the first chapter in the Bible, it says there: 'Whomsoever sheddeth man's blood, by man shall his blood be shed.'. . . I don't know what else we can do, but I do know this: if we don't live up to the laws and rules of society, then there's no hope at all for this society. And one of those rules is, 'Thou shalt not kill.' Tell them, people on the jury. Tell everybody out there that from this day forward, 'thou shalt not kill.'"

The atmosphere in the courtroom was tight and strained when, at 4:22 in the afternoon, the jury retired to deliberate on Kenneth Brock's life or death.

* * *

At 6:15 p.m. a note came out of the jury room, signed by the foreman: "What would be the ruling or result if we cannot reach agreement on one of the issues?"

Jacobs read this note, and his heart sank. It meant that the jury was divided. It was the prelude to a hung jury. The case would have to be tried all over again from the beginning. A retrial might well cost the people of this State a million dollars, counting everything, and it was frustrating to think of the positive things such an amount could be used for; but the cost was the least of Jacobs' worries. When there is a horrible murder case, it should be resolved. Whether the resolution is a sentence of life imprisonment, or the death penalty, or whatever, this case should not have to wait another year or two before another trial could be held. And before the decade-long sequence of appeals could begin. But quite properly, the jury could not consider those kinds of questions. That would distract them from their duty, under the law, which was to "render a true verdict." And so under the law, the judge could not answer the jury's question at all.

All the judge could do was to have the jury brought into the courtroom and give them a written order saying, "You are directed to continue your deliberations in accordance with the court's original charge." Burk, ever mindful of his possible appeal, filed a written objection to even this apparently innocuous communication, on the ground that it was "coercive of a verdict." It was his job to fight, to be loyal to his client, to avoid ever giving in.

The minutes stretched by and became hours.

At 8:00 p.m., the buzzer sounded. The jurors had reconciled their differences. The bailiff announced that they had reached a verdict.

A few of those watching had left. But the room was still full of spectators.

They tried to guess at the verdict as the jurors filed in. It was a life imprisonment verdict, most of them thought. The note they had sent out could only mean that several of the jurors had strong doubts, and it would be easier for those jurors to persuade the others that their view was reasonable than to be persuaded, themselves, toward the harsher verdict. But a veteran probation officer saw the jury come in, and he offered a different insight. "They had their faces down and their chins on the ground," he said. "I knew they had given him the death penalty."

The judge studied the verdict for what seemed an eternity.

Then he read the questions and the jurors' answers.

"Do you find from the evidence beyond a reasonable doubt that the conduct of the defendant, Kenneth Albert Brock, that caused the death of the deceased was committed *deliberately and with the reasonable expectation that the death of the deceased or another would result?*

"To which the jury answered, 'Yes.'"

Everyone waited. That was the "deliberateness" question, and maybe it was the easier of the two questions to answer. The next question, the "violence" question, would tell the story.

The judge read it. "Do you find from the evidence beyond a reasonable doubt that there is a probability that the defendant, Kenneth Albert Brock, would commit criminal acts of violence that would constitute a continuing threat to society?

"To which the jury answered, 'Yes.'"

The jurors looked straight ahead, soberly, or at the judge, or down at their feet. They were exhausted. Once the judge released them, several of them wept.

In accordance with the jury's verdict, Judge Walton directed Kenneth Albert Brock to stand.*

"Under the law, and under the jury's verdict, I fix your sentence at Death."

---

* The following names in this chapter were changed, without alteration of the incidents in which the persons were involved: Jean Pace, Warren Nettles.

Chapter 7

The Aftermath

When the judge first announced that the jury had answered "Yes" to each of the penalty questions, Linda Brock had not understood what that meant. But when the judge pronounced the death sentence from the bench, she began to scream and had to be removed from the courtroom. It was, in fact, the second time that that had been necessary: the first had been when she had interrupted Jacob's final argument in the penalty hearing with cries of "Stop it! Stop it!" until a bailiff had had to take her by the arm and lead her to the hall. The Brock family had been miserable throughout the trial. Quite understandably, they were miserable over the sentence.

Adrian Burk, tough old fighter that he was, was shaken by it too. But Burk, with a courage that was in character with his conduct of the defense, walked over and shook Jacobs' hand. And he did not by any means give up after the verdict. He engaged another lawyer on the appeal, and he worked to get the sentence overturned.

For Burk's services during the trial, Judge Walton approved a fee in excess of $8,000, to be paid by Harris County since Brock was indigent. But lest it appear that he made money on the case, it should immediately be added that that sum was small in relation to the energy, skill and time that the big defense lawyer had devoted to the case. Later, Adrian Burk became the general counsel to the Houston Oilers football team. He almost certainly lost time and treasure from his practice because of his representation of Kenneth Brock. In many ways, it was a thankless task; and certainly there was no adequate compensation for the pressure he went through over the trial and verdict.

George Jacobs continued his duties as a prosecutor in the District Attorney's Office. In a few months, he would try another capital case, another robbery-murder—the killing of an eighty-year-old woman who was bludgeoned to death in her own home with a pipe. As far as the Kenneth Brock case was concerned, Jacobs had felt throughout the trial that a sentence of death was the only just resolution. Now that the verdict had come in, he had a curious feeling: it was not an occasion for rejoicing, or for satisfaction, or for congratulation, but it was an event that did give a sense that some justice had been salvaged from a sorry situation. He spent the next day, and most of the next week, answering a flood of telephone calls from people who believed the restoration of capital punishment was necessary, and who complimented him on a job well done.

For Judge Walton, the trial of the Brock case had been a burden. It had been a long trial; his docket had done nothing but increase. If every case took as long, he would be able to handle only eight or ten of them a year. The judge went back to work, in earnest, on his docket.

For Kenneth Brock, the verdict meant the distinction of being sentenced to death under the Texas capital murder statute.

A few weeks after the verdict, Brock was transferred to Huntsville, Texas, and incarcerated on death row. It would take years for the process of appeal to run its course, and during that time he would be held there. If the Texas Court of Criminal Appeals did not reverse his conviction and sentence, his lawyers would undoubtedly take the case to the Supreme Court; and all things considered, the question whether Kenneth Brock would die in the electric chair was still very much in doubt. After the appeals, his lawyers would start all over again, by bringing arcane kinds of lawsuits under the habeas corpus statutes, starting first in the same state court where he was convicted, and appealing to the highest state court, then filing a similar suit in the federal courts, and appealing yet again to the Supreme Court—and then, probably, if they lost, starting over again with new habeas corpus claims, in a repeated loop that sometimes seemed endless from the vantage point of the state's lawyers. But to those later-loop defense lawyers, the habeas claims would seem like scary, heart-pounding brinksmanship, as they sought stay after stay and tried to keep their client alive. That is, if the case ever got that far. Maybe one of the many courts that would review the case would reverse the conviction, or reduce the sentence; maybe the governor would commute it to life. Whatever happened, it would take years. Maybe it would take decades.

Perhaps for that reason, the defendant showed little emotion at the verdict and none at his sentencing. When someone suggested that he should invite George Jacobs to his execution, Kenneth Brock just nodded his head and smiled.

* * *

Kenneth Brock's victims did not fare nearly so well. Warren Nettles took nearly 200 stitches to close the stab wounds Brock had inflicted on him, not to mention the operations that were necessary to repair his internal damage. His ability to lift objects and to move his body was permanently impaired. As a result of his hospitalization and his infirmity, he lost his job, his marriage and most of what he had in the world. In the space of a few seconds, Kenneth Brock had ruined Warren Nettles' life.

And in the space of an even shorter instant of time, Michael Sedita's hopes and dreams had gone down the drain. The murdered storekeeper had worked his way through college, had graduated with a business degree, and had begun what appeared to be a promising career in management with the Southland Corporation. But instead, the life he had labored so hard to build had ended for no reason in this improbable place on Surry Road by a man who had nothing to live for and nothing to lose, and a gray stone with a spray of flowers marked the final resting place of Michael Sedita.

* * *

In every state, the details of capital sentencing differ, but they all resemble the procedure in Kenneth Brock's case in their broad outlines. In Georgia, for example, the jury must consider during the penalty phase whether there is a statutory "aggravating circumstance" present, and whether circumstances favoring death outweigh those favoring life. California uses an analogous procedure.

In Florida, the judge does the sentencing. The jury renders an "advisory" sentence, favoring either life or death, which the judge normally must follow, but which he can reject in an extreme case. Florida's method is supposed to produce greater consistency and predictability. In Ohio, a panel of three judges decides the sentence. This method also may have the advantage of consistency, but the down side is that Ohio has removed the check of direct community control, represented by the jury.

All of the capital trial procedures are like Brock's case, in that they all use a separate sentencing hearing. And everywhere, the sentencing hearing allows broad admissibility of evidence but guidance of the judge or jury, narrowly, on the legal issues that control the death decision. Unlike Ohio, most states reserve a central role for the jury not only in determining guilt but in sentencing too. And so the kinds of jury argument that the prosecutor and defense lawyer used in Brock's case are normal, throughout the country.

* * *

What then, finally happened? What happened to Kenneth Brock? Was his sentence carried out?

We're going to tell you. Later in this book. It took many, many years. And it is a story with twists and turns that will surprise you. It is a story about courtroom dramas spread over a decade, with stays of execution pushed to the edge, and with skillful teams of prosecutors battling dedicated and selfless attorneys for the defense in a mind-numbing series of habeas corpus claims.

What happened to Kenneth Brock? We want to tell you, just as we want to tell you what happened to *all* of them—all of the different defendants in this book. In every case, the process was slow. Deliberate. Excruciatingly slow. Frustratingly deliberate. But probably, that is the way it has to be, the way it always will be; because no one—not even the most ardent supporter of capital punishment—wants the courts to handle these cases any way other than deliberately.

In the meantime, there are other cases. Other terrible stories, other dramatic courtroom scenes, other murders, and other verdicts. Other defendants and other trials. Each one is as fascinating, as chilling, as terrifying, as instructive, and as capable of producing insights into criminal justice as Kenneth Brock's story. We want to tell you those stories, now.

Kenneth Brock was on death row. He stayed there for years. We shall return to him; but for now, let us leave his story there.

Let us tell you, next, about John Stiles Griffin, and his strange case. And Ronald Clark O'Bryan—the defendant they called "The Candy Man."

PART TWO

The Jury and the Life or Death Decision

WE DON'T WANT to leave the impression that the Kenneth Brock case was the only kind of capital murder case in America, or even that it was a typical case.

There is no "typical" capital murder. The capital murder law was designed in the first place to apply only to murders of exceptional brutality, and nearly every case tried under it has been extraordinary in one way or another.

And since the cases defy easy categorization, it is difficult to predict the outcome in any given case. Will the jury opt for life or for death? That depends on the total picture the case presents — and it depends on the personalities of the jurors themselves.

That is what we will look at next.

First, there is the case of John Stiles Griffin. Griffin escaped from a federal prison in California and committed a series of crimes in at least two states. He committed two grisly murders — combination rape-robbery murders. He was actually a multiple-time ex-convict, and his efforts to escape from the jail where he was kept were unceasing as his trial approached. Would he be convicted on the circumstantial case the prosecution had built up? And if so, would he be sentenced to death — or to life in prison?

Ronald Clark O'Bryan's case was completely different in motive, in the method of murder, and in the personality of the killer. O'Bryan was an upper-middle-class suburbanite who had a professional career as an optician. He was deeply religious, and he had a spotless record. But with financial troubles closing in on him, he took out a policy of life insurance on his son, and then — according to the prosecution — he put cyanide in the boy's Halloween candy. During funeral services, O'Bryan sang a solo in the church for his son — after a crime in which he had sold his soul to the devil, if the prosecutors were right. The case became known as the Halloween Candy Murder case, and it received news coverage far and wide. Would the "Candy Man," as O'Bryan came to be called, be convicted, and would he be sentenced to life — or death?

79

These are two extraordinary capital murder cases, each quite different from the other.

The outcomes may not be what you would expect.

Counsel for the Prosecution

Stu Stewart "beats you fair and square, or not at all," as one lawyer put it. But even Stewart was non-plussed by the judge's pre-trial rulings in the "Brady Bunch" case.

Doug Shaver, in the trial of Gerald Bodde, presented a witness who was so fright-ened she had to be dis-missed. The witness was five years old.

Vic Driscoll told the jury that Ronald O'Bryan "sac-rificed his son not on the altar of God as Abraham might have done, but on the altar of his own greed."

The authors, George Jacobs (left) and David Crump, are shown here standing in the court-room where Richard Vargas was tried and sentenced to death.

Counsel for the Defense

"People are going to have a low regard for life if we take life," said Victor Blaine to the jury that decided Richard Vargas' fate. "... The only question is, if you don't burn him, would he do it again?"

Stuart Kinard's client, Bernardino Sierra, confessed on television to six brutal murders —one of which he committed inside the county jail. "Is the death penalty a deterrent?" Kinard asked a defense witness.

Does [Ronald O'Bryan] sound like a man who'd knock off his son for a few gold coins?" Marvin Teague asked the jury emotionally. (He also headed the defense team for Gerald Bodde.)

Al Thomas (standing) and his co-counsel, Fred Heacock, defended John Stiles Griffin, who was accused of a bloody rape-robbery murder. "I tried to put the Bible where the jury would have to see it," said Thomas. "It's a question of strategy."

Chapter 8

The Richmond Avenue Murders

It was two o'clock in the afternoon when Patricia Hixson got out of the car.

She waved goodbye as her tennis partner drove away, and she walked toward her apartment.

For pretty, 22-year-old Patricia, these April days were long and pleasant. She had been married to her husband, Walter, for just two months, and she was enjoying just being a housewife for a while. Today, for instance, was an especially beautiful, warm sunny day. She had plans to stay outdoors and make the most of it.

The plans included going bicycle riding with her good friend, Louise Ponder. Louise was going to come over this afternoon to visit. Patricia Hixson and Louise Ponder were very close. They had a lot in common: They were both newly married, they had worked together at the same job, and Louise had been a bridesmaid in Patricia's wedding.

Marriage had changed Patricia's life, but there were many parts of it that remained the same. Walter had moved into the apartment where she had lived while she was single—apartment number 144, at 5127 Richmond Avenue. There were advantages to living in the same place. For one thing, she knew her neighbors, and many of them were friends.

Now, as she climbed the steps toward her apartment, Patricia passed the window of one of her friends—a neighbor named Robin Couch. Robin looked out and saw Patricia for an instant. The two women's eyes met, and they smiled at each other.

Robin Couch had no way to know, at that moment, the significance of that brief glance.

There was nothing to direct her attention to the muscular man in his late twenties who was watching, with curious interest, as Patricia climbed the stairs. And Robin could not have realized, then, that she would be the last witness to see Patricia alive.

* * *

That had been two o'clock, when Patricia Hixson had returned to her apartment.

83

It was now 6:30.

Detective Carolyn Stephenson was sitting at a desk in the homicide division office of the Houston Police Station, finishing her paperwork. Her shift was over. It had been over since 4 o'clock. She would finally be able to leave for home, she thought, two and a half hours late—as soon as she finished this report.

"Stephenson!" she heard a voice call. It was her supervisor, Lieutenant Crittenden.

She stepped into his office.

"You got one," Crittenden said. "Go make the D.O.A. at 5127 Richmond, apartment 144."

Stephenson's shift was not ending after all. It was a double murder, Crittenden explained.

Not much was known about the case yet. The husband of one of the victims, Walter Hixson, had reported it to the police. The dead women were Patricia Hixson and Louise Ponder. The lieutenant added that it appeared a rape might have been involved. The next shift with a rape investigator had not come on yet, and so Stephenson would have to go.

Detective Stephenson was used to shifts that didn't end on time. She was a veteran of fourteen years on the force. She had come up through the ranks the hard way, starting in juvenile and working in vice, narcotics and in the city lockup. She had been assigned to homicide later, after police departments throughout the country had begun to realize the necessity of having female officers in traditional police positions. And that was also when she had earned the rank of detective.

Carolyn Stephenson certainly did not look like everyone's stereotype of a police detective. She was an attractive redheaded woman—well dressed, petite, and with delicate features. She was cheerful and feminine —so much so, in fact, that her male counterparts could address her with the words, "Hi, kid," and get away with it. But Stephenson also had something else. She had the stomach for police work.

"I like police work," she was fond of saying, "because it's not routine. Every day's a new situation." Sometimes the job got to her, but she could handle it.

And that was why she was leaving, now, for the Richmond Avenue address Lieutenant Crittenden had given her. She found herself in the company of two other veteran Houston officers, Detectives L. W. Henning and J. M. Roescher.

Carolyn Stephenson could sense it already. She had a feeling, she would later say, that the murders of Patricia Hixson and Louise Ponder were going to be "as bad a homicide scene as I've ever made."

* * *

Apartment number 144 at 5127 Richmond was moderately expensive and immaculately kept.

The floor was covered with a cheerful yellow shag rug.

It was 6:44 p.m. when Detectives Stephenson, Henning and Roescher walked in the door. They immediately saw the young man who was sitting on the floor in the living room, crying softly.

While Henning and Roescher went into the hallway and back toward the bedrooms, Carolyn Stephenson went to the young man on the floor and spoke to him. "I'm Carolyn Stephenson. I'm a detective with the Houston Police Department," she said. "What's your name?"

"Walter Hixson," the man answered, with difficulty.

Walter Hixson was holding a throw pillow in his hands. He was twisting it, wringing it, back and forth.

"I know this isn't a good time to talk to you, but I have to," Stephenson said. She paused. Then she said, "Can you help us? Can you tell us what you know?"

Walter Hixson said that he would try.

"Are you the one who reported this to the police?"

"Yes."

Haltingly, Walter Hixson told Carolyn Stephenson that he had come home from work and walked into the apartment. It had been unlocked. He had taken his coat and tie off and sat down. A moment later, when he still hadn't heard anything from Patricia, he had called her name. There had been no answer. And so he had walked back to the bedroom.

There, he had seen his wife and her friend Louise Ponder lying on the floor. There had been a lot of blood. He hadn't touched the bodies. Instead, he had come back to the living room and called the police.

"Do you know anything about who killed your wife?" Carolyn Stephenson asked quietly.

"No."

"Do you know of any reason why anyone would want to kill her?"

"No."

With that, Carolyn Stephenson went to join the other two detectives in the bedroom.

She was totally unprepared, even with all her experience, for what she saw. Patricia Hixson lay in the corner, her torso resting on a crumpled cardboard box. There was blood on the wall behind her. She was still wearing her tennis dress, but it was pulled up around her stomach.

Stephenson had her notebook out.

She wrote that the dead woman's bra "was completely soaked in blood, and detectives were unable to determine its color."

Patricia Hixson's right arm was "extended straight to the south, along and touching the west wall, palm up—hand in a fist." And Stephenson's notes went on to record a bizarre detail: "There were white shoe strings tied around the right wrist, and there was a defense wound on the right wrist."

The victim's wrists had been bound. There were constriction marks on the flesh under the strings. The attacker had been a powerful man who had tied his victims, hand and foot, while killing them. And he had kept stabbing them, and kept stabbing them, long after they were dead.

The "defense wounds" that Stephenson noted were slashes on the hands and wrists, characteristic of the wounds a person fending off a knife attack will receive. They were silent testimony to Patricia Hixson's pathetic attempts at self-preservation.

Patricia Hixson's fingernails were broken. She was riddled with red gaping holes in her arms, neck and chest.

A few feet away lay the other victim, Louise Ponder. And in the same businesslike jargon, Carolyn Stephenson described her body, too.

Louise Ponder, she wrote, "was face down, and a brown leather strap was around her neck. And what appeared to be a coat hanger was also visible around the complainant's neck."

It was not just brutal. It was incomprehensible. The attacker had circled the woman's throat with the leather strap. Then he had tightened it by twisting the coat hanger wire.

And the attacker had made sure Louise Ponder was unable to cry for help. "The complainant was gagged," Carolyn Stephenson wrote, "with 1/2 inch adhesive tape across her mouth, under her chin and up both sides of her face."

Evidently, death had come slowly for this victim. The crisscrossing straps of adhesive tape would not have been necessary otherwise.

Louise Ponder's hands were tied behind her back "with what appeared to be nylon hose at the wrists." Again, the bindings had been tightened with "a piece of what appeared to be coat hanger" wrapped around them.

And Louise Ponder had been raped.

Her attacker had left her nude from the waist down, and barefooted. Her bicycling shorts had been cut off her body. Her bra had been severed in two. Later, the medical examiner would report that there were remnants of spermatozoa in her vagina.

Her breasts were crisscrossed with rows of stab wounds, parted into ugly red semicircles.

There would never be any way to be sure exactly how it had happened, but Carolyn Stephenson thought she knew. The attacker had used some pretext to get Patricia Hixson to let him into the apartment. There had been a struggle, and he had tied her. Then, perhaps, Louise Ponder had knocked at the door.

In a frenzy, Stephenson thought, the man had killed Patricia when he heard Louise. Then he had overpowered the second woman. And, the detective thought, he had tortured and raped her. There were small, non-fatal "pick" wounds on Louise Ponder's extremities. There were burn marks on her elbows.

There was no way to know how long it had taken. Carolyn Stephenson fought to keep control of her stomach. It took three pages just to fill in the standard wound description, because Patricia Hixson had twenty-nine separate stab wounds and Louise Ponder had eleven.

Outside, the press was on the scene. The detectives stopped the photographers at the door, with cameras clicking. It took effort to keep them and the reporters from entering the apartment.

Carolyn Stephenson was disgusted. "They don't care if justice gets done," she said later. "They like it better if it isn't. It makes a better story." Right now, she just wanted to be left alone so she could do her job.

The photographers congregated outside the bedroom window. They tried to take pictures through the curtains.

Carolyn Stephenson kept writing. She described the hands of the two victims. Each of them had a gold watch, and a gold wedding band set, still in place undisturbed.

But the most surprising development in the case was yet to come.

* * *

Carolyn Stephenson was interviewing a witness — a man in uniform.

"I saw him walking around on the parking lot," the security guard said. "He looked like he was in a daze."

The security guard was talking about Walter Hixson. And what he was saying was that Hixson had been near the apartment, near the scene of the crime, during the time when the murders were probably committed. It was in conflict with Hixson's own statement, because he claimed to have been at work.

Carolyn Stephenson thought hard.

Could Walter Hixson have committed these murders?

It seemed almost inconceivable — a husband who could kill his wife, rape and kill her friend, tie them both and then pretend to know nothing after calling the police. Was it possible? But as soon as she asked herself that question, Stephenson knew the answer.

It was possible. Stranger things had happened. In more than seventy percent of homicides, the attacker and victim know each other, and a husband is often a logical suspect for the murder of his wife.

Detective Stephenson took Walter Hixson into custody.

Early the next morning, she released him. She had talked to Walter Hixson at length, and she was satisfied that he was telling the truth. Most of his afternoon could be accounted for by independent witnesses. And the officers had discovered, by now, that the killer had probably changed his own bloody clothes for clothes in the apartment, belonging to Walter Hixson. That might explain the security guard's error.

Walter Hixson was innocent.

But he had spent most of the night of his wife's murder in police custody, away from the solace of family and friends.

* * *

Carolyn Stephenson seemed to be a long way from a solution to the Richmond Avenue Murders.

There was no solid suspect and there were few leads. What was to be done?

There were at least two things the detectives knew to do immediately. They needed to cover the crime scene like a vacuum cleaner. And they needed to talk to everyone in the area who might know anything.

Shortly after the detectives had arrived, the crime scene had given up the first clue that might help to track down the killer. There was a pair of checked pants lying on the bed. Walter Hixson said they did not belong to him.

There was blood on the front of the trousers.

Maybe, Carolyn Stephenson thought, the killer had left these trousers. He would have known he could not wear them; the bloodstains were too conspicuous. He had probably exchanged them for a pair of trousers in the apartment.

And inside the trousers pocket was another lead.

It was a bus ticket—a ticket from San Diego, California, to Houston. The date was April 25. It was now April 27. It was a two-day bus ride from San Diego to Houston. The killer probably had been just passing through.

And there was something else in the pants pocket. It was a key—a key with a red tag that said "Astroworld Hotel." The Astroworld was a medium sized hotel near a giant amusement park in southeast Houston.

Perhaps the killer had been to the Astroworld, either to stay there or to break in. Perhaps someone could identify him. Detective Henning left immediately to go there, to the Astroworld, leaving Stephenson and Roescher at Richmond Avenue.

For hours, Stephenson and Roescher worked on the physical evidence. They secured and described everything they could see.

Step two was to question everyone who might have seen anything—anything at all.

Carolyn Stephenson found that witnesses around the apartment complex could add relatively little. There was only one promising lead—and it was a strange one.

A neighbor named Paul Manteris told the detectives that he had been accosted at his door by a man with a U. S. Customs identification card.

The man had asked to be admitted to Manteris' apartment, and Manteris had let him in. They had had a short conversation and the man had left. It was around 2 p.m. And the man had headed toward the Hixson apartment.

It sounded as though a Customs agent had been near the Hixson apartment. Or maybe it was someone posing as a Customs agent. That might explain how the killer had gotten inside the apartment without attracting attention.

Manteris said he thought he would be able to recognize the man if he saw him again.

Carolyn Stephenson spent six hours at the crime scene. Then she kept at work, for the rest of the night, trying to put together the parts of the puzzle. When the sun came up, and 8 o'clock rolled around, she started her next day's shift.

And she remained on the job, hour after hour, trying to solve the Richmond Avenue Murder Case. Could there be a lead to be found from the bus ticket, she wondered—the ticket from San Diego?

* * *

The San Diego Police Department gets hundreds of crime reports a day.

One of them, Carolyn Stephenson thought, might provide a link between the clues she already had and the killer she was trying to find.

Detective work is hardly glamorous. It starts with the tedious step of collecting miscellaneous facts, and it progresses into the equally tedious step of making sense out of the clues those facts provide. And so detectives spend a great deal of their time plowing through crime reports in an effort to find a common thread.

Carolyn Stephenson got on the phone to San Diego.

Hours later, it paid off. On April 25th, the date of the bus ticket, San Diego had reported a burglary in a hotel room. The victim had been a businessman named Arnold Merrill. That was significant to Stephenson, because the name "Merrill" had been found on the register of the Astroworld Hotel, corresponding to the room number on the key found in the Hixson apartment.

The killer had apparently burglarized Merrill's room in San Diego. And then he had used Merrill's identity when he had gotten to Houston.

The bus ticket. The San Diego burglary. The Astroworld key. The name on the register. The trail of the Richmond Avenue Murderer led from California to Houston. But where did it go from there?

For two days, Carolyn Stephenson's leads varied with no recognizable pattern. The description of a Chicano man furnished a possible suspect for the San Diego burglary. Was he the Richmond Avenue Murderer? Was it a bellboy from the Astroworld, or one of Louise Ponder's old boyfriends who had given her some trouble, or a drifter from Pennsylvania who was arrested near the Hixson apartments? Each of these possibilities had to be considered. But each evaporated as quickly as it appeared.

The detectives needed a break in the case.

*   *   *

When the breaks finally came, in the week following the Richmond Avenue Murders, they came as a result of chance.

The first break involved a robbery in Galveston, fifty miles to the southeast.

The homicide division got a call from a University of Houston student who had been at a fraternity party in Galveston. He had been staying overnight at a hotel, and he and one of his friends, together with their dates, had been accosted by a man with a shotgun. The man had tied them up, he said, and robbed them. The man had been frightened off by a knock at the door. He had stolen a car, some clothes and a few dollars in cash.

Might it have been the same man, the caller wondered? Since he had fit the description that had been printed in the papers for the Richmond Avenue Murders, and he had tied up all these people and gagged them, could it be the same man?

Carolyn Stephenson shuddered when she heard it. That fortuitous knock on the door had left the intruder no time to kill his victims. The students had no idea how close to death they might have been. Stephenson put Galveston on an imaginary map in her mind; and she drew a mental line, representing the path of the killer, through that city.

That was a break in the case.

But the biggest break was yet to come. It would begin with a call to the police about a man who was acting strangely inside a motel in Port Arthur, Texas, and it would end with the arrest of a man carrying the credentials of a U.S. Customs official.

It turned out that the man's name was John Stiles Griffin. And the events leading to the arrest were unusual. They began when Griffin stopped to go to the bathroom.

*   *   *

"Acid's worse than heroin when I come down off it," John Stiles Griffin said later. "So I was jumpy as hell.

"I was in the bathroom for about fifteen minutes. I was running like a horse—all jacked up."

Griffin was coming down from a very long trip. The LSD he had dropped was treated with "speed," and that gave a better high—but it also made him even more paranoid than usual. He fought, now, to keep his bearings.

He was inside a motel room in Port Arthur, Texas, going to the bathroom.

He had come here in the first place because he was in desperate need of money. He was nearly out of cash. Motels were the easiest places to get money, for Griffin, because the doors were easy to open and people from out of town generally had money lying around. But the odd thing was that he was too shaky, now, to pull it off. Besides, his bladder was bursting. The call of nature had taken precedence over his finances for the moment.

It was dangerous, he knew. The LSD was making him act strangely. The guest in this room was a woman who had opened her door in response to his knock and had let him in to use the bathroom. She was obviously frightened. What an inconvenient time to have to take a piss—!

Finally, he finished. Now, to get out of there.

But as he stepped out of the bathroom, John Stiles Griffin saw that there was a bellboy in the room with the woman. That was a bad sign. She had been frightened enough to call the motel office. That meant that she had probably been frightened enough to call the police.

John Stiles Griffin thought fast. He had not spent half his life in prisons without learning a few things. And one of those things was how to imitate police talk. He could do it so it sounded better than the cops themselves, at times.

He fingered the Customs I.D. in his pocket.

"Let me introduce myself," he said to the bellboy. "I'm with the U.S. Customs Service, and we're here on a stakeout."

He fished out the Customs I.D. and held it up. The bellboy gave a visible sigh of relief.

"You just took a load off my mind," said the bellboy. "Somebody just reported seeing somebody with a gun."

"Oh," Griffin said casually, "that was me." He had left his rifle in the bushes outside.

Almost apologetically, the woman said: "Well, I've already called the police."

That was going to mean trouble, Griffin knew. But he heard himself say, "No problem. I'll just call in and cancel it."

John Stiles Griffin had been free for a week. When he had gotten to Houston, he had been in a fog, blazing on LSD. He hardly remembered hitchhiking to Galveston, and his memory of the visit to his mother's home in Beaumont, where he had picked up the shotgun, was hazy. Now he was in Port Arthur, Texas—heading for Florida—and he needed money—

But he had to do something fast, or he was going to get arrested.

As soon as he finished retrieving his gun, he saw that the patrol car was there.

It was a good thing he had been thinking ahead.

Officer M. A. Hebert was startled to see this disheveled man, carrying a rifle, who walked out of the bushes. He looked even more surprised when Griffin showed him the Customs I.D. and told him he was a federal agent working a narcotics case.

"Please," Griffin said with authentic confidentiality, "look. Let's get away, because you're in a marked car. And it'll blow our stakeout."

Officer Hebert believed him. Griffin bent down to get in the car. He urged the officer, again, to drive away. When they got far enough away, Griffin thought, he could turn the gun on the officer if he had to. His mind raced. He could take the car. And it might be necessary to kill the cop—

Hebert drove around the corner, with Griffin in the passenger's seat. He parked the car.

Moments later, a second patrol car arrived. Then there was a third. And suddenly it became clear that Griffin's cover wasn't going to work. The other officers had to be told what was happening. Griffin kept talking. But the officers began to realize something was wrong. It was an instinct, a sixth sense—the smell of danger in an otherwise innocuous situation, born of a thousand street encounters. The officers asked Griffin where he was stationed. Who else worked out of that location? Who was with him now?

Come to think of it, why hadn't he called in to alert the locals in the first place so the stakeout wouldn't get blown? That was what Customs always did when they had a deal going down in Port Arthur. Then it developed that Griffin had never heard of the D.E.A.—the newly-formed federal Drug Enforcement Agency.

The officers weren't sure what they had. But Officer Hebert was suspicious enough, by now, to arrest John Stiles Griffin.

A day later, Carolyn Stephenson sat in the homicide office in Houston. She went over the arrest report from Port Arthur P.D.

The charge was "impersonating a federal officer."

Carolyn Stephenson turned it around in her mind. It all fit, she knew. A forged Customs I.D. badge. A muscular young man. A description identical to the one Paul Manteris had given—of the man who had shown him the I.D. and then walked toward the Hixson apartments.

And there was something else that fit.

John Stiles Griffin was an escapee from the federal correctional facility in Los Angeles, California. That was only a short distance from the city of Anaheim, California. Griffin had escaped last Monday, April 23, just a few hours before an Anaheim hotel maid had been found tied up, raped and stabbed to death. And that crime had been a carbon copy of the Richmond Avenue murders.

Carolyn Stephenson needed more evidence, though. For example, if she could match the arrested man's fingerprint to one of those found in the Richmond Avenue apartment, it would do wonders for her case.

*   *   *

"With all that adhesive tape," Carolyn Stephenson said, "You know there has to be a print somewhere." She was counting on Leblanc to find it.

L. N. Leblanc was one of HPD's best identification experts. He was fond of saying, "Finding a usable fingerprint is the exception rather than the rule." What he meant was that when prints are lifted from a crime scene, the majority of them are not suitable for identification, and the odds are high that all that will turn up among those that *are* suitable is prints of the victims themselves.

Leblanc had gone to the Hixson apartment and laboriously dusted every surface that seemed promising. He had covered the bathroom counter-tops, the doors, the knobs, the walls.

Gingerly, with a set of forceps, he had picked up those items that were moveable and brought them back to his laboratory for testing with a variety of chemicals and powders. Laboriously, one by one, Leblanc tested each of the tiny smudges he had found against the known print of John Stiles Griffin.

None of them seemed to fit.

Leblanc could get prints from improbable places, if they were there. Using a substance called Ninhydrin, he could develop them on paper surfaces. Ninhydrin reacted with fingerprint oils to produce a bright orange color pattern. There were even new techniques for bringing out fingerprints from dead human bodies.

But nothing worked.

Leblanc covered every inch of the adhesive tape that was recovered from the body of Louise Ponder. As he pushed his brush delicately across the tape surface, oval shapes appeared and flickered before his eyes. But none of the prints was usable for an identification.

Failure.

Finally, Leblanc applied his chemicals to the tape dispenser, which he had collected in a sample bag from the Hixson apartment. A piece of a print appeared.

It arched slightly, and it looked, in its basic configuration, like one of the prints that had been taken from John Stiles Griffin's right thumb after his arrest.

Would it be large enough for a comparison? It was nothing more than a scrap.

Under a microscope, Leblanc looked at the two prints — the known one from John Stiles Griffin's arrest papers, and the unknown scrap from the tape dispenser. Leblanc was looking for "points," or fingerprint char-acteristics—the small similarities that would let him say that the two prints had, or had not, been made by the same person. Fingerprint experts do not look at the overall pattern for this purpose; that is an unreliable guide for matching single prints. Instead, they looked for what they call "forks," "ridge endings," "dots," and other tiny patterns. And if they find a sufficient number of these in the same positions in the two prints, they are able to say that the two came from the same person.

Leblanc looked at the arch of John Stiles Griffin's known thumbprint, and he compared it, point by point, with the scrap he had lifted. Here was a ridge ending on the unknown scrap that matched, exactly, with the same point on John Stiles Griffin's known print. Here was a fork, and there was another ridge ending.

The similarities mounted quickly.

And a few seconds after he had begun the comparison—for it does not take a professional print examiner long—Leblanc was certain.

John Stiles Griffin, who had been in prison in California until April 23, had left his fingerprint to be found in the Hixson apartment on April 27.

He had left it on the same tape dispenser that he had used to gag Louise Ponder. It was the best evidence that could possibly have been found. John Stiles Griffin was the killer.

*   *   *

The fingerprint left no doubt whatsoever to Carolyn Stephenson. But there was a great deal more, she knew, that needed to be done. There was a large number of witnesses to interview. And it would be important to test their identifications of the subject in a properly conducted lineup.

That was why Carolyn Stephenson panicked, the day after Griffin's arrest, when she saw the picture the *Houston Chronicle* had run.

There, prominently displayed in a major Houston newspaper, was a photograph of John Stiles Griffin. The story beside it was about the Richmond Avenue Murders.

There was good reason for Stephenson's panic. She had not yet had a chance to conduct a lineup to see whether her witnesses—Paul Manteris, the people from the Astroworld, and the Galveston victims—could identify John Stiles Griffin. The fingerprint, of course, had been a milestone in her case, but she needed these eyewitnesses too.

The problem with the newspaper picture was that a lineup had to be just like a laboratory procedure. It was as delicate a process, Carolyn Stephenson knew, as a chemical test or a fingerprint identification. The reason was simple: the decisions of the United States Supreme Court required it to be. Those decisions were directly to the point and quite explicit. If the testimony of any witness was tainted by "suggestion," the testimony of that witness could not be used in court.

That was the reason, for instance, that a suspect always had to be displayed to witnesses in a group. The group had to include other people with the same general appearance as the suspect's. There could be no individual features that set the suspect apart from the others in the lineup, whether they were age, weight, height, dress, hair color or something else.

And certainly, a lineup identification by a witness who had seen this *Chronicle* picture would create problems in court. It was more than "suggestive." It identified John Stiles Griffin as the suspect.

Stephenson got Paul Manteris on the telephone. She was relieved to hear that he had not seen the photograph. "Don't even look at a newspaper today," she said emphatically.

Manteris, impressed by her insistence, agreed.

More phone calls told Stephenson that none of the witnesses had seen the picture. She breathed a sigh of relief. But she decided to hold the lineup immediately, to avoid further problems.

The lineup room was like a tiny theatre. The five men—one suspect and four stand-ins—mingled about on the stage. Ironically, several of the stand-ins were police officers wearing casual clothes; for with his husky build, short hair and clean-cut appearance, John Stiles Griffin looked more like a police officer than like anyone else available. It was customary to let the suspect choose his position in the row, and Griffin chose position number two.

The bright lights were on. An officer working the front gave commands to the five men behind the one-way glass: "Turn and face left." "Turn and face right." The process was repeated for each of the ten witnesses. And each was taken outside, individually, and asked whether he or she had seen any of the men before.

"I see him," said Paul Manteris. "It's the man in position number two."

The Galveston witnesses came out of the room, nodding their heads before Carolyn Stephenson could ask the question. Eight of the ten witnesses were positive in identifying John Stiles Griffin. They would make good witnesses in court.

But the lineup also provided examples of the fallibility of eyewitness testimony.

Two hotel workers were positive in their identifications of the men in positions 4 and 5, respectively, as the one who had rented the room under the name "Merrill." Actually, positions 4 and 5 were both filled by stand-ins—who happened to be vice officers with the Houston Police Department. The witnesses were simply mistaken. It happened sometimes.

* * *

Now came the hardest part: fitting all the details together and filling in the gaps.

Bit by bit, it all came together.

—Handwriting analysis showed that the register slip signed with the name "Merrill" at the Astroworld Hotel matched other writing by John Stiles Griffin.

—John Stiles Griffin had had a pocket knife in his possession when arrested. The medical examiner said that the murder weapon was a knife with a blade 3 to 3 1/2 inches long. That fit the red-handled pocket knife Griffin had been caught with.

—A watch found on Griffin's person at his arrest had come from the San Diego burglary.

—Various items belonging to Walter Hixson were found in the hotel room rented by Griffin. And a pair of trousers belonging to Hixson were found in the car Griffin stole and abandoned in Galveston. They could only have gotten there because he had taken them with him from the Hixson apartment.

—The red shirt that Griffin had been wearing was identified by the Galveston victims. He had stolen it from them.

The assistant district attorney at the intake desk accepted two capital murder charges against John Stiles Griffin. One accused Griffin of the murder of Louise Ponder during the course of a rape. The other charged him with the murder of Patricia Hixson during the course of a robbery.

Carolyn Stephenson had made her case.

But she had only made it on paper, of course, and that could turn out to be illusory.

What would the jury do? That was the real question.*

---

* The following names in this chapter were changed, without alteration of the incidents in which the persons were involved: Patricia Hixson, Walter Hixson, Louise Ponder, Robin Couch, Paul Manteris, Arnold Merrill.

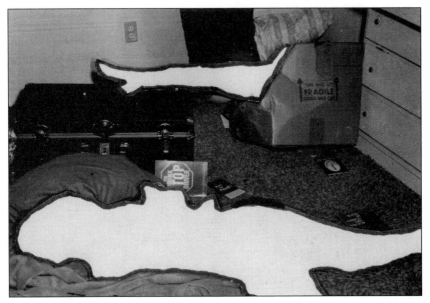

The John Stiles Griffin Murder Case. The homicide scene, according to Detective Carolyn Stephenson, was "as bad as I've ever made." The body of Louise Ponder is in the foreground, nude from the waist down. The body of the other victim, Patricia Hixson, is partially obscured by pillows and a crumpled cardboard box. The original photograph depicted the nature of this murder in a way that is conveyed only partially by this edited version.

The John Stiles Griffin Murder Case. Detail from original photograph of crime scene. This picture shows the bindings on the wrists of Louise Ponder (the body in the foreground). The killer tied her with nylon hose, then tightened that with a coat hanger. He also tied the victim's feet, circled her neck with a leather strap and coat hanger, gagged her with crisscrossed strips of tape, and raped her.

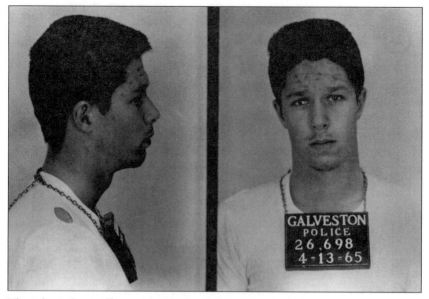

The John Stiles Griffin Murder Case. This booking picture was taken in 1965, just before one of Griffin's earliest prison sentences. He was seventeen years old and on his way to the Texas Department of Criminal Justice.

The John Stiles Griffin Murder Case. Detective Carolyn Stephenson of the Houston Police Department Homicide Division, one of Houston's best police officers. "You can't do anything with Carolyn," said the lawyer who defended Griffin. "She knows what she's doing." Her peers in the police association agreed; they named her Police Officer of the Year. (Photograph courtesy Nancy Redding).

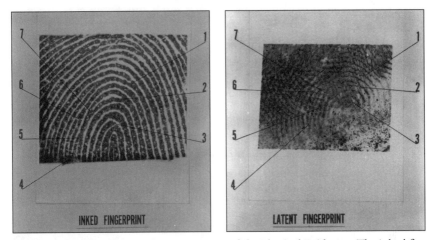

The John Stiles Griffin Murder Case — Part of the Physical Evidence. The inked fingerprint was taken after John Stiles Griffin was arrested, during the booking procedure. The latent fingerprint was developed by dusting the dispenser of the tape that was used to gag one of the victims, Louise Ponder, immediately before she was murdered. A fingerprint expert would analyze these prints by comparing "points," some of which are labelled in these photographs. Point number 1, for instance, is a "fork," point 3 is a "ridge ending," etc. Usable latent prints are hard to find. This one is smeared and overlaid with another print, but is sufficient for an identification.

The John Stiles Griffin Murder Case. The photographer took this picture through a small window in the courtroom door. Detective James Pierce testifies before a jury against John Stiles Griffin, who sits with the back of his head to the camera, behind his attorneys. (Photograph: Nancy Redding).

The John Stiles Griffin Murder Case. Officer M.A. Herbert of the Port Arthur Police Department arrested John Stiles Griffin. Griffin produced a U.S. Customs I.D. and told a story that "sounded convincing," but upon closer questioning Officer Herbert found that the suspect knew no other federal officers and had never heard of the newly formed D.E.A. (Drug Enforcement Agency). Griffin was carrying a knife that fit the measurements of the murder weapon used in the Richmond Avenue Murders, a shirt from a Galveston robbery and a watch from a California burglary. (Photograph courtesy Nancy Redding).

The John Stiles Griffin Murder Case. Wound chart compiled by detectives for one of the victims. Detectives graphed the wounds to Louise Ponder on this chart, which uses unemotional images in a way that nevertheless symbolizes the savagery of the crime. It also illustrates the way in which criminal investigators must professionally approach the most shocking kinds of tasks: thoroughly, and with an unusual degree of detachment.

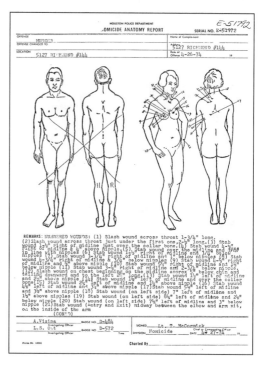

Chapter 9

The Trial of John Stiles Griffin

Homicide prosecutors get used to discussing the clinical details of murder cases in frank, professional terms.

They learn to suppress their revulsion because they have to, long enough to get the job done. But prosecutors are people too, and the revulsion is always there, under the surface.

You could see it now on Ted Busch's face, as he talked about the Richmond Avenue Murders.

"It was senseless, and it was horrible, and it was completely random," Busch said. "And you can make up just about any scene your mind can think of for those four hours, for what those two girls went through, and there's nobody who can call you a liar."

Busch was a veteran prosecutor. He came to Texas from his native Minnesota because "the army brought me here," and he stayed because he liked it. When he became a lawyer, he didn't like private practice. He became an assistant district attorney because "I wanted to be on the side of the angels," and he stayed "because I was satisfied."

He had started prosecuting in misdemeanor court. Now, he was chief of the trial division. That made him responsible for most of the operations of the district attorney's office.

Busch was around forty, but he looked about twenty. His clean-cut, youthful appearance was at odds with his reputation as a courtroom fighter. When the Griffin case had come up for trial, the District Attorney, Carol Vance, had assigned Busch to handle it. "I'm just horrified at some of the cases we've had involving sadistic crimes of violence," Vance had said, sounding like an outraged citizen himself. He had wanted to try the case personally, the District Attorney had said, but other commitments would prevent him from doing so.

Now, a year later, Ted Busch looked down at the glass top on his desk and he began to talk about John Stiles Griffin: Griffin the man, Griffin the defendant, and Griffin the Richmond Avenue Murderer.

"It was about as bad a murder case as I've ever seen," Busch said.

"And just about as bad a defendant."

* * *

John Stiles Griffin was the eldest of four children born to a juvenile probation officer and his wife in Beaumont, Texas.

He once told a prison case worker, "My father is as honest as I am dishonest." And it was true: his parents were hardworking, middle-class, ordinary people.

There was nothing in Griffin's past to show exactly where he departed from his parents' example, but he was 13 years old at the time of his first arrest. Three years later, he had his first institutional commitment as a juvenile: he was sent to the State Reform School at Gatesville, Texas.

At the age of 17, Griffin earned his first prison sentence as an adult. It was on a conviction for burglary. He was paroled from that sentence; but within a year, he was back again for burglary.

From that day forward, John Stiles Griffin spent all but a few months of his life inside prison walls. The time he spent on the outside consisted of brief interludes, created by paroles or escapes.

Eventually, he received a 6-year federal sentence for interstate car theft and he was sent to the Federal Reformatory in El Reno, Nevada. From El Reno, he went to the Federal Corrections Institute in Seagoville, Texas. He failed on a work-release program there and was transferred to the higher security Federal Correctional Institute at Texarkana, Texas. From there, he went back to El Reno; and in 1970, he was paroled. The parole did not last long. Within a matter of months, Griffin was on his fourth adult trip to prison, this time to serve a sentence for theft at Seagoville. Again within a matter of months, he escaped. During the time he was free, he committed a burglary in Las Vegas.

And that burglary was a preview of the Richmond Avenue murders. John Stiles Griffin tied up the woman he found inside the room he had entered, and he left her while he stole her car.

Federal prison authorities failed to recognize this signal of Griffin's violent character. They thought of him as a burglar and a thief. He had not killed the victim that time.

For his most recent offenses, Griffin was given a sentence of 5 years. And in spite of his escape history, he was sent to a minimum security facility in Los Angeles.

A prison psychologist's report described Griffin's behavior as "classically antisocial," and a Bureau of Prisons staff report said, "He has been in repeated conflict with society and seems to have his own set of values. He is tremendously impulsive and irresponsible."

But John Stiles Griffin was intelligent. He boasted an I.Q. of 135. And he had learned, from being in prison most of his adult life, how to manipulate the system and the people who ran it. For instance, the same psychiatrist who called him "classically antisocial" believed Griffin's representations of good intentions. He wrote, "It is not anticipated that he will experience as much difficulty in the institutional setting as he previously had because of a desire to cease taking drugs, maximize chances for release, and live within the institution as comfortably as possible."

In addition to his manipulative abilities, Griffin had an accomplished expertise at obtaining drugs on the inside. At times during his prison terms, he supplied pills to other inmates. While in Los Angeles, he laid in a supply of LSD.

But he was a model prisoner there. He worked in the refrigeration shop, plumbing shop, group activities center, and electronics cable shop, and got excellent work reports everywhere. He even used his leisure time for self-improvement programs. After he had finished earning his high school degree, he began going to motivation classes. Soon he was running those classes. His caseworker wrote, "There have been definite noted positive changes in Griffin's character traits over the past 25 months."

Social work in prisons often has an Alice-in-Wonderland quality to it. That quality was certainly present in the reports Griffin received just four months before the Richmond Avenue Murders. His caseworker concluded, "Although Griffin has had five major periods of confinement, it is felt he has matured a great deal over the past 25 months. At this time, he definitely has the ability to remain in the community without violating the law."

It was a strange way of thinking. And Patricia Hixson and Louise Ponder would pay for it with their lives. Four months later, on that ill-fated April 23, Griffin stopped "maturing," escaped from the minimum security facility, and took his LSD with him.

He apparently travelled to the city of Anaheim, just a few miles away, and murdered the hotel maid there.

That same afternoon, he travelled to San Diego, stole Arnold Merrill's identification, and bought a bus ticket to Texas.

He arrived in Houston on April 25th, took a room at the Astroworld Hotel, and had been in Houston only a few hours when he murdered Patricia Hixson and Louise Ponder.

On April 27th, he surfaced in Galveston. That was where he tied and gagged the people in the motel room. He did not have a chance to kill them, because a knock on the door frightened him away.

And on the 28th, just five days after his escape, he was arrested in Port Arthur — on the grounds of another motel.

* * *

A few days after charges had been filed against him, John Stiles Griffin agreed to talk to the Houston Police.

Carolyn Stephenson, together with Detective James Pierce, located him comfortably in an office, turned on a tape recorder and listened to him for the better part of an hour.

He remembered standing in the San Diego Bus Station—

"Where did you get a ticket to?" Pierce asked.

"I was going to go to Dallas," Griffin replied. "I reorganized my thoughts. And I decided, well, I'll go to Beaumont." He had gone to Beaumont by way of Houston and Galveston.

"I dropped two hits of acid in San Diego," Griffin went on, "which—one hit, or half a hit, will really get you wasted. So I blazed for the next 36 hours." By the time the bus trip ended, he said, "I might as well have been on a plane."

"You were on two trips, the bus trip and the other trip," Pierce said. Griffin laughed and agreed.

He admitted to the burglary of William Merrill's hotel room. And he described the robbery in Galveston.

"Oh, by the way," Pierce said, "what about that Customs identification? Where'd you get that?"

"I worked for Westlake Moving Company," Griffin answered. "We were movers for the FBI, Customs and so forth." This had been one of Griffin's jobs when he was on work-release in California.

During one of the moves, he explained, a box containing blank Customs identification cards and folders had dropped out and spilled. He had taken "two or three" of them. " I filled it out, and took a little picture, and put it on there," he said. "We all did it, you know. It was a joke. It was just a joke."

So that was where the Customs I.D. had come from.

But for all his talking, Griffin said he could neither confirm nor deny that he had murdered Patricia Hixson and Louise Ponder. He just couldn't recall. He had been on LSD the whole time, and he couldn't remember anything. "For me to sit here and actively tell y'all everything," he said, "would be impossible."

"Outside of Sunday, or outside of Wednesday, that was the only day I was straight; and I was just coming down then."

Pierce wanted to know what effect the LSD had had on Griffin. Did it make him belligerent? Did it make him feel strong?

"Did it make you feel like you could pick somebody up and throw 'em down?" Pierce asked.

"Oh, I could pick somebody up and throw 'em anyway," Griffin answered promptly. He had been a weightlifter in prison, he explained. "I've done over 1200 pounds in three lifts, three power lifts. I can bench press over 300, dead lift over 500, and squat over 400."

That, the officers thought, explained a lot of things.

They thought about the riddled bodies of Patricia Hixson and Louise Ponder. And they shuddered.

* * *

The men who were appointed to defend John Stiles Griffin had no rapport with him as they began to build a case to save his life.

"I didn't like him at all," says defense lawyer Al Thomas. "And he didn't like us either."

That was a problem, Thomas knew. Theoretically, it might be possible to defend a man under these conditions. But it would be hard. As a practical matter, you can't defend a man very well if he won't talk to you, and you can't protect him if he won't follow your advice.

Thomas did criminal defense work almost exclusively. He was good at it. And there was no doubt he was one of Houston's more colorful defense lawyers. He had a revealing nickname: Everyone called him "The Indian."

Just how The Indian came by his name was a matter of conjecture. Many of his friends believed he was called that because he was one, but that, Thomas said, was "an old wives' tale." The nickname may have come from his Oklahoma origins. Or it might have been because of his ruddy complexion and dark curly hair. Or it might, conceivably, have been a result of his lifestyle. Thomas was unpretentious, erratic, and fiercely independent.

In any event, the name stuck so tightly, said Thomas, that "Back home in Oklahoma, even the Indians call me 'The Indian.'"

He didn't have a secretary.

He did have an office, but he avoided going to it except on Saturday ("That's when I collect my fees"). A person who asked to make an appointment with The Indian would be told, "I'm usually at the courthouse. You can catch me there."

When Thomas was appointed to defend John Stiles Griffin, his first official act was to try to get his client to remain silent. "He was running his mouth to anyone who'd listen," the lawyer explained. This was the first confrontation between lawyer and client. Thomas kept insisting, and Griffin kept refusing, until, said Thomas, "we finally got him to dummy up."

But there was one subject Thomas was careful not to discuss with his client.

"I never did ask if he did it," The Indian said. "I didn't want to know." And he added that all John Stiles Griffin told his lawyers about the crime itself "was that he was blazing on acid the whole time he was in Houston and he didn't remember anything."

* * *

It was not until jury selection was actually underway that John Stiles Griffin seemed to settle down and cooperate with his attorneys.

"I asked him one day, 'Are you right with the Lord?'" Al Thomas says.

"He answered, 'I don't know.'" Griffin seemed concerned enough to think about it.

That unusual exchange led to a visit by Thomas' mother, who delivered a Bible to John Stiles Griffin. The whole incident, for some reason, led to a greater degree of trust between this strange, highly intelligent prisoner and his lawyers. "I tried to put the Bible where the jury would have to see it," Thomas adds. He regarded it as a way to enhance his client's defense.

"Y'all are playing poker with my life," John Stiles Griffin said to his lawyers during one hard-fought day of jury selection.

"I guess you could say that," Thomas answered. "It's all a question of strategy."

For the first time, Griffin seemed to sense that this was a game that could be won — and, more importantly to Thomas, he seemed to care about it. "Well," he said, "let's play cards."

*   *   *

Jury selection did not go well for the prosecutors.

Ted Busch felt uncomfortable with the jury that was finally selected. So did Alan McAshan, the prosecutor who was assisting him.

Jury selection is only loosely related to the law. It is actually an exercise in a kind of applied psychology. It depends, more than anything else, upon an understanding of people — and of how they are likely to vote when they become jurors.

And unfortunately, it has little to do with the romantic ideal of an "impartial" jury. Each side is trying to get a favorable jury, not an impartial one. Much of it is founded on stereotypes, and the stereotypes, at times, seem to approach pure prejudice. Are white collar workers likely to vote for conviction in a given case? If so, the defendant's lawyers will strike them. Are construction workers, as a class, more likely to acquit in a given type of case? Then prosecutors may tend to follow the percentages — and strike them.

Polls show, for example, that women are far less likely to support capital punishment than men. A jury with a majority of women is far more likely, on the average, to acquit or assess a life sentence in a death penalty case than one composed of a majority of men. It is not quite that simple, of course, because the statistics do not apply to all women or to all men. But nevertheless, both Ted Busch and Al Thomas recognized the significance of the composition of the jury that would try John Stiles Griffin.

There were seven women and five men.

"All these women qualified," Ted Busch said. "It amazed me that they all did." In spite of the strength of his case, it made him uneasy.

And there was something else that troubled Busch. There had been a large proportion of potential jurors who had indicated adamant opposition to the death penalty, initially, but who had changed their answers and qualified under persistent questioning by the judge. When this would happen, Al Thomas would grin and punch his fist through the air like a cheerleader. "I knew Busch would have to strike all those people," he said. " I was just saying to myself, 'come on, baby, use up those strikes."

The faster Busch used his peremptory challenges, Thomas knew, the faster he would run out of them, and the faster he would have to begin accepting jurors who were opposed to his case. And although it was an intangible thing, Busch had a sense that that had happened to him by the time jury selection was over. It was one of the reasons he was uncomfortable.

Across the table from Busch and McAshan, Thomas — and his co-counsel, Fred Heacock — were happy when jury selection ended.

"We won the battle of the strikes," Thomas said.

"We even snuck one past Busch," Thomas adds. "We had one lady who was a Pentecostal. One of their tenets says that we are in a state of grace here and now. They believe that any sin can be forgiven." The Pentecostal lady was going to be a problem for the prosecutors where the death penalty was concerned.

"Fred and I were extremely satisfied with that jury," Thomas said. "We even started getting downright friendly with John Stiles Griffin."

* * *

The State's first witness was Walter Hixson.

It was visibly hard for him to testify. He had to relive the day he had found his wife's body in his apartment. But that, by itself, was not the hardest part of his testimony. The hardest part came after Busch had finished questioning the witness, and the strategy that Al Thomas had mapped out for the case began to emerge.

Thomas had a simple theory of the case: John Stiles Griffin hadn't killed Hixson's wife. Hixson had.

Griffin had been there in the Hixson apartment. That had to be admitted, Thomas decided, because there was no way around the fingerprint on the tape dispenser. But Thomas had also concluded that there was no reason Griffin could not have left while the two women were still alive.

"Our theory was that John Stiles Griffin had got in there and tied 'em up," Thomas explained. The fingerprint made that much undisputable. But the theory went on from there. "Walter Hixson came home, saw them tied up, and freaked out. And he killed 'em both. It's a terrible thing to accuse him of," Thomas added, "but his actions were strange."

It was not only terrible; it seemed ridiculous. And it was inconsistent with the physical evidence — the bloody pants with the bus ticket and Astroworld key in them, for one thing. But it was Thomas' defense. And he was skillful in developing it.

He was gentle, polite and restrained as he made the awful insinuation start with the first witness — Walter Hixson himself.

"What time did you go to lunch?" Thomas asked.

Hixson told him.

"What time did you leave lunch? And where did you go from there?" Using this technique, The Indian pinned Hixson down on the details of his day. And he established that there was a period of time, during the mid-afternoon, that Hixson had been "running errands." No one else had been with him to say that he had not gone home to his apartment.

Thomas pointed out that Hixson had been taken into custody by the police. And he pointed out that the apartment security guard had seen someone whom he had identified as Walter Hixson, wandering around near the apartment "as if in a daze."

The defense lawyer did nothing to anger the jury. He simply left the monstrous accusation hanging, like a will-o'-the-wisp, in the air. When Walter Hixson was finally excused from the witness stand, it remained in the air — too vague and undefined for Busch to answer. Thomas wanted the jurors to flesh out the idea for themselves. And yet none of them could fail to grasp the point he had made.

Reasonable doubt.

Paul Manteris was one of the next witnesses Ted Busch called to the stand. As Busch puts it, Manteris was as "strong as horseradish."

Manteris told the jurors about the strange man who had come to his door, showed him a Customs I.D., and asked to come inside his apartment.

"Is this the man?" Ted Busch asked, indicating John Stiles Griffin.

"Yes," the witness replied without hesitation.

And Griffin had walked in the direction of the Hixson apartment afterward, Manteris added.

Al Thomas' cross examination, again, was careful and controlled. It was designed to raise questions, not to answer them. And it was designed to exonerate his client.

Thomas pointed out that the direction the man had taken could have led him to the freeway and out of the apartment complex just as easily as to the Hixson apartment.

"You didn't see where he actually went?"

"No."

"You didn't see him actually go *into* any apartment?"

"No."

"The last time you saw him, he was heading in this direction, which could have been toward the freeway?"

"Yes." The questions and answers meant nothing, really, except that the witness had not continuously observed John Stiles Griffin. But once again, the cross examination invited the jurors to discover an alternative explanation. And it could seem, to some of them, to create a reasonable doubt.

Carolyn Stephenson was on the witness stand, testifying for the prosecution, for over two hours.

Ted Busch led her through a description of the bodies, the scene, the bloody pants, the Astroworld Hotel key, the bus ticket and every other feature of the apartment.

Before passing the witness, the prosecutor asked her: "And did you take copious notes?"

'Yes," she responded.

Al Thomas' first question on cross examination was, "What are 'copious notes?'"

Everyone smiled a little at the phrase. Thomas, secretly, was hoping the witness wouldn't know what the word "copious" meant. If she didn't, he could follow up with a question like, "Well, why'd you testify you took copious notes, then?" and perhaps it would make the whole prosecution case look a little foolish.

Carolyn Stephenson paused momentarily.

Then she said, "It means I took a lot of notes."

"You can't do anything with Carolyn," Thomas said afterwards. "Heck, she knows what she's doing. She knows what she's about.

"We just sort of ragged her around a little bit."

Thomas' cross-examination did considerably more than that. It uncovered every possible point one could have thought of to help his "Walter-Hixson-did-it" theory. Was there a laundry mark on the pants, he wanted to know? Had Stephenson looked to see whether there was any sort of mark, or anything else, that might have showed that the pants belonged to Hixson?

Thomas, says Carolyn Stephenson, was "completely professional" in front of the jury. He didn't take any "cheap shots." That was the mark of a good defense lawyer.

Carolyn Stephenson was on the witness stand for several hours more. She was re-called to testify on three separate occasions.

* * *

Thomas built his defense with consummate skill. But he was trying to build bricks without clay.

His points of doubt, viewed realistically, seemed only to underscore the case Ted Busch was building.

Through nearly two dozen witnesses, Busch fought to get all his evidence before the jury. Thomas fought to keep as much of it as he could from being heard. When Thomas objected to testimony Busch offered about "extraneous offenses," Busch showed the judge why the testimony was admissible. He got most of the pictures of the crime scene admitted, over Thomas' objections and motions for a mistrial. And he built a proof of John Stiles Griffin's guilt that was simply overwhelming.

Finally, the parade of witnesses fit together like a mosaic. Busch's talent was that he made the mosaic emerge, from the various bits of knowledge, like ragged stones, that each witness could contribute.

Manteris' identification of Griffin as the man with the Customs identification. Griffin's arrest with the I.D. in his possession, trying to use it. The hotel key in the Hixson apartment. The property belonging to Hixson that had been found in the Astroworld Hotel room. The identification of Griffin as the man who had rented that room. Griffin's handwriting on the hotel register. The name "Merrill" on the register. The California burglary of Arnold Merrill's room. The watch from the California burglary in Griffin's possession. The knife, which fit the wounds. The Galveston robbery, and the car Griffin had stolen. Hixson's trousers, which were found in that car after Griffin abandoned it.

And Griffin's fingerprint on the tape dispenser.

"My guess was that one or two of the jurors had a reasonable doubt," Thomas said later. But, he admitted, "with all that evidence, you just couldn't find him not guilty."

It was early the next morning that the jurors returned, with a verdict that bore out Thomas' prediction.

They had found John Stiles Griffin guilty of capital murder.

* * *

The penalty hearing was short.

The prosecutors introduced into evidence John Stiles Griffin's prior criminal record. The five periods of confinement, and all the multiple convictions that supported each of them, were all set out before the jury.

And it was time for jury argument—on the issue of life or death.

Jury argument, especially on a volatile issue like the death penalty, is a strange thing. Sometimes juries respond to logical reasoning. But sometimes they do not. A jury is not, and it has never been intended to be, a mere factual computer. And it was Al Thomas' genius that he recognized this principle as he stood before this jury, for the last time.

His argument was unconventional.

"You've convicted the wrong man!" he all but shouted at the jury, with an expression of contempt on his face. "You should have found him not guilty.

"And since you shouldn't have convicted him in the first place," the defense lawyer went on, "I'm not going to plead for his life now!"

That, in substance, was Thomas' whole argument. It lasted about thirty seconds. But it was perhaps the single most effective thirty seconds of the trial. Thomas understood jury psychology; he knew that most human beings feel uncomfortable finding anyone guilty in a court of law. The whole process, he recognized, could subtly make the jurors themselves feel guilty for rendering a "guilty" verdict. Thomas knew the jurors' inner guilt. And he was using it against them.

From head to toe, the defense lawyer radiated disgust—disgust at the jurors' dereliction of duty in finding his client guilty.

Ted Busch, the veteran prosecutor, had the last word. He answered Thomas' argument: there was no question of guilt, none at all, and there was no question the sentencing questions should be answered "Yes." Logically and forcefully, he summarized the evidence.

And he concluded by saying, "If this isn't a death penalty case, then there's no such thing."

* * *

The jurors were out for two hours. Then it was three.

" I know I'm either going to die or spend the rest of my life in prison," John Stiles Griffin said to Al Thomas. "Maybe I can do something to help somebody.

"Maybe," he added, "I can help keep them from making my same stupid mistakes."

It was the same sort of thing he had said to manipulate his case workers in prison.

Silently, the fourth hour of deliberations passed.

"If the death penalty was ever called for, this is the time," Ted Busch thought to himself, as the time dragged by.

Five hours.

Suddenly, the buzzer sounded from inside the jury room.

The jurors had reached a verdict. They filed out and took their places in the jury box. The foreman handed the verdict sheet to the bailiff, who handed it to the judge.

Judge Joseph Guarino held the sheet in his hand. Two "yes" answers would mean a sentence of death, while one, or more, "no" answers would mean a sentence of life imprisonment. Everyone wondered what those two words were—the words that the jury had written, that made the life-or-death difference.

The judge read the first question, slowly and with emphasis. It asked the jury whether John Stiles Griffin had committed the murders deliberately.

"Yes," was the jury's answer.

Everyone in the courtroom sat forward in his chair.

The judge read the second question. Was there a probability that John Stiles Griffin would be a continuing threat to society?

The judge read the answer.

"No."

"No." The second answer was "no." It was a sentence of life imprisonment. That was the jury's verdict—that John Stiles Griffin was not a continuing threat to society. It meant that he would get a sentence of life imprisonment for the murders of Patricia Hixson and Louise Ponder.

Al Thomas had won the case for the defense.

* * *

Soon afterward, John Stiles Griffin was in prison in Huntsville. Law enforcement officers in California tried to put together enough evidence to convict him of the Anaheim Hotel murder, but they were unsuccessful. They linked his name to other crimes there, and they saw his method of operation in at least one more grisly murder. But there wasn't enough evidence. And as time went by, it became more and more unlikely that John Stiles Griffin would ever be tried for any of those crimes.

Griffin did not stop breaking the law after his arrest. On one occasion, he got a hacksaw blade smuggled into his jail cell and cut nearly through a steel plate before guards caught him. On another occasion, he improvised a knife with a two-inch blade inside the cell, using a cigarette rolling machine to make it. Griffin was dangerous, in or out of prison.

Although it seemed improbable, Al Thomas maintained that Griffin was sincere about his newfound interest in religion. And Griffin began improving himself, again, in prison; he started going to school. "He has just about a 4.0 average," said Thomas. "He's had two things he's written published, and he's working on a novel."

He would be eligible for parole after he had served 20 prison "years." But that time limit is misleading, because it was possible, then, with "good time," to serve 20 "years" in ten calendar years or fewer, in the Texas prison system. If that had happened in John Stiles Griffin's case, he would have emerged from prison at the age of 38.

It wasn't likely that parole would come that early. But it was fair to anticipate that a parole for Griffin might someday be possible. Courtroom observers guessed that Patricia Hixson and Louise Ponder might have been in their graves somewhere between eight and fifteen years when the parole board first considered whether to release John Stiles Griffin.

* * *

Why did the Griffin case come out as it did?

Why, for example, did John Stiles Griffin get a sentence of life imprisonment when Kenneth Brock had been sentenced to death? What was the difference between the cases?

Ted Busch knows part of the answer. It lies in the twelve people who rendered the verdict. "Wishy-washy, pussycat jury," he says. "We had a really weak jury."

But Busch is equally hard on himself. "Wishy-washy prosecutor, too," he says. " I didn't get down into the trenches and go through the horror of the crime with them again during final argument. I just, calmly and coolly, said, 'This is what the evidence shows, and this is what you have to find.' I didn't get wrought up. And they need that."

Busch's self-criticism is far too harsh. A good trial lawyer always, without fail, blames himself whenever anything goes wrong; it is a characteristic of the breed. Actually, the verdict was surprising precisely *because* Busch had tried the case so well. The jury just didn't respond to his proof.

It came down to this: Al Thomas' final argument—or rather, his final non-argument—was more effective than Busch's analysis of the evidence. In a logical world, perhaps, it should not have been; nevertheless, it was.

Carolyn Stephenson agrees. "The defense did an A-number-one job," she says. "They didn't miss a single chance to bring out any incident that was in their favor."

And she adds, "It was the Indian. He did it."

Still, Stephenson was shocked by the verdict. "If you can't get the death penalty in this case, then you can't get it in any case," she said. And she would be right, if it were not for the jury system—a system that allowed twelve people to listen to the kind of evidence they heard in the Griffin case, and then return a verdict pronouncing that the defendant was not a threat to society.

But characteristically, it was Al Thomas who had the most unusual insights into the verdict.

In the first place, Thomas denied that the verdict was really in his favor. "We didn't win the case. A not-guilty verdict would have been what we would have gotten if we had won it."

The murders, Thomas conceded, were "as brutal as any I've ever seen, as sensational as any I've ever seen." But by his inferences that Walter Hixson could have done it, and by his spectacular argument technique, Thomas had succeeded in planting that seed of doubt that makes a juror hesitant. Not hesitant enough to acquit, perhaps—but hesitant enough to be unable to sentence the convict to death.

And so the jury did not return a death penalty verdict, Thomas explained, because "the jurors had a reasonable doubt that John Stiles Griffin did it." Of course, to have that reasonable doubt after all the evidence they had heard, the jurors had to be a certain kind of people.

Thomas had chosen them carefully.

The last word in the case belonged to The Indian. He collected the final payment of his fee for John Stiles Griffin's defense from the county. It was a sizeable sum, and with his lack of overhead, it seemed even more substantial. The Indian left a note for Ted Busch as he walked from the courthouse. It was scrawled in a cramped hand that was hard, at first, to read; but on second glance, it left no doubt about what it was saying.

"Busch," the note said, "I just got $6300.00 for Griffin case. Thank you very much. Al Thomas."

*   *   *

The Griffin case, with that, was over.

Within a few months, the sensational publicity connected with the case would subside, and others would take its place. There was one case in particular, involving a murder committed seven months after Griffin's crime, that would seize the public's attention in a way that seemed to eclipse even the Richmond Avenue Murders.

It was called the Halloween Candy Murder Case.

The Halloween Candy Murder bore no resemblance to John Stiles Griffin's crime. The motive, the victim and the method of commission were all different. And the final suspect in the case was the last person anyone would have suspected.

The story of that case begins on October 31, on Halloween — the night when Ronald Clark O'Bryan's son was murdered in Pasadena, Texas.

Chapter 10

The Halloween Candy Murder Case

After his son's death, Ronald Clark O'Bryan wept.

"He was all boy," the grieving father said. "He loved baseball, football —anything. He never met a stranger.

"But I have my peace in knowing that Tim is in heaven now."

O'Bryan's fellow citizens in Pasadena, Texas, shared his shock and outrage. So did the rest of the country, because the case had attracted the attention of the national press. A small army of reporters was camped on the doorstep of the Pasadena Police Building.

But there was no one so spectacularly affected as the boy's father.

On the evening after the boy's death, a memorial service for Tim O'Bryan was held at the Second Baptist Church. Ronald O'Bryan sang a solo in the boy's honor. It was a Baptist hymn called "Blessed Assurance."

As the father's strong, clear singing voice filled the church, listeners realized that he had changed the hymn as a tribute to his son. The usual words went, "This is my story/—This is my song;" but instead, O'Bryan sang, "This is Tim's story/—This is Tim's song."

The distraught father had tears in his eyes as he sang. So did many in the congregation. It was profoundly moving. But Ronald Clark O'Bryan obviously had the full strength of his religion sustaining him, because he told the congregation that his eight-year-old son had "given his life to Jesus."

* * *

The autopsy report was standard.

It began with a section called "History." Here, in succinct and unemotional terms, the report told of the unusual way in which Timothy Marc O'Bryan had met his death.

"This 8-year-old boy," it said, "arrived at Southmore Hospital Emergency Room at 9:20 p.m., where he was pronounced dead at 10:30 p.m. on October 31, 1974.

"Earlier, the decedent had been out trick-or-treating. He became ill after ingesting some candy obtained earlier that afternoon."

October 31. Halloween. Timothy O'Bryan, a normal eight-year-old boy, had received and eaten some candy that made him sick. In fact, it had made him very sick; it had made him vomit violently. The autopsy report described the volume of "red-gray frothy material exuding from each of the external nares."

Inside the morgue, Dr. Joseph A. Jachimczyk took personal charge of the autopsy. He was the county's chief medical examiner, and he was known throughout Houston as "Dr. Joe"—because of his unpronounceable last name. Dr. Joe was not only a medical doctor; he also had a law degree and was a licensed attorney. He knew the difficulties a case such as this could present in court. And so he was handling it himself.

The abundance of frothy material—so thick that it clogged the boy's bronchial tubes—was not caused by any of the ordinary lethal agents that Dr. Joe and his cohorts saw every day. It was not caused by an infection. It was not caused by hemorrhaging. And it was not the result of blows or "trauma."

It was a case of poisoning.

Dr. Joe's immediate task was to find out what the poison was and how much of it had been used.

He used a small circular saw to cut through the bone of the skull, completely around it. Then he removed the severed portion of the scalp like a skull cap. This procedure allowed the medical examiner to remove, section and inspect the brain. It was called "reflecting" the head. There was nothing unusual about it; dissecting the brain was part of a standard autopsy.

But Dr. Joe's findings from the brain in this case were not ordinary. Instead, they were highly unusual.

Almost immediately, he noticed the bright, glistening network of blood vessels that crisscrossed the top of Tim O'Bryan's brain. He saw that they glowed with an abnormal color and intensity. Something, he knew, was very wrong. And he thought he knew what it was.

It was cyanide.

This deep, cherry color was characteristic of cyanide poisoning.

Dr. Joe paused to speak into the microphone that was recording his report. "The surface vessels of the brain," he dictated, "were strikingly hyperemic red."

Liquid taken from the boy's stomach had a bitter smell, like almonds. That, too, was characteristic of cyanide. And when Dr. Joe tested the stomach washings with a reagent called prussian blue, it gave the color change that was a positive indication of cyanide, before his eyes.

Next, the doctor needed to know how much cyanide there was.

Dr. Joe took a measured sample of the stomach washings. He carefully noted the fraction the sample represented of the whole. And then he "titrated" it with silver nitrate.

The "titration" technique is a familiar tool of analytical chemistry. Here, it consisted of pouring a measured amount of another chemical, silver nitrate, into the sample—drop by drop, with a special glass column equipped with a sensitive valve—and waiting for the milky color that indicated it had reacted with all the cyanide in the sample. The doctor knew the concentration of the silver nitrate solution; and from this concentration, together with the volume of reagent he had used, he would be able to calculate exactly how much potassium cyanide was present.

Now, he had the result. Sixteen milligrams of the deadly poison had been recovered.

That was a huge amount to find in stomach washings of this kind.

The autopsy report was now complete.

Of course, the autopsy did nothing to tell what sort of person had given the poison to Timothy Marc O'Bryan in the first place. The key to the killer's identity was not to be found in this laboratory. It would be discovered, if it was to be discovered at all, in the streets and homes of Pasadena itself.

Somewhere in Pasadena, there was someone on the loose who was willing to kill an eight year old boy by giving him a piece of Halloween candy laced with enough potassium cyanide to kill him several times over.

* * *

Within minutes of Timothy Marc O'Bryan's death, the Pasadena Police Department had located the murder weapon.

It wasn't a gun. It wasn't a knife. It was a piece of candy.

A lot of people in the larger city of Houston, frankly, look down their noses at suburban Pasadena. Although it is located only a few miles from one of the nation's most populous metropolitan centers, Pasadena has the atmosphere of a small town. It is a blue-collar, refinery-and-factory city.

But Pasadena certainly had at least one thing to boast of. It had one of the finest investigative police departments in the United States.

Now, as Pasadena's homicide detectives looked at the "weapon," they were struck by its innocuous appearance. It was a plastic tube of purple-and-white powdered confection. It had the trade name by which it was sold, "Pixy Stix," printed on the tube. It was brightly colored, to appeal to children.

But the tube was lethal.

Ronald O'Bryan told the detectives that he had permitted his son to eat part of the Pixy Stix before going to bed. Within minutes, Timothy had complained of abdominal pain. Soon he had convulsed, vomited and lost consciousness. O'Bryan had called an ambulance, but the boy had died within a short time.

With characteristic thoroughness, the Pasadena officers interviewed the ambulance driver and hospital personnel. The boy's father had been "pretty shook," they said. When an ambulance driver had told him, "The boy isn't going to make it," O'Bryan had beaten his arms on the hospital wall and screamed, "Oh, God! Don't let my boy die!"

In fact, the doctors added, it had seemed for a moment that O'Bryan himself might have been poisoned, too.

It had been strange. O'Bryan had complained of the same symptoms his son was exhibiting. He had even lain on a stretcher for a few minutes. But when the doctors had offered to pump his stomach as they were pumping Timothy's, O'Bryan had said he didn't feel that bad. He had seemed more secure in his refusal of this service than one would have expected him to be, after showing the same symptoms that had so spectacularly killed his son. Perhaps it could have come, somehow, from being near his son — ?

In any event, it was a mystery.

But where had the Pixy Stix come from? That was the real question.

The events preceding the boy's eating of the candy were not nearly so easy to trace as the events at the hospital. It turned out that the entire O'Bryan family — O'Bryan, his wife Daynene, their son Tim and their daughter Lane — had gone over to the home of their friends, Andy and Michelle Rourke, to go trick-or-treating. The Rourkes' children, Philip and Anne, were also in on the trick-or-treating.

The O'Bryan children had been excited and happy. Tim had been dressed as a warrior from the Planet of the Apes. Lane had had on the costume of a female from the Planet of the Apes.

The two fathers, Ron and Andy, had accompanied the children as they made the rounds of the neighborhood. Some of the candy had been collected by the fathers, to be given to the children later. Some had been accepted by the children themselves.

When they had gotten back to the Rourke home, after trick-or-treating, Ron O'Bryan had passed out the candy he had collected. The children's eyes had lighted; it had included five giant Pixy Stix. One had gone to Tim, one to Lane, one to Philip, and one to Anne.

There had been a fifth one left over. Ron O'Bryan had joked with the children, saying, "I'll just keep it and eat it myself." It had been amusing then, but it was frightening now. For O'Bryan, by not eating the Pixy Stix, had narrowly averted death himself.

There had been a young boy, a friend of the Rourke children, who had come to the door, O'Bryan told the detectives; and he had given the fifth Pixy Stix to the boy.

The Pasadena officers were aghast. O'Bryan was telling them, in essence, that there were four more Pixy Stix in circulation — one of which had gone to a boy whose name O'Bryan did not know.

Immediately, the police department made a public appeal: any parent whose child had received Halloween candy that seemed suspicious at all should turn it in. Worried parents responded by handing in dozens of pieces of candy. And this public appeal resulted in the finding of the four missing Pixy Stix.

These four Pixy Stix, the medical examiner reported, were as lethal as the one that had killed Tim O'Bryan. Each one was stuffed with potassium cyanide.

Now, the Pasadena Police recognized the need for a systematic investigation of the route the trick-or-treaters had taken. They used a helicopter to take aerial photographs of the neighborhood, showing every house on the blocks O'Bryan and Rourke said they had covered. It was typical of Pasadena P.D.'s thoroughness. These aerial photographs would enable the detectives to interview witnesses with more precision. They could have each witness point out exactly where he had been and what he had seen.

And so on November 1, the day after the murder, Andy Rourke took the Pasadena detectives through the steps that the trick-or-treaters had followed. One by one, he identified the residences where they had stopped. The critical passage, it seemed, was on Pasadena's Donerail Street — a horseshoe-shaped residential lane with neat, new houses on it, located in an expensive new development called Bowling Green.

The group had stopped at 4126 Donerail first, Rourke said.

Then 4124 Donerail, next door.

Then 4122 Donerail.

From there, Rourke thought, the party had crossed the street to 4119 Donerail. The lady who lived there made it an annual custom to dress as a witch and serve "witches' brew," which in reality was Kool-aid.

Witches' brew. The detectives found it all chilling in spite of themselves. It was only play-acting for children. But it made this case, which was macabre enough already, seem just a little spookier.

The children had had some of the witches' brew.

The trick-or-treaters had then crossed back to the even-numbered residences and continued west. 4114 Donerail; 4112 Donerail —

After that, Andy Rourke was not sure. But apparently, there had been another crossing, to 4111. In any event, Andy Rourke was sure of one thing: Ron O'Bryan had had the Pixy Stix in his hand before they had gotten to 4111 Donerail. He thought it had been on the even-numbered side of the street.

Was it 4112? Or maybe 4114?

Silently, the officers wondered: Which house was it?

Which of Andy Rourke's neighbors was the murderer?

*   *   *

The next day, November 2, the officers talked to the grief-stricken father, Ronald Clark O'Bryan.

They had waited an extra day to interview him thoroughly. Now, they apologized for disturbing him at such a tragic time. The investigation, they felt, had to get underway. They hoped he understood.

"I'll help in any way I can," Ron O'Bryan said earnestly.

They started in with the neighborhood aerial photographs. O'Bryan, as it happened, remembered the journey much the same as Andy Rourke had. But he could add something Rourke had been unable to.

He remembered the residence where he had gotten the Pixy Stix. And he described it for the detectives.

It had been brown in color, O'Bryan said, with a brown wooden door of lighter color. It had small plants and bushes and some sort of hanging ivy in front.

He had gone to the door of this house with the children, he said. But the children had run back to the sidewalk, leaving him alone at the door when it opened. It had been a man with giant Pixy Stix in his right hand who had opened it.

"How many of you are there?" the man with the Pixy Stix had asked.

"Four or five," had been O'Bryan's answer.

"Here!" the man had said. And he had handed O'Bryan five Pixy Stix. Immediately he had shut the door behind him.

O'Bryan, now, told the detectives he could describe the man's clothing, but he was vague about the man's face. "I only saw it for a moment," he said.

And so the next step, it seemed, was to go out and find the house.

With O'Bryan in the car, the Pasadena officers drove slowly down Donerail Street. When they neared the bend in the horseshoe, O'Bryan pointed. "That looks like it," he said.

It was 4112 Donerail.

They turned and passed the residence again. This time, said O'Bryan, he was positive. That was the house. 4112 Donerail.

Now the officers had a solid lead. It coincided with what Andy Rourke had said the day before.

As the police car passed the house for the second time, everyone looked at the group of people who were standing in the front yard. O'Bryan reacted suddenly. He pointed out one of the men in the yard.

That was the man who had given him the Pixy Stix.

"I'm almost positive," O'Bryan said.

Within the next few hours, the officers covered 4112 Donerail—and all its inhabitants—like a glove. The man O'Bryan had pointed out was their first concern. He was the prime suspect. His name, it happened, was William Hudspeth. It seemed likely that the case was solved, and all it would take was follow-up investigation.

But almost immediately, there were problems with this simple solution.

The officers found that the man O'Bryan had identified had not been home at all on Halloween night. He had been at work. William Hudspeth worked at the Houston Airport, and his job required special skills. A large number of people had seen him there, and his work records showed that he was there all night. There just wasn't any question about it; the man O'Bryan said had done it actually hadn't been there at all.

And then the officers discovered something else that surprised them.

The children didn't remember seeing a man at that house. They hadn't seen anyone come to the door of 4112 Donerail. And neither, when he thought about it, had Andy Rourke. The way they all remembered it, there had been no one at home.

Something, the detectives knew, was terribly wrong.

And in any event, the investigation was back to square one.

"What kind of person do you think the killer is?" Ronald O'Bryan asked Officer W. D. LaNier.

"Some kind of perverted, abnormal, sadistic maniac," LaNier responded. "He'll kill again if we don't catch him."

O'Bryan burst into tears.

* * *

It was Friday, November 4.

The Halloween Candy Murder investigation had occupied most of the resources of the Pasadena Police Department for four days.

Assistant District Attorney Michael Hinton was in charge of legal matters connected with the investigation. He was in constant touch with the officers, because there were new developments almost by the minute. But he was also trying to handle his usual duties. It wasn't easy.

This afternoon, Mike Hinton happened to be teaching a class in the Pasadena Police Academy. Every year about this time, he came here to lecture new police recruits on the Texas criminal code. Ironically, he had covered the law of homicide in his lecture this morning. The Halloween Candy Murder, of course, had been on everyone's mind.

This morning, in fact, Hinton had had half a dozen interruptions having to do with developments on the Halloween Candy Murder Case. Now, at 1 o'clock in the afternoon, he had just resumed his lecture, and he was launching into an explanation of the law of theft.

"The crime of theft consists of taking property from another person 'without his effective consent,'" he began.

Suddenly, the door to the classroom opened and the lecture was interrupted once again. It was one of the officers in charge of the murder investigation, Lieutenant Goad. He asked to see Hinton privately, outside the classroom.

"We just received information that Ronald Clark O'Bryan took out insurance on his son just before he died," Goad said. "I think you'd better come see what we have."

Hinton was numb with surprise. He could hardly hear his own voice as he dismissed the class.

* * *

From 1 p.m. until 5 p.m., Assistant District Attorney Mike Hinton studied the evidence the Pasadena Police Department had collected.

Finally, he concluded—as the officers had already concluded—that Ronald Clark O'Bryan must have killed his own son.

First, Hinton thought, there was the Pixy Stix itself. The Rourke children said one had been given to Timothy and one to each of them. Strangely, the Pixy Stix that had killed Timothy—like the others—had been stapled at one end of the tube. It was not sealed, as it would have been at the factory, but stapled.

Why had O'Bryan given stapled Pixy Stix to the children?

Then there had been O'Bryan's accusation of the man at 4112 Donerail. The accusation against William Hudspeth was false, Hinton saw. The children and Rourke said no one had come to the door. O'Bryan could be excused, of course, for mistaken identification. But how could it be a mistake, Hinton thought, if no one had come to the door at all?

Now something else had come up.

The insurance.

Mike Hinton read, once again, the affidavit that O'Bryan's insurance agent had given to the detectives. "To the best of my knowledge," the affidavit said, "Ron O'Bryan called me at the office and stated that he thought he needed some more insurance on his children."

O'Bryan had said, at first, that he wanted $20,000 worth of coverage on each of his children, but he bought even more than that. "To the best of my knowledge," said the affidavit, "he never asked what the premium would be."

O'Bryan had been in an unusual hurry, the affidavit said. "Ron paid me $108.00 in cash for both policies that day. I thought this method of payment was unusual because I've had Ron's insurance business since about 1971 and he always paid on a monthly draft basis."

The affidavit was signed by O'Bryan's insurance agent, Gilbert Cartwright. It also pointed out that O'Bryan had made a strange request: he had not wanted his wife told about the policies. He had been quite insistent.

It was five o'clock now. Hinton had been going over the evidence for four hours. He and the officers decided that the next step would be to get Ronald and Daynene O'Bryan down to the police station and talk to them again.

* * *

When the O'Bryans arrived, the officers immediately separated them.

Daynene O'Bryan was questioned by Officers H. J. Nassif and Evelyn Lancaster. Ronald Clark O'Bryan was taken into another office and interrogated by Detective D. N. Mullican.

For her part, Daynene O'Bryan seemed almost relieved to be able to talk to the police. "This is the first time anyone has really talked to me since Timothy's death," she said.

She added, "God will eventually give the person who committed this crime the strength to come forward."

"Mrs. O'Bryan," Detective Nassif asked, "How much life insurance did you and your husband have on your children?"

Daynene O'Bryan answered that each member of the family was insured for $10,000. The insurance was provided through their bank for a token monthly payment. But she wasn't sure they had even that much, because Ron had told her that he was reducing the insurance on her and the children.

Gently, Nassif explained to her that Ronald Clark O'Bryan had indeed rewritten the policy on the children. But he had not reduced it. Instead, he had increased it—to a total of $65,000.

And he had paid for the coverage in cash.

"Oh, my God,—no," said Daynene O'Bryan softly.

She lowered her head.

It took a moment before she recovered her composure. But when Daynene O'Bryan was able to talk again, she told Detective Nassif everything she knew that might help the officers to convict her husband for the murder of her son.

Her husband, she said, had good qualities, but he was a chronic liar, a dreamer, an exaggerater. She told the officers that the O'Bryans had received an overdraft notice on their account at the First Pasadena State Bank a month ago. They were almost broke and their car was about to be repossessed.

Ronald O'Bryan was thirty years old. He was an optician by trade, employed by the Texas State Optical Company. It was a decent living, Daynene O'Bryan said, but her husband was a spendthrift. He had held and lost 21 jobs in the last few years, and the family had lived in five different cities. They had had constant financial worries. Even the necessities of life had been in doubt.

O'Bryan had done some strange things, and his wife had sought psychiatric help for him. She described one chilling incident to show what she meant. Her husband had been in bed, abnormally tense, and she had suddenly realized that he was holding a bayonet under his pillow—pushing it in and out of its scabbard. She had had a harrowing feeling that he might use it on himself or her. But she had not been able to find a "good Christian" psychiatrist, so she had given up on this venture and decided "to just seek the help of the Lord."

And Daynene O'Bryan told the detectives something that made the whole case a little clearer.

She explained how her husband had collected fire insurance on their furniture when they had lived in Baltimore years ago. She was sure he had set the fire or had knowledge of it. And there had been another insurance fire after they had moved to Texas.

So that was why it had happened, the officers thought.

The murder of Tim O'Bryan was brazen to the point of stupidity. But insurance frauds are often brazen to the point of stupidity, and most of them succeed. Ronald Clark O'Bryan was a habitual liar, and he was unbalanced enough to do it. He had probably said to himself, So what? The insurance company will pay. On two occasions in the past, he had filed claims so transparently fraudulent that his own wife had seen him for what he was—and yet both insurance companies had paid like slot machines. Seen in this perspective, Ronald Clark O'Bryan's murder of his son was nothing but an extension of the pattern he had always used to deal with his finances when they became acute. It was nothing but another insurance fraud—of monstrous proportions. An insurance fraud. The child's body for the insurance money, just as he had exchanged his furniture for the insurance money in Baltimore. Death by cyanide poisoning is excruciatingly painful. The boy's nostrils, flaring with blood and mucus; the glowing vessels in his brain. It was just a matter of finances, a matter of degree. Ronald Clark O'Bryan just had graduated to a bigger kind of insurance fraud.

Finally, the interview of Daynene O'Bryan approached its end.

"I feel that he needs help," she said of her husband. "I feel that he is dangerous. I feel that he cannot be allowed to walk out of this place for the sake of other children, for Lane's sake and for my sake."

Meanwhile, in a separate room, Detective Mullican was talking to the man who had killed little Timothy O'Bryan.

* * *

"Mr. O'Bryan," asked Detective Mullican, "how much insurance did you have on Timothy, and how long was it in effect prior to his death?"

O'Bryan looked startled. At the commencement of the interview, Detective Mullican had warned him of his constitutional rights: "You have the right to remain silent. . ." That had surprised him, but this startled him. The police weren't supposed to know about the insurance.

Mullican was using an effective interrogation technique, one that is used throughout the United States and, indeed, the world. Textbooks on police interrogation stress the importance of making the subject realize that his statements are but an elaboration of what the investigator already knows.

Talk to the subject politely, sincerely and patiently, the textbooks say. Be understanding. But be firm. And let him know that you know the facts. That was the effect of Mullican's first question.

O'Bryan paused before answering.

"Well," he said nervously, "I had a $10,000 policy with the New Outlook Club at the bank. Then I had a small policy or two, worth a couple of thousand dollars or so. I don't remember exactly how much the small ones are worth."

Detective Mullican knew that this was a lie.

When the subject lies, the textbooks say, show him the facts that disprove the lie. And have him explain them.

"Mr. O'Bryan," said Mullican politely but firmly, "isn't it true that around the first of October, just a few weeks ago, that you took out a $20,000 policy on your son and daughter?"

The suspect flinched.

Mullican pressed him. "Mr. O'Bryan, isn't it true that about four weeks ago you called a Mr. Gilbert Cartwright, an insurance agent in Galena Park, and asked him to come to your office at Meyerland, where you work, and told him that you wanted to take out $20,000 policies on both your children?"

Finally, O'Bryan capitulated.

"Yes," he said. "He came over, and we discussed what kind of policy was needed and decided that one was best."

Again, O'Bryan was lying.

"Mr. O'Bryan," said Mullican patiently, "according to Mr. Cartwright, there was no discussion at all."

O'Bryan, flustered, knew that the officer knew he was lying. "Well, yes, I decided this one was best. I didn't want the other one."

O'Bryan explained his cash payment: "I just happened to have enough money on me." He had kept the policies secret from his wife even to the extent of insisting that they not be mailed to him. "Well, I make all the decisions," he said. "She was real busy with church work."

Mullican asked why O'Bryan had been in such a hurry to file his insurance claim. Before the funeral, before the autopsy, in fact, within eleven hours of his son's death, O'Bryan had been calling the bank to get benefit forms. That was at 9:15 a.m., just a few minutes after the bank opened on the day after his son's murder.

Unseemly haste in collecting the money is a red flag. It is one of the telltale signs of insurance fraud.

"Well, Mr. Mullican," said O'Bryan, "I am in a very poor financial condition. And I didn't have the money to pay for the funeral."

"You are in a very poor financial condition, yet you could afford to pull over a hundred dollars out of your wallet and institute an excessive amount of insurance coverage?" said Mullican incredulously.

O'Bryan said that didn't seem unusual to him.

Mullican began to concentrate on the details of the killing. He asked whether O'Bryan had ever bought any Pixy Stix. Yes, said O'Bryan, he had; he had bought some just before Halloween, in fact. Mullican next asked whether O'Bryan had poured the candy down Timothy's throat. Well, O'Bryan answered, he had just sort of held the tube for Tim "so he wouldn't spill it." He didn't recall whether the Pixy Stix was stapled or factory sealed. He just hadn't paid any attention to that. When he was asked whether he had purchased a stapler recently, O'Bryan said "Yes," then said, "Well, no," and then changed his mind again and admitted that he had.

The interview had started at 5:30. It was now nearly 8 o'clock.

"Mr. O'Bryan," said Mullican, "do you feel like Timmy is better off being dead, since you feel he already is in heaven?"

"Yes," said O'Bryan, "I do."

Detective Mullican's report concluded with the following words: "After talking to Mr. Ronald O'Bryan for some two and a half hours, noting that he remained almost completely calm during this time even when asked a direct question about taking his own son's life, and after noting several very obvious lies, it is my opinion that Mr. O'Bryan is the prime suspect in the murder, by cyanide, of his son Timothy Marc O'Bryan."

*   *   *

It was one thing for Detective Mullican to write those words in an internal police report. It would be quite another if Mike Hinton said the same thing in a criminal indictment and then presented it to the grand jury.

Normally, Assistant District Attorney Mike Hinton was no shrinking violet. In fact, he was one of the most colorful, boisterous prosecutors the Houston District Attorney's Office had ever seen. His infectious laugh, his booming voice and his taste for good Scotch whiskey were legendary to those who knew him. He was a decisive man, with plenty of experience to back him up.

Hinton had been a prosecutor since he got out of law school. His formative years were spent in Randall County, Texas, where he was the District Attorney's only assistant. It was like being a country doctor. "There, you did it all," Hinton said. "Everything from going with the officers to make a bust to arguing the case in the Court of Criminal Appeals."

But on this case, Mike Hinton didn't know quite what to do.

"I'm grown up enough to make my own decisions," he said. "But this thing was bizarre.

"I was so shocked, I called Carol."

Carol Vance was the elected Criminal District Attorney of Harris County. Although the position he held made him Houston's top prosecutor, he didn't routinely participate in investigations. The reason was simple: It took all of his time to make the policy decisions that ran his office. The workload of the Houston office was huge, and Vance had over 100 lawyers working for him as assistant district attorneys.

But Carol Vance still tried cases when he could, and he was capable of making investigative decisions quickly when the case needed him.

Now, Mike Hinton had Carol Vance on the telephone.

He told the district attorney the strange turn the case had taken. It was the father, Ronald Clark O'Bryan. The evidence was circumstantial. O'Bryan was persistent in denying his guilt. There would have to be a great deal more investigation before the case would be ready for trial. There was no doubt in Hinton's mind O'Bryan was their man, but this was a case with national attention focused on it. All the wire services were there. A father who had killed his own son—

"Do you want me to come out, Mike?" Vance asked.

"Yes," said Mike Hinton unequivocally.

It was near midnight when Carol Vance drove out to the Pasadena Police Building. Once again, the officers went over the evidence they had gathered—this time, with the district attorney himself. It was early in the morning when Vance had heard enough. He agreed with Hinton's assessment. The man was a murderer. He should be charged. And it should be done tonight.

Together, the prosecutors drew the indictment charging Ronald Clark O'Bryan with the capital murder of his son.

It was not just murder; it was capital murder. The capital murder statute said that murder for "remuneration" was a capital offense. Life insurance proceeds were remuneration. And so the money that had been Ronald Clark O'Bryan's motive was also the reason his crime was a capital one. He would face the death penalty because of it.

Later, Hinton drew up four more indictments. Each of them charged O'Bryan with an offense of attempted murder.

There was one for each of the Pixy Stix.

Stripped of their legalism, these last four indictments told an amazing story. Ronald Clark O'Bryan had tried to kill his own daughter. He had tried to kill the two Rourke children and a boy from the neighborhood who just happened to be at the door. Had he succeeded, it would have seemed a random, purposeless act. And that, strangely enough, was precisely the purpose behind it. Ronald Clark O'Bryan, the indictments said, had been willing to kill all these children merely to obscure the trail that led to him through the insurance policies, the Pixy Stix and the body of his poisoned son. This man had been willing to commit four more murders of children to cover up the first one.*

---

* The following names in this chapter were changed, without alteration of the incidents in which the persons were involved: Andy Rourke, Michelle Rourke, Philip Rourke, Anne Rourke, Gilbert Cartwright, William Hudspeth.

The Halloween Candy Murder Case. The funeral of Timothy O'Bryan. The murdered child's head is visible in the open coffin. His death was caused by a large dose of cyanide, which has the effect of accelerating breathing, rushing blood to the brain, and finally inducing vomiting, convulsions and death. His father, Ronald O'Bryan, sits in the front row; he commenced the process of collecting $20,000 worth of insurance on the child's life before the funeral was held. (Photograph courtesy Houston Post).

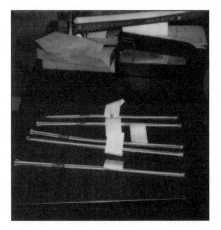

The Halloween Candy Murder Case. The murder weapon was a plastic tube filled with an innocuous-looking confection called a Pixy Stix. O'Bryan handed out five of them, one of which was eaten by his son Timothy. The candy tube had been slit open and partially filled with poison. Tags on each tube contain exhibit numbers.

The Halloween Candy Murder Case. Daynene O'Bryan testifies against her husband. At lower left, in front of the witness, sits court reporter Ann Rossberg. This shot was taken during the entry of a spectator into the courtroom, while the door was ajar. The photographer had stationed himself outside for precisely that purpose, and snapped the shutter before the door closed again. (Photograph courtesy Houston Post.)

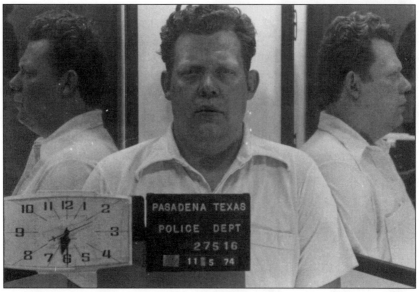

The Halloween Candy Murder Case. Booking photograph of Ronald Clark O'Bryan, taken shortly after his arrest for the capital murder of his son. Part of the evidence against him was his false accusation against an innocent stranger, whom he was willing to blame for the crime in order to avert suspicion from himself. On death row, he still proclaimed his innocence.

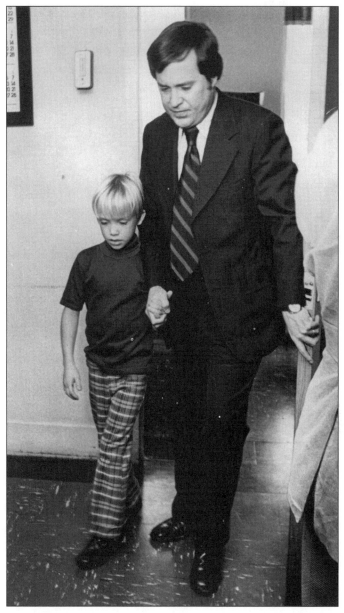

The Halloween Candy Murder Case. Assistant District Attorney Michael Hinton walks toward the Grand Jury Room holding the hand of one of the trick-or-treating children (Photograph courtesy Houston Post). Ronald Clark O'Bryan not only murdered his son, he attempted to murder his daughter and three other children by giving each a piece of Halloween candy containing cyanide.

Chapter 11

The Trial of Ronald O'Bryan

Richard Harrison must have emerged from that three-hour conference with an awareness that his client's future was bleak.

But the veteran defense lawyer did not show it.

He met with the press and made a statement: O'Bryan was not a murderer. Instead, said Harrison, his client was "heartbroken over the boy's death."

He had been hired by relatives, Harrison explained, and the family might hire other counsel later. "But in the meantime," he said, "I am trying to protect this man's rights."

And Richard Harrison proceeded vigorously to do just that.

One of the first steps Harrison took was to file a request for an examining trial. An examining trial, in Texas, is a preliminary hearing; it is a procedure designed to determine whether there is sufficient evidence to warrant grand jury action on the case. Similar procedures exist in most other states.

Why an examining trial demand in this case, since it seemed clear the prosecution could put on enough evidence to secure an indictment? The reason was simple. The prosecutors might be able to show probable cause, but they would have to put on their case to do it. And they would have to expose their witnesses to cross examination. That would give a good defense lawyer a chance to pick apart their testimony.

Harrison also filed a petition for habeas corpus. It requested the release of his client on a small bond.

As matters developed, only a single hearing was held—on the habeas corpus petition. The State's case was complicated. Hinton called witness after witness. As Harrison cross-examined them, he began to learn what he needed to defend his client.

It became painfully obvious that the complexity of the case would require more than one lawyer for the defense. And Ronald Clark O'Bryan was indigent. He would not be able to pay the cost of a defense even by a single attorney.

And so Judge Frank Price, to whom the case had been assigned, appointed Harrison to represent Ronald Clark O'Bryan at county expense. He also appointed a second lawyer, to assist Harrison. Marvin Teague, a criminal lawyer with a reputation for excellence in getting convictions reversed by appellate courts as well as for vigorous defense at trial, joined the defense team.

Teague brought a distinctive flavor to the case. He had a crew cut and eyes that twinkled behind rimless glasses. He looked like what some courthouse practitioners call a "book lawyer," and in fact he was good with the books; but that wasn't all he was. He could be alternately scholarly and folksy. And he was a veteran of the rough-and-tumble of criminal trials. His experience included the defense of hundreds of serious criminal cases.

Mike Hinton was going to have a difficult time of it.

Hinton had secured the indictment he had sought from the grand jury, and he had succeeded in getting the judge to order Ronald Clark O'Bryan held without bond. But there was a great deal more he needed to do before the took his case to trial. And a lot of it would be unglamorous, plain hard work. It would involve digging for more evidence. Mindful of the circumstantial nature of his case, Mike Hinton wanted to be sure he had found all the evidence there was to find.

* * *

Assistant District Attorney Vic Driscoll was the perfect foil to Mike Hinton.

Hinton was boisterous; Driscoll was quiet. Hinton was the fiery orator before a jury, while Driscoll was the calm voice of reason.

Early in the case, Hinton had recruited Driscoll as co-counsel for the state. The two prosecutors formed the core of the team. Together, they kept in close touch with the Pasadena detectives. Together, they reviewed the evidence and looked for new leads.

The investigation continued without a pause after O'Bryan's arrest. The Pasadena detectives, very early, searched the O'Bryan house and car. They asked for, and got, the permission of Daynene O'Bryan, who signed a standard consent-to-search form.

The search of the O'Bryan car did not turned anything up. But the search of the house did.

Officer Evelyn Lancaster found a knife belonging to O'Bryan that had minute traces of purplish substance on it. There was also a pair of scissors in the house with the same traces.

The Pixy Stix had contained powdered candy that was about the same color.

Lancaster submitted the knife and scissors to the medical examiner's office for identification of the substance. If it matched the Pixy Stix candy, Hinton and Driscoll thought they would have some useful evidence.

The defense lawyers would probably attack the evidence on fourth amendment grounds, claiming that it was the result of an illegal search and seizure. They would try to get it suppressed. But they probably would not succeed, Hinton thought; a wife could lawfully consent to the search of a home jointly possessed by her and her husband. The Supreme Court had said so.

Meanwhile, a surprising development was beginning. The Pasadena Police Department was beginning to get calls from citizens who had something to add to the investigation. And quite a number of people, as it happened, had something to say about Ronald Clark O'Bryan's curious interest in cyanide.

Arthur Don Moseley was a typical example. A 42-year-old chemist with an oil company, he had known Ronald O'Bryan for four years. When he read in the newspapers about the Halloween Candy Case, he wondered about a conversation he had had with O'Bryan a few days earlier. Now that O'Bryan had been arrested, he called the police department to tell what he knew.

Now he was dictating an affidavit to the detectives.

"Some time in the early part of September—I think it was on a Tuesday night—Ron called me about 9:00 p.m.," he said.

"He indicated that he was taking a chemistry course at San Jacinto College and had a discussion with his instructor about cyanide compounds."

O'Bryan had wanted to test his instructor's knowledge, Moseley said. At least, that was why he had told Moseley he was calling. The conversation had been lengthy, and O'Bryan had wanted to know how many cyanide compounds there were, what the most common ones were, whether cyanide was detectable in the body, and where it could be purchased. Moseley had told him that The Curtin Company, an industrial chemical sales company, was one of the biggest suppliers in the area.

"He then asked me how much cyanide it would take to be fatal," Moseley said. "I asked him why he wanted to know all this. It ran through my mind that his was not the kind of question that a grown man would ask."

Within hours, the Pasadena detectives were calling on the Curtin Company.

"He asked me if we carried potassium cyanide," said Curtin employee Sam Ricks, after identifying a photograph of O'Bryan. "I told him yes. I think the man wanted the one pound size, but we were out. And he asked about the five pound size."

Apparently O'Bryan had not bought the five pound bag because it cost too much. The price had been fifty dollars. He had gotten the name of another company, a company that sold cyanide in smaller lots, and he had walked out of the store.

The detectives got several other calls linking O'Bryan with cyanide.

Fred Hinman had been a patient of O'Bryan's at Texas State Optical Company. O'Bryan had been carrying a new pocket stapler with him. And after he had explained to Hinman what the visit was going to cost him, he had asked Hinman an odd question: "Say, what do you know about cyanide?" Hinman had told him that a small amount could be fatal.

Hinman had not realized the significance of the conversation until he had seen film clips of O'Bryan's arrest on television.

At about the same time Fred Hinman came forward, a co-worker of O'Bryan's gave an affidavit that said: "Approximately the last two and a half weeks in October, Ronald approached me on different occasions when we were not too busy at work and asked me questions about potassium cyanide such as the lethal effects, and was it the most deadly poison.

"Also somewhere in the conversations he brought up the effect of arsenic, and was it as powerful as cyanide," the affidavit went on. "He seemed to be trying to decide which was the most powerful."

As Mike Hinton and Vic Driscoll read these affidavits, they marveled at Ronald O'Bryan's cold-bloodedness.

There was one more thing.

The medical examiner's office had written a report about the substance on the knife and scissors. It was identical to the substance in the Pixy Stix. These two items, found in O'Bryan's home, were the implements that had been used to open the candy and to remove enough of it to put the cyanide inside.

* * *

The investigation was over.

The trial had finally begun.

As they plodded through jury selection, Hinton and Driscoll used extreme care to see that every juror could accept their case if they proved it. The case was circumstantial; would the jurors be able to believe circumstantial evidence? Could they decide in favor of the prosecution if that evidence was strong enough to overcome all reasonable doubt?

Jury selection had been going on, now, for over two weeks. Ten jurors had been selected. It was clear the process could not last much longer. There were only two more positions to fill, and besides, both sides were running out of challenges.

The man who might be the eleventh juror walked into the courtroom.

Hinton read his name from the jury list. "Dan Kirktrane," it said. Hinton knew that these last two jurors were crucial. When it got down to both sides' last challenges, and both sides were taking risks in accepting jurors for fear someone less acceptable might be the alternative, the case could quickly be won or lost on the choices that were made.

Hinton and Driscoll looked intently at Dan Kirktrane. He was carrying a motorcycle helmet. He had gold jewelry around his neck. His appearance radiated an anti-establishment attitude, a countercultural bias, that seemed sure to go deeper than the clothes he was wearing. Hinton and Driscoll knew that such nuances as this were the very essence of jury selection. And Dan Kirktrane did not look like the sort of man who would be comfortable voting as the prosecution wanted him to.

The examination was brisk. Dan Kirktrane answered the questions and was qualified. His answers were short and to the point.

Hinton whispered to Driscoll, "Do you think we ought to keep him?"

Paradoxically, Driscoll thought so. "He's a risk," Driscoll admitted. "We're taking a chance." But the prosecutors did not have enough challenges to remove everyone they might want to.

Finally, Driscoll—who had been examining this juror—stood. "The State will accept Mr. Kirktrane, your honor," he said.

Across the table, the defense lawyers reacted with surprise. But they were happy to agree. With satisfaction, they accepted the juror, too.

Dan Kirktrane became juror number eleven.

The drama of the moment overshadowed the strategy that had gone before it. Hinton and Driscoll had examined Dan Kirktrane with care. Could he accept circumstantial evidence? In asking the question, the prosecutors had brought out all the uncertainties that circumstantial evidence evokes, just to test the potential juror's reaction. Could the juror accept circumstantial evidence in a death penalty case, provided it was strong enough?

Kirktrane had said that he could accept the prosecutor's case if they proved it to him. He could also find in favor of the defense if there was a reasonable doubt. All four of the lawyers in the courtroom had believed him. Now, each of them watched as juror number eleven walked from the courtroom with instructions to return when the jury was complete.

Across the table from the prosecutors, Marvin Teague permitted himself a nervous chuckle. "He's one for the defense, I hope," he said softly to the prosecutors.

*　*　*

Andy Rourke was one of the State's first witnesses.

"He said he wanted to buy a home in the Bowling Green addition, where I live," Rourke said of O'Bryan.

O'Bryan had been nearly broke at the time. "He said, 'I've got some money, but I'll have some more coming in before the end of this year.'"

Rourke took the jury through the route the trick-or-treaters had followed that Halloween night. And he described how O'Bryan had waited at the dark door of 4112 Donerail—a door that never opened.

Rourke's son, Philip, was simple and childlike. "We rang the doorbell, and yelled 'Trick or treat!'" he said, "but nobody answered the door, so me and Tim ran on to the next house."

The defense lawyers tried to cross-examine Philip, but they were singularly unsuccessful. As often happens with children, it only showed that he lacked the age and sophistication to lie.

The chemical salesman, Sam Ricks, told how O'Bryan had tried to buy cyanide from him.

The ambulance driver recounted O'Bryan's mysterious illness and miraculous recovery at the hospital.

Dramatically, the man O'Bryan had framed—William Hudspeth—told the jury where he had been Halloween night: at work, at the Houston airport. His co-workers corroborated his testimony.

A succession of Pasadena detectives told about O'Bryan's statements, half-truths, and falsehoods during the investigation. The interview with Detective Mullican, with its damning lies and evasions, was not admissible, because an oral statement of a suspect in custody could not be told to the jury in Texas. Amazingly, Texas was the only state that excluded this kind of confession. But the previous statements of the defendant, before he was a suspect, were damning enough in themselves.

A vice-president of the company that manufactured Pixy Stix testified that the candy was heat sealed at the factory. "We do not use staples," he said, "because it would be too easy for a staple to get into the candy and be eaten by a child."

The funeral director who handled the services for Timothy O'Bryan told of the grieving father's strange request: O'Bryan had wanted not one, but six, certified copies of the death certificate—for use, he said, in collecting insurance.

Officer Evelyn Lancaster told about the knife and scissors she found in O'Bryan's home.

The insurance agent, Gilbert Cartwright, testified about O'Bryan's cash payment, his strange secrecy, and his insistence upon buying straight life policies rather than the more logical juvenile policies.

O'Bryan's banker testified that the defendant's bank account was nearly empty. O'Bryan was about to have his car repossessed.

Daynene O'Bryan related to the jury how she had discovered the existence of the policies: from Detective Nassif. And she told how O'Bryan had held the Pixy Stix and poured it down Timothy's throat.

Arthur Don Moseley, the chemist, and Fred Hinman, the Optical patient, described their conversations with O'Bryan—and his unusual interest in cyanide.

But the best witnesses of all were the children. Their testimony made it clear that no one but O'Bryan had been responsible for the Pixy Stix. He had not gotten them from 4112 Donerail. That house had been empty, with no lights on and no one at the door. Ronald Clark O'Bryan had had the Pixy Stix all along. And he had given them out, one by one, to each of the children. The Pixy Stix had come from Ronald Clark O'Bryan's own hand.

A prosecutor who rests his case always feels some anxiety. It is easy to make a mistake and to leave something out. But this was one time when Mike Hinton did not hesitate to stand and say, "Your honor, the state rests."

* * *

If the defendant chooses to testify, it is always the high point of a criminal trial.

So it was in Ronald Clark O'Bryan's case.

The tiny courtroom in Judge Price's 209th District Court was cramped anyway, and today it was packed to the rafters. The reporters had all gotten there early and had the best seats. People from Pasadena ran them a close second. All the aisles were crowded with lawyers. No one could move. It was hard even to breathe.

The defense lawyers questioned their client for nearly three hours. They drew from him the story of his life, from his birth to the present moment. They had him describe how someone — an "unknown" person, he now said — had given him the Pixy Stix. Ronald Clark O'Bryan insisted that he had no idea who had given him the candy, and he denied that he had ever told the detectives it was the man at 4112 Donerail. "It could have been a man, woman, boy or girl," he said. He didn't know.

As the examination neared its end, Richard Harrison spoke earnestly to his client. The points he was about to make now were crucial.

"Did you ever put cyanide in a Pixy Stix and give it to your son, Mr. O'Bryan?"

"No, sir, I did not," the defendant replied firmly from the witness stand.

"And did you know that the Pixy Stix you gave that child had poison in it?"

"Good God," said O'Bryan emphatically. "If I had, I'd never have given it to him."

Finally, Harrison passed the witness.

Mike Hinton's cross examination would come next.

Why had O'Bryan needed that much life insurance on his children, Hinton wanted to know?

"The two $20,000 policies were not taken out as life insurance, but to build up a cash value on them," O'Bryan said. When Hinton pointed out that the juvenile policies would have had a better cash value for the money, O'Bryan said he thought the ones he bought were just a better buy.

And then Hinton pointed out that O'Bryan, who had overinsured his children, had no insurance on his own life.

As to the cyanide conversation with Hinman, O'Bryan said, it probably did not occur—because "we're not supposed to talk to patients." He had talked to his friend Arthur Don Moseley about cyanide, but it was just out of curiosity.

O'Bryan admitted that he had not been taking a chemistry course at the time, as he had told Moseley.

"Isn't it true," Hinton asked finally, "that from the very beginning of your marriage you lived beyond your income?"

"Yes, I have lived beyond my income," O'Bryan said. "I always wanted my wife and children to live well.

"Yes, I dream. I dream of the very best for me and my family."

*   *   *

The case was almost over, but not quite.

Mike Hinton had some rebuttal witnesses.

Robert Parkinson had attended the funeral. He had spoken with O'Bryan there. "I told him that Timothy looked so peaceful and so good that he might open his eyes and say something to me," Parkinson testified.

"O'Bryan replied that he, himself, had committed Timothy to the care of the Lord."

Parkinson also quoted O'Bryan as saying he envied Tim because he would not have to "go through the trials and tribulations" that his father had had to face. "That was the first time," Parkinson said with evident revulsion, "I have ever heard anyone say they envied someone who was a corpse."

The jurors listened to arguments and heard the judge's instructions. Then they left to deliberate.

Ninety minutes after the jury retired, it was back with a verdict. The judge read it with a clear voice: "We, the jury, find the defendant, Ronald Clark O'Bryan, guilty of the offense of capital murder, as charged in the indictment."

O'Bryan had been convicted of the murder of his son.

*   *   *

The penalty hearing was short.

The defense called a string of character witnesses for Ronald Clark O'Bryan. One by one, they testified that O'Bryan would not be a threat to society if given a life sentence. And one after another, they said they thought he was innocent in this case.

"If a person has been incarcerated," said one of the defense witnesses, "it is the state's job to rehabilitate him—not to take a life."

The prosecutors had no additional evidence in the penalty hearing. The reason was that they had put all of the evidence they needed into the trial on guilt or innocence.

The crime spoke for itself.

When it came time for jury argument, Vic Driscoll stood for the prosecution. And it quickly became clear that for this case, at least, Driscoll was not going to be scholarly.

O'Bryan, said Driscoll, "did not have the truth in him, even when the truth would do him better.

"He has used his friends, his family and his church," the prosecutor went on. "He has sacrificed his only son—not on the altar of God as Abraham might have done, but on the altar of his own greed."

Marvin Teague saw the case differently.

"Sure, they lived high on the hog," the defense lawyer said. "Sure, they lived beyond their means—just like you and me.

"Maybe it's a crime if you don't have tears flowing like the Brazos in a flood," Teague went on, answering charges that his client had been cold and unemotional when accused of his son's death. "But does that sound like a man who'd knock off his son for a few gold coins?"

In the second defense argument, Richard Harrison told the jury not to lose sight of the "real" issues in the case. As he saw it, the real issue was that the prosecution hadn't proved anything. Not only had the prosecutors failed in their burden to prove the issues in the punishment phase of the trial; they hadn't even proved that Ronald Clark O'Bryan was guilty.

"Has the State proved that he ever bought cyanide?" Harrison asked emotionally. "No. Has the State proved that he bought Pixy Stix? No."

"And that's what this case is all about."

Harrison sat down.

Now Mike Hinton would give the final argument, the closing argument for the prosecution.

"It is the most despicable crime I ever heard of, to take the life of your own flesh and blood for money—to kill a kid for money," he shouted.

And Hinton did not hold anything back. He told the jurors that O'Bryan "ought to be damned for what he did."

Was O'Bryan dangerous? Was he a threat to society? Hinton's answer to that was an emphatic "yes." He reminded the jurors of the defendant's willingness to see another human being, William Hudspeth, falsely accused for his own crime. And he told them "not to forget for one minute" that O'Bryan had been perfectly ready to poison a group of other children "to cover up his tracks."

The courtroom was hushed as the jury filed out for the last time.

* * *

Dan Kirktrane's motorcycle helmet looked like a big plastic bowl. It was propped up on a chair in the jury deliberation room.

Kirktrane was colorful. The other jurors liked him. He was a man of judgment, and he had some influence with them. Now that they had discussed the evidence, they were ready to vote.

One by one, they filed by — and they dropped their slips of paper into Dan Kirktrane's motorcycle helmet.

It was an unorthodox ballot box, but it was the most functional one the jurors could find. Furthermore, they were not an orthodox jury. There were young people and old, blacks and whites — liberal and conservative. And there was Dan Kirktrane. It was a jury — and as juries always are, it was unorthodox. It was different from any other collection of twelve people.

On the first ballot, the jurors were unanimous.

They filed into the courtroom and handed the verdict sheet to Judge Price. The judge read it; then he announced that it was in order.

The jury's answer to the first question, he read, was "Yes."

Ronald Clark O'Bryan had killed his son deliberately.

The courtroom was hushed.

The answer to the second question, too, was "Yes."

There was a probability that Ronald Clark O'Bryan would commit future crimes of violence, and he would be a continuing threat to society. That was what the jury had found.

Judge Price, in accordance with the jury's verdict, assessed the defendant's sentence at death.

At his cell on Huntsville's death row, O'Bryan continued to protest his innocence. Marvin Teague, his lawyer, visited him in jail, and later said, "He told me he hopes the actual killer is caught before next Halloween, so this doesn't happen again."

And the minister of the Second Baptist Church said, "His religious faith is probably the only thing" carrying O'Bryan through the ordeal.

O'Bryan's fellow prisoners on death row seemed to like and accept him; none had a harsh word to say about this man who had used church and family to shield his act of murder. But in their cynicism, they gave O'Bryan a nickname that fit his case.

They called him The Candy Man.

*   *   *

What had produced the death sentence for Ronald Clark O'Bryan?

Why did O'Bryan receive a sentence of death when John Stiles Griffin, for example, had been sentenced to life imprisonment?

What was the difference between the two cases?

The O'Bryan prosecutors had selected the jury with painstaking care. They had done a superb job—not just in the jurors they had selected, for that is largely guesswork, but in the way they had questioned them.

And the case that Hinton and Driscoll put on was compelling. They, and the Pasadena detectives, had left no stone unturned. There had been fifty-one prosecution witnesses in all. Each one had told a small piece of the story, but the prosecutors had made them into a mosaic, a whole picture—and the pieces had come to life. Certainly the jurors had thought so; they had been completely convinced. As the foreman said, after the case, "The evidence of guilt was just overwhelming."

But it was more than that; the prosecutors had successfully made the jury feel the full horror of the crime. The helpless dependence of the victim on his father, the remorseless hypocrisy of the defendant, and his willingness to kill four other children made the offense stand out in any person's mind.

But even that was not all of it.

Ronald Clark O'Bryan had done more than commit murder. His was an act of desecration.

Ever since the dawn of time, the world's greatest literature has said it clearly: murder within the family is the worst kind of homicide. The ancient Viking legends condemn it as the most heinous of all possible offenses. The song of Beowulf glorifies violence, but it heaps contempt upon the "killing of kin." The Bible's strongest condemnation is reserved for Cain, who murdered his brother.

But there is another ancient story that fits Ronald Clark O'Bryan's case even better. It is the Faustian legend.

The Faustian legend has taken many forms, and it appears in different guises in different civilizations. For English-speaking peoples, the most famous version is Christopher Marlowe's play—in which Doctor Faustus bargains for earthy riches with Mephistopheles and Beezlebub, using his own soul as currency.

Ronald Clark O'Bryan was a modern Doctor Faustus. He invoked the name of Jesus and wept at the memorial service for his son. But his death sentence was a recognition of the fact that he also came as close as mortal man can come to selling his soul to the devil.*

* The following names in this chapter were changed, without alteration of the incidents in which the persons were involved: Arthur Don Moseley, Fred Hinman, Sam Ricks, Dan Kirktrane, Robert Parkinson.

PART THREE

The Evidence and the
Life or Death Decision

THERE ARE SOME CAPITAL MURDER CASES IN WHICH the result is determined by the jury.

But there are other capital murder cases, too, in which the outcome is determined by knotty, technical rules of law, or by the availability of the evidence. In such a case, the question may come down to this: how much can the jury hear? What can the jury be told? What facts are there that remain hidden from the jury, either because they are not obtainable or because they are kept out of the trial by technical rules?

In this part of the book, we will look at two extraordinary cases.

The case of Gerald Bodde was a capital murder in which the prosecution had an unusual problem. As the trial got underway, the prosecution's evidence slowly began to disappear. The question was whether there would be enough left for the jury to see what had happened. Would Gerald Bodde be convicted of beating an elderly woman to death? And if he was, what would his sentence be?

And there was another extraordinary case that had serious problems about evidence—the cases of a bizarre group of men who called themselves the Brady Bunch. That was because one of their first murders was committed on Brady Street. These four men seemed to have overwhelming cases against them—they confessed to a group of television news reporters, who filmed the confession and broadcast it on the six o'clock news. The members of the Brady Bunch were credited with six brutal murders, and their confessions described most of their crimes in detail. But would they be convicted? That depended upon whether the confessions would stand up in court.

Again, as with Ronald Clark O' Bryan's case or John Stiles Griffin's case, the results may not be what you would expect.

Chapter 12

The Murder of an Old Woman

The people who were involved:

Gerald Bodde	The defendant. He was accused of murdering his landlady with a pipe.
Jean Dodd	The defendant's former live-in girlfriend. When she discovered what he was like, she moved out as quickly as she could.
Roberta (Bobbie) Dodd	She was five years old, and she called Gerald Bodde "Jerry," until she saw what he had done to Bernice Hartsfield.
Bernice Hartsfield	The victim. She was eighty-one years old.
Lieutenant Hiram Contreras	The Houston police officer who arrested the defendant and helped rescue the kidnap victim unharmed. The discovery of the murder came as a complete surprise to him.
The Houston Police Department Property Room	In addition to Gerald Bodde, it was the villain of the piece.
The Honorable Dan Walton	The judge. He finally decided that Bobbie Dodd couldn't be allowed to testify.
Marvin Teague, Donald Rogers and Frank Shepherd	Counsel for the defense. One of their arguments was that Bernice Hartsfield might have loaned her diamond rings, silverware and bond certificates to the defendant.
George Jacobs, Doug Shaver and David Crump	The prosecutors. They started the case with plenty of evidence, but during the trial it started, mysteriously, to disappear.

The jurors   At times they must have seen the case as a
                             modern-day Whodunit, but their final decision
                             was about a brutal murder.

                                     *   *   *

Jean Dodd walked from room to room in her apartment. There had
been no word from the kidnaper for two days, and she couldn't stop looking at the telephone.

Her daughter, Bobbie, was five years old. But Bobbie had been missing
since Friday, and no one knew whether she was still alive.

The last thing Jean Dodd had heard had been on Saturday, January 4.
That was when Jerry Bodde, the man she had once lived with, had called
to tell her that he had taken Bobbie and wanted a thousand dollars' ransom. He had said he would call again. But now it was nearly seven o'clock
on January 6, and no word had come yet.

Suddenly, the telephone rang.

The two police officers who were in the room with Jean Dodd were
immediately alert. One of them turned on the tape recorder. The electronic
instrument that would attempt to trace the call was already operational. Jean
Dodd's heart was pounding as she picked up the telephone.

"Hello?" she said.

The kidnaper's voice was relaxed and casual. "Do you want Bobbie
back?" Jerry Bodde asked.

The tape reel was turning. Jean Dodd paid no attention to it as she
answered, eagerly, "I got your money. I had it since Saturday."

"One thousand dollars?" the kidnaper asked.

"Where is my baby?" asked Mrs. Dodd desperately.

The kidnaper, though, was insistent. "You got a thousand dollars?"

"Yes," she answered. "I've had it since Saturday."

The kidnaper was still not satisfied. "Have you done called the law on
me?" he asked. "Did you call the law?" With the two police officers standing beside her, Jean Dodd earnestly denied that she had. She tried to convince him, to reassure him.

"Well," said Jerry Bodde, "I'm going to send Bobbie back in a pine box
if you called the law on me."

The officers watched as the tape turned on its reel. The conversation, they
reflected, would have been humorous had it not concerned the child's life
or death. "I'll send her back in a pine box?" It sounded like something
straight out of the movies.

Actually, the whole kidnaping was hard to understand. Why would
anyone hold a child for ransom and then make a demand for only one
thousand dollars? And why would anyone take the child of a woman

whom he knew—especially when he also knew, as Gerald Bodde surely knew, that Jean Dodd didn't have a thousand dollars?

Mrs. Dodd was at the edge of poverty, and the ransom demand might as well have been for a million dollars. But she reassured the kidnaper—and hoped that if she met him at the payoff place, he would lead the police to her daughter.

The officers shook their heads. But they were hearing it with their own ears. And there was no question that the man's threats had to be taken seriously.

"Jerry, please," Mrs. Dodd breathed into the telephone. "I want my baby. I got you the money."

"Listen," said Gerald Bodde. "I'm taking care of Bobbie. I'm feeding her three meals a day and I'm taking good care of her. But I want a thousand dollars. I'm hard up."

And he gave her the instructions that told her where, and how, to make the payoff.

* * *

Three hours later, Mrs. Dodd took a seat in a crowded restaurant on Houston's west side. It was more crowded than usual, because it was filled with plainclothes police officers.

Mrs. Dodd had been seated only a short time when she was paged for a telephone call—a call she was expecting.

It was the kidnaper, Gerald Bodde. He had some new directions for her. There was a set of apartments up the hill from the restaurant, he said. Yes, Jean Dodd answered, she could see them.

"Go to apartment number 53 in those apartments," Bodde said. There would be someone there to take the money. And, the kidnaper reminded the distraught mother, if she didn't bring the money, he would send Bobbie home "in a box."

"I've already killed an old lady," the kidnaper added casually, as if in passing. "It was easy. And I'll kill Bobbie too." Jean Dodd, concerned about the child above all else, reassured him. The remark about "killing an old lady" didn't catch her attention.

She spoke to the officer in charge, Lieutenant Hiram Contreras. Then she left for the apartment complex. And within minutes, the police contingent had left the restaurant and had regrouped at unit number 53. Lieutenant Contreras stationed himself, along with two others, inside the apartment.

A few minutes later, Gerald Bodde arrived. He evidently planned to collect the ransom personally.

Jean Dodd saw him first. "Where's my baby?" she asked urgently.

"Where's the money?" Bodde answered.

Lieutenant Contreras stepped out of the door. "You're under arrest," he said. Another officer handcuffed Bodde and took the pistol that was in his pocket. The kidnaper had his hand on the pistol, and there were five live rounds in it.

"Where's the little girl?" Contreras asked.

"In San Antonio," Bodde answered. "And she's safe."

Within hours, the little girl was rescued from the boarding house in San Antonio where the kidnaper had left her. It seemed that the work of the police on the case was nearly over. The victim was reunited with her mother. And there was little further investigation needed to solidify the kidnaping case, because the suspect's voice was on tape, he was known to the victim, and he had been arrested in the very act of collecting the ransom.

But the case was not solved yet.

And the reason it was not solved was that the kidnaping was only the tip of the iceberg.

When Gerald Bodde had been arrested, there had been a set of keys in his pocket. One of them fit the car he was driving: a green Chevrolet, which was parked near the apartments. The car was filled with a curious set of items, including clothing, a radio, a set of silverware—and other personal property. There was a name on some of the articles: "Bernice Hartsfield."

"I've already killed an old lady," the kidnaper had said to Jean Dodd. But the distraught mother had been so concerned about getting her daughter back that she had attached no significance to it. The course of the investigation might have been different if she had.

*   *   *

A few hours later, little Bobbie Dodd was telling her story.

"Then we got on a freeway and drove a long ways." She was describing the trip to San Antonio. "Jerry never did play nasty with me or take my clothes off."

Officer Mary Tobar was listening to the little girl and taking down her statement. Throughout the interview, Tobar asked the child questions to guide her through the kidnaping. For the most part, the story seemed simple and coherent. But there was one thing that Bobbie had said that came as a surprise, and it needed to be investigated right away.

"Before we left to get on the freeway," the little girl said, "Jerry went to some apartments. And Jerry told me to get in the closet because he was going to kill somebody."

That got Tobar's attention. He was going to kill somebody?

"There was an old lady there," Bobbie went on. "And Jerry got an iron rod from under the bed. And I heard him hit the old lady on the head. When 1 came out of the closet she was down on the floor and her head was bleeding."

Tobar wondered at it. The little girl did not seem to be inventing the incident. She could talk about it in detail. She even told Tobar how the kidnaper had wrapped the body in a blanket, locked it in a closet, and covered the blood on the floor with two small rugs.

Could there have been another crime involved in this kidnaping? Could there have been a murder too?

Mary Tobar asked Jean Dodd about it.

Something stirred in Mrs. Dodd's memory. "Jerry told me over the phone that he had killed an old lady," she said. And she added, "Bobbie doesn't lie." The child was not in the habit of making up stories.

Tobar thought about it. The car that Gerald Bodde had been driving at the time of his arrest was registered to a Mrs. Bernice Hartsfield. And some of her property had been found in the car.

Earlier, the Houston Police Department had run a "make" on the car, routinely. But the NCIC—the National Crime Information Center—had reported no "stolen or wanted" on it. Now, suddenly, it dawned on the officers that there would not have been any stolen-or-wanted on the car if the owner had been killed before it was taken.

Someone looked up Bernice Hartsfield's number in the telephone book, dialed it and listened to the ring for several minutes. There was no answer.

Within minutes, a team of detectives was knocking at the door of the modest white frame house that was the Hartsfield residence. The door was locked, and there was no answer. The officers took it from its hinges and went inside; They searched each room, one by one. The master bedroom, they saw, had a safe in it. The safe had been opened and ransacked.

Finally, the officers struggled to open the hall closet.

"Jerry wrapped this old lady up in a blanket that he killed," Bobbie Dodd had said. "And locked her up in a hall closet."

Now the closet door was open. There, on the floor, was a rolled patchwork blanket. It was rolled around something bulky and soft, and the ends of it were tied—tied with electrical cords. Immediately, the officers knew what it was.

Because there was blood oozing from one end of the blanket.

Inside, there was the body of an elderly lady. Her name was Bernice Hartsfield. But a friend who came to identify her remains found that Bernice Hartsfield was hardly recognizable, because her face had been misshapen by a severe beating with a blunt instrument. It was blackened on both sides. Her skull was crushed, and chips of bone were imbedded in her exposed brain. Her head was mottled with dried blood.

She had been dead for several days.

In the kitchen, the officers found a pair of small rugs. Underneath them, there were bloodstains—just as Bobbie Dodd had said there would be.

This was where the murder had been committed.

In the front room, the detectives found an iron pipe. There was a waste-basket filed with bloody tissue, which had evidently been used to clean the pipe and wipe it for prints.

The child was telling the truth. The kidnaper, it seemed, was also a murderer.

Who was this Gerald Bodde, the officers wondered? And what had impelled him to commit this gruesome crime? The answer was imbedded in a history that had begun more than a quarter-century earlier.

* * *

Gerald Lee Bodde had been born twenty-seven years earlier in Rock Rapids, Iowa. He was the byproduct of a broken home. His first act of outward rejection of society came at an early age, when he set fire to a neighbor's garage. His mother and stepfather decided, shortly after that, to move to another neighborhood.

They relocated in Houston, Texas. But they found that young Gerald's conduct did not improve significantly. As soon as he started school, he began to have obvious difficulties getting along with other pupils. He also had difficulty with school work, and even special education classes failed to reach him.

Gerald Bodde quit school at the end of the seventh grade because, as he would later explain to a court-appointed psychiatrist who examined him, "I did crazy things. I felt like I had a little devil in my head." He frequently carried such things as snakes and spiders to school with him. He had a history of cruelty to animals, and he simply could not establish any relationships with other students.

At age fourteen, Gerald Bodde was committed to the Austin State Hospital, where he remained for nearly six months. His problem was diagnosed as an "adjustment reaction" of adolescence, and psychological testing also indicated a "prepsychotic personality configuration." It was a warning of his conduct in the future.

Gerald Bodde was not a bright boy, but he was not abnormally dull, either. Intelligence testing later showed that he had an I.Q. of 85, which was within the normal range for the adult population—the lower end of the range, to be sure, but normal nevertheless.

It was as a youth that Gerald first began to have trouble with the police. His first conviction as an adult came when he was seventeen. He was convicted twice for theft, once for a firearms violation and once for the uncommon crime of bigamy.

But Gerald Lee Bodde's history was not as forbidding as that of many accused murderers. He had no known history of drug abuse, for example, and he apparently had no serious problems with alcohol. And although his home was a broken one, he was raised during most of his childhood by his mother and stepfather—a stepfather, named Bodde, who gave him his name.

The young man was attractive enough to women to be married five times (two of the marriages were at the same time, and that was the reason for the bigamy conviction). And he was able to secure some interesting employment on occasion. He earned part of his income singing in nightclubs, as the featured performer in a group called "Jerry and the Four Speeds."

But for the most part, he had difficulty succeeding at anything. As one of his lawyers would later say, "The only accomplishment we were ever able to find out that he made was that he memorized all of Elvis Presley's records." That had apparently been when he was with the Four Speeds.

The young man's wanderings eventually led him into the life of Jean Dodd, a divorcee and mother of three children. They met while she was working as a gas station attendant in an attempt to provide a living for her family. Gerald Bodde was down on his luck, and he was looking for anybody that would be a friend. Jean Dodd was looking for any man who could take on some of the crushing burden of supporting three children.

Soon they had set up housekeeping in a little apartment on Houston's north side. But almost as soon as they had moved in together, the relationship was near its end. Jean Dodd began to recognize Gerald Bodde's self-centeredness and immaturity. The man, she learned quickly, shared absolutely nothing. As Jean Dodd would later recall from the witness chair in open court, "Gerald would lock all his personal belongings in the closet. He got violently mad if one of the children touched his property, and he even locked up his cokes and candy bars."

Gerald Bodde probably never realized the real reason Jean Dodd walked out on him. It is likely that he saw it as one more failure in a life to which failure was the norm rather than the exception. But this failure was one too many, and it broke a thread that had been holding his life together.

During the first few days of the separation, Gerald Bodde responded to an advertisement in the newspaper and rented a room from an elderly lady, a widow living in a white frame house. His landlady's name was Bernice Hartsfield. From all outward appearances, it seemed that she too lived on the edge of poverty, since the house was an old one and the furnishings were worn.

But Bernice Hartsfield was not poor at all.

It was on the morning of January 3 that Gerald Bodde discovered how wealthy Bernice Hartsfield actually was. He stepped out of his room, walked through the breakfast area and went into the kitchen. His landlady was sitting with an elderly man in her breakfast room. She introduced the man to Bodde.

She had more than ten thousand dollars worth of bonds spread out on the table.

She was preparing to re-write her will, Bernice Hartsfield explained. The gentleman with her was her attorney. He was helping her to record the bond certificate numbers.

Bernice Hartsfield was 81 years old, but still healthy and active. She was a widow, and had spent most of her adult life as a mathematics teacher in the Houston public schools. Her husband had been a teacher and an athletic coach. The salaries for their positions had been modest, but the combined incomes of husband and wife had been enough to allow them to save considerable amounts each year. Bernice Hartsfield had never given up her habits of thrift and modest living, and by now, she had accumulated an estate of over three quarters of a million dollars, simply by saving and investing wisely throughout her eighty-one years.

She banked at Houston's First City National Bank, one of the area's largest. But she did not park her car at the bank when she visited. That was too expensive. Instead, the frugal schoolteacher left the car at the edge of town, on Houston's Polk Street, and rode the bus to the bank. That was the kind of thinking that had made Bernice Hartsfield rich in the first place. It was also the kind of thinking that made her take in a boarder for rent.

Her life came to an end on January 3, the day Gerald Bodde saw the bonds.

Before murdering his landlady, Gerald Bodde kidnaped little Bobbie Dodd from her home. He then returned to Mrs. Hartsfield's house for the last time, and he beat her to death with a steel pipe. He took her bonds, and the diamond rings from her fingers, and her silverware—and he drove, in her car, to San Antonio. It was from there that he made his ransom demand to Jean Dodd by long distance telephone.

The entire criminal episode was stupid. No one could have hoped to get away with it. But there was something even more stupid about it than that, because the bonds were nonnegotiable. The certificates for which he had killed Bernice Hartsfield were of no value to anyone but her. As one of his attorneys would later say, everything Bodde took was "nonsalable, traceable or valueless—pure junk. If you got $200 for what he took, you'd be doing good."

And Gerald Lee Bodde was stupid enough to leave an unmistakable trail of physical evidence behind him, stretching from Houston to San Antonio—evidence that would eventually be used to convict him of capital murder.

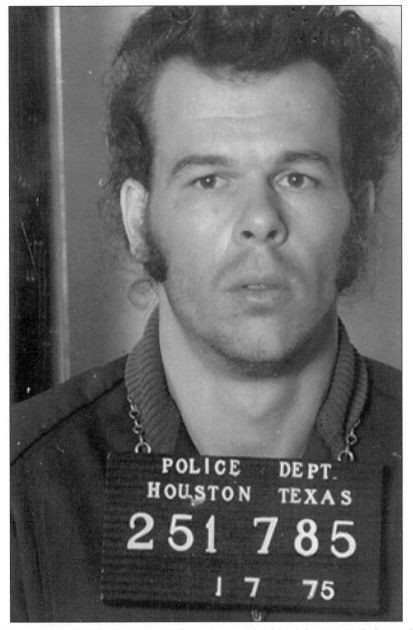

The Gerald Bodde Murder Case. Booking photograph of the defendant. He kidnapped Bobbie Dodd, and he took her with him when he entered Mrs Bernice Hartsfield's house and killed her with a pipe. He then took the dead woman's rings and bond certificates. Defense lawyers argued, at trial, that she could have "loaned" the property to him.

The Gerald Bodde Murder Case. The victim (left), Mrs. Bernice Hartsfield, was 81 years old. The defendant beat her with a pipe, wrapped the body in a blanket tied with electric cords, and left it in a closet (top). He took her car, which was parked outside her house (bottom right) and drove to San Antonio with his kidnap victim, Bobbie Dodd, and Mrs. Hartsfield's rings, silverware and bonds. The elderly woman lived simply and modestly, but accumulated an estate that was inventoried at $789,000; Gerald Bodde killed her after she took him into her home as a boarder.

Chapter 13

The Trial of Gerald Lee Bodde

A little girl, who was now six years old, sat on the witness chair in the 178th District Courtroom.

A little over a year had passed since the murder of Bernice Hartsfield, and the trial of Gerald Bodde was finally under way. There had been six weeks of pretrial motions, during which Gerald Bodde's lawyers—there were three of them: Marvin Teague, Donald Rogers and Frank Shepherd —had tried to challenge as much of the evidence against their client as they could. There had been a month of jury selection. Now, the trial itself was in its second week.

This was the crucial moment. The prosecution's only eyewitness, little Bobbie Dodd, was about to testify.

But before the child uttered a word, Marvin Teague stood and asked the judge to excuse the jury. Teague had been one of the Halloween Candy Case lawyers, and he was known for his technical expertise. He now showed the reason for his reputation. With a witness this young, he explained, there was always a question whether she understood the oath she was required to take. And she might be too young to separate fact from fantasy, or to relate her testimony coherently.

The judge should listen, first, to see whether she was qualified, Teague argued.

As it happened, this suggestion was the best defensive strategy of the entire trial. The events that followed it seemed to shake the prosecution's case to its foundations. Judge Walton, a cautious judge, agreed with Teague that the child should be examined first with the jury absent. In fact, he had already removed the jury in anticipation of this request by the defense.

The hearing began as Assistant District Attorney Doug Shaver began to question the child in an attempt to demonstrate to Judge Walton that she was qualified to testify. His questions were gentle and slow, because the little girl's nervousness was obvious.

"What's your name?" Shaver asked first, in this unusual hearing before the judge.

"Roberta," said the witness hesitantly.

So far so good, the prosecutor thought. "What's the rest of your name?" he asked.

"Roberta Dodd."

"Do you know what it means to tell the truth?"

And with that question, the prosecutor suddenly reached an absolute impasse. There was an embarrassing, awkward silence. The witness sat in her chair, twisted her tiny hands, covered her eyes—and looked at Gerald Lee Bodde.

Shaver tried again. "Do you know what the difference is between the truth and a lie?"

There was no answer. The witness seemed to be frozen with fear. Shaver repeated the question again.

Finally, Roberta Dodd said, "The devil will get you if you don't tell the truth."

Shaver breathed a sigh of relief. That was part of what was needed to qualify the witness; it showed that she knew the difference between truth and falsehood, and she could therefore take the oath. But the hardest part was yet to come. Could Shaver get the little girl to talk enough so that Judge Walton could see that she was a competent witness?

Roberta Dodd sat with her lips pressed tightly together and her hands covering her eyes.

"What school do you go to?" Shaver asked. "What grade are you in? What room do you go to when you go to school?"

There was no answer.

At the defense table, Gerald Bodde looked on in impassive silence. Teague, Rogers and Shepherd all watched the little girl intently. At the prosecution table, three lawyers for the State—George Jacobs, Doug Shaver and David Crump—all stared at the witness. And Judge Walton, leaning to his left, looked down at the little girl—who, by now, was toying with her hands.

Roberta Dodd was afraid of the defendant. She began to cry.

Shaver had anticipated that he might have difficulties of this sort. He had carefully let the child get to know him before the trial, and he had brought her into the courtroom so that it would be familiar to her. But the problem was far worse than he had hoped. It seemed that the little girl would not be able to tell her story—the story that she had related so completely and so accurately to Officer Mary Tobar on the day of her rescue. It seemed she would not be able to talk at all with the defendant present. And the defendant had a right, guaranteed by the United States Constitution, to sit in the courtroom and confront her.

"Do you remember last Saturday, when we took you out and got you a Dilly Bar?" Shaver asked now. "Do you remember when we brought you up here to the courtroom, and let you sit in the chair?"

The witness did not answer.

Twenty minutes passed. Shaver repeated, over and over, his gentle questions. For the entire time, awkwardly, the child cried.

"Just nod your head or shake your head," Shaver suggested at one point. But the child continued to cry, and occasionally she glanced at the defendant.

It was excruciating to watch. And it was cruel to keep the child on the witness chair. But what choice was there? Should Gerald Lee Bodde be released? Shaver kept trying, for what seemed an eternity.

"We'll take a recess," said Judge Walton finally.

When the recess was over, Shaver brought the witness back. Three more times he tried to get her to speak, and three more times he was met with silence and weeping. Judge Walton had a reputation for patience, and he was true to that reputation. Each time, he took a recess and waited.

"Are you going to take another run at her?" Teague asked, at the end of the last recess. "Yes," Shaver answered grimly.

The child was seated in the witness chair once more. Judge Walton leaned down and said gently, "Bobbie, are you ready to answer their questions now? Nobody's going to mess with you or bother you."

The child rubbed her eyes, cried and fidgeted.

The judge looked at the prosecutors. He had made a decision. "I'm going to have to excuse the witness, Mr. Shaver," he said.

The child was led from the courtroom for the last time. The State's case seemed to collapse with her.

During the recess that followed, Bailiff Angelo Passante took Gerald Lee Bodde to the lockup behind the courtroom. The defendant was pleased at what had happened. "Aw," he said, "I've got this case beat."

He turned to Passante, and he added: "I'll be drinking coffee with you on your front porch by tomorrow afternoon."

*   *   *

The prosecutors pondered what to do next.

Was the loss of their only eyewitness going to mean that Gerald Bodde would go free?

That was certainly possible, they knew. But the case was, as yet, far from lost. Actually, there was still a formidable collection of evidence that was admissible before the jury. Jean Dodd had already testified about Gerald Bodde's confession: "I've just killed an old lady." The pipe and bloody tissue had been found in Bodde's rented room. The defendant had stolen the victim's car and had been arrested with the keys to it, which were on a ring that included all the dead woman's other keys. In the San Antonio boarding house where Bodde had stayed, Bernice Hartsfield's bonds had been recovered. So had her diamond rings, taken from her fingers. Marvin Teague was maintaining that the recovery of these items constituted an illegal search and seizure from his client, but it seemed likely that they would be admissible in evidence.

Then there were the items in the car—the silverware and other property belonging to Bernice Hartsfield.

There had even been a witness who had seen Gerald Bodde, together with Bobbie Dodd, driving the car from the house at the time of the murder. When the witness had asked him about it, Bodde had lied and claimed that the car was his.

And the killing itself had been accomplished in a locked house that showed no sign of forced entry. That was because Bodde had access to it.

In their research, Jacobs and Crump found several cases in which convictions had been obtained with similar kinds of evidence. *The State of Texas versus Jones; the State of Texas versus Pulido*—these were cases in which circumstantial evidence alone had been held to be enough for a conviction. Lawyers know a famous saying about it: "Sometimes circumstantial evidence can be persuasive, such as when one finds a trout in the milk." The finding of a trout in the milk, in any reasonable person's mind, would support an inference that the milk had been improperly prepared.

The case against Gerald Bodde seemed equally convincing, even without Bobbie Dodd's testimony.

But even as they thought that to themselves, the prosecutors knew that their own evaluation of the case might be misleading. It was not they who would decide. It was the twelve people in the jury box. And jurors, by and large, do not find it natural to accept circumstantial evidence. The loss of the little girl as a witness might, for the jury, create an intolerable gap in the prosecution's case.

The prosecutors decided that it would be best if they could have the child's story told to the jury, even indirectly—through some other witness, perhaps.

* * *

The three prosecutors had divided their responsibilities during the trial.

Jacobs was the lead counsel, and he was in charge of the overall case. Doug Shaver was co-counsel: he would question some of the key witnesses, such as Bobbie Dodd, and share the jury argument with Jacobs at the end. David Crump was the silent partner: he would help by dealing with technical legal problems in presenting the case.

In this trial, that was a job that kept all three lawyers busy. And now, even more than before, technical points were going to matter. Crump and Jacobs began to consider whether there was any legal means to bridge the gap left by the loss of Bobbie Dodd's testimony.

"The Gerald Bodde case was a frustrating experience," says Crump. "With lawyers like Teague, and Rogers, and Shepherd defending him, we knew we were going to have to dot our i's and cross our t's on every technical point. The defense lawyers would make us. We knew we were going to have to fight to get every piece of evidence before the jury.

"It was going to be hard enough anyway, but when we saw what happened to our main witness, the little girl, it really took the wind out of our sails."

Crump was a former Assistant District Attorney, but now he was a professor and he taught in law school. He was assisting Shaver and Jacobs in the Gerald Bodde case as a special prosecutor, by appointment of the Houston District Attorney's Office. One of his specialties was the law of evidence—the complicated, confusing rules that determine what a jury can and cannot hear in the courtroom.

"Courtroom procedure doesn't always make sense," says Crump. "And if you want to understand how a trial works, you have to keep that fact in mind. A lot of the rules aren't there because of any sensible reason; they're there because they developed centuries ago, and they've been handed down from judge to judge until the present day."

A lawyer has to know all of these rules—and know how to use them. There are rules against hearsay, rules about expert witnesses, rules about confessions, and rules about almost every phase of testimony in a case. And there are exceptions, too, to every one of the rules. There are even, in some instances, exceptions to the exceptions.

"It's sort of like the Internal Revenue Code," Crump says.

"A great deal of the time," he adds, "the rules have the result of *hiding* the truth, rather than bringing it out." But although a lawyer might not like the rules, there is no question he has to learn how to deal with them if he is going to be a trial lawyer, because they can cause a case to be won or lost.

Now, Crump and Jacobs were confronted with a very practical problem. Since the main prosecution witness could not testify, was there any other way to get her story to the jury?

"The first thing we thought of," says Crump, "was getting Officer Tobar to repeat to the jury what the little girl had said to her when they brought her back from San Antonio. The problem was, repeating something someone else has said is hearsay. And hearsay can't usually be used in a trial. That's one of the oldest rules in the books.

"But there are exceptions to that rule against hearsay. A spontaneous statement by a victim of a crime, made close in time to the crime itself, is sometimes admissible in evidence. And sometimes that kind of hearsay *can* be used. It comes within an exception to the usual rule against hearsay."

The prosecutors thought it through.

Could Officer Tobar relate, from the witness stand, what the little girl had told her a year ago? Might that be a way in which her story could be conveyed to the jury?

Crump and Jacobs were skeptical about the idea. But it might be possible. And if so, that would solve the problem.

The two lawyers went to the books. They found several cases decided by the Texas courts dealing with the issue, and some of the decisions looked promising. For example, there was a case, in 1964, in which a man named Hudgeons was accused of a sex crime with a little girl. The case was called *The State of Texas versus Hudgeons*. The interesting thing about the case was that the little girl had run home and told her mother about the crime, and then, when the case reached court, the mother was allowed to testify what the child had told her. Hudgeons was ultimately convicted, and he appealed. But the higher courts said the Mother's testimony was valid. The Texas Court of Criminal Appeals, in particular, said that the little girl's statement to her mother, even though it was hearsay, could properly be told to the jury — because it was spontaneous and close in time to the crime.

Crump and Jacobs nodded their heads to each other. Perhaps this precedent could be used to persuade Judge Walton to do the same thing in the trial of Gerald Bodde.

There were other cases. For example, there was a 1973 case in which a man named Beam was charged with robbery. This case was called *The State of Texas versus Beam*. What interested Jacobs and Crump about it was that the robbery victim had told a police officer what had happened, at the crime scene; and at the trial, the officer was allowed to repeat to the jury what the victim had said. The statement had been spontaneous and close in time to the crime.

A lawyer's reasoning process works by analogy. And the prosecutors felt that these cases were analogous to the trial of Gerald Bodde, in many respects. There were some dissimilarities, to be sure, but the prosecutors also saw a good many points in common. And so maybe Judge Walton could, indeed, be persuaded to let officer Tobar testify concerning what little Bobbie Dodd had told her about the murder of Bernice Hartsfield. It would be a difficult legal argument to make, the prosecutors knew. But it might work. And now that the judge had ruled, finally, that the child herself would not be allowed to testify, what else could be done?

Crump and Jacobs collected the cases they had read, and they wrote a brief for Judge Walton.

*   *   *

Several hours later, the judge sat in the courtroom. He was studying the cases and evaluating the prosecutors' argument.

Finally, he was ready to rule.

"The court commends counsel for the state on the work they have done," the judge said. "But I do not consider these decisions applicable to the case."

That was the end of the matter. The little girl's story would not be heard by the jury, directly or indirectly. It was a judgment call, and Judge Walton had made a reasonable decision; in his view, the statement had simply not been spontaneous enough, or close enough in time to the crime, to fit within the exception to the hearsay rule. It was not analogous to the other cases.

The prosecutors pondered their case again. And they prepared to proceed with the evidence that was left.

The case was still not lost. The circumstantial evidence was compelling. And actually, there was a great deal more than circumstantial evidence. There was a clear confession of guilt, out of the defendant's own mouth. The statement that he had made to Jean Dodd about killing an old lady, together with all the physical evidence and the other testimony in the case, ought to be enough to convince the twelve citizens who were sitting in judgment of Gerald Bodde—even without the little girl's eyewitness testimony.

* * *

But as it happened, the prosecutors' difficulties were only just beginning.

Suddenly, there was a new development in the case that made Jacobs gag with frustration.

He had just returned from his office, where he had been in touch with HPD. "Do you know what those guys in the property room have done now?" he asked Shaver and Crump incredulously. "They've lost the tapes of the kidnaping demand."

The Houston Police Department's property room was a mammoth cavern where evidence was retained for safekeeping. Hundreds of weapons, dozens of items of bloody clothing, thousands of pieces of stolen property—all were kept under lock and key, with a sign-out system that was supposed to account for every item that was taken out.

But somehow, things were constantly getting lost in the property room.

The tapes, it seemed, had simply been misplaced. Trying to find them would be literally like looking for a needle in a haystack. The property room had already been turned upside down, and the tapes were not to be found.

In a way, it was understandable that losses would occasionally occur, because there were tens of thousands of separate items there. And with criminal court dockets being what they were, property was frequently checked out and returned over and over again. But still, Jacobs was thinking, in this case, a capital murder case, with a tape of a kidnaping ransom demand that was involved with the murder—it just seemed that that kind of evidence should not have been lost.

The defense, without a doubt, would lambast the prosecutors for this latest development. It was even conceivable that it might result in a dismissal of the case. In any event, Marvin Teague's job would be to try to persuade the judge that a dismissal was necessary.

Teague rose from his chair in the courtroom. He had considered the possibility, he told the judge, that the tapes might exonerate his client. They might show that Jean Dodd was lying. They might show that Gerald Bodde had not said anything about killing an old lady, after all.

Besides, Teague went on, "The jurors could listen to the tapes and decide whether it was really this defendant." But now, without the tapes, Jean Dodd "would have carte blanche to say whatever she wanted about what was in the conversations, and all we could do would be to say: 'Did that really happen?'"

The only fair thing to do, Teague said, was to suppress the testimony of Jean Dodd.

Fortunately for Jacobs, Judge Walton refused to do that. But he addressed the prosecutor sternly. "If it is found that this defendant's rights are prejudiced in any way, the result will be that any conviction will be set aside. This court will not hesitate to do so."

And there was one other danger that Jacobs had to consider in connection with the missing tapes. He had to consider the effect that this new development would have on the jury.

Even in the best of circumstances, an occurrence such as this would raise a red flag in any juror's mind about the prosecution's entire case. Some of the jurors were old enough to remember the Watergate case, which ruined the Presidency of Richard M. Nixon. There had been an eighteen-minute gap on one of the tapes — an erasure — that might have been accidental, but it was one of the most damning pieces of evidence against the President. And so losing this tape was certainly not the thing for a prosecutor to do. It made the state's case against Gerald Lee Bodde look about as credible as Richard Nixon's defense.

If the loss of Bobbie Dodd had not already ruined the prosecution of Gerald Bodde, it seemed entirely likely that this newest development would be the end of it.

But even that was not the final difficulty for the prosecutors.

The HPD property room was also unable to find some of Bernice Hartsfield's stolen property. Her silverware, which had been found in Gerald Bodde's possession at the time of his arrest, was missing. And HPD had even lost a bronze eagle statuette, stolen by Bodde, that had the dead woman's name on it. These important pieces of evidence, which linked the defendant to the victim, were going to be unavailable to the prosecution.

"My God," said Crump to Shaver. "Those guys can't keep track of anything over there."

And when the prosecutors learned *how* the silverware had been lost, the explanation left them even more dumfounded than the disappearance itself. It had happened when Gerald Bodde's father had come to the police station to pick up his son's personal effects. The man had had no intention to remove evidence, as such; he had simply made a routine request for the return of property belonging to a relative who was being held in police custody. But the officer in charge of the property room had given him everything he could locate that had been found in Gerald Bodde's possession. Without realizing it, the officer had surrendered several items of property that had happened to be there because Gerald Bodde had stolen them from Bernice Hartsfield. Those items had included the silverware.

Each of the prosecutors asked himself the same question. "How could this sort of thing be happening to us?"

Actually, it was unfair to blame it all on the police. There had been many difficult things that the Houston Police Department had done extraordinarily well. Houston police officers had disarmed and arrested a kidnap-murderer, without a single shot having been fired. They had treated him professionally while he was in their custody, so that there was no substantial question of any violation of his rights. They had recovered the victim, unharmed, within days of her capture. And they had solved a murder case almost as soon as they had learned of its existence.

HPD had done an excellent job of the things most citizens would think were important. It only remained to be seen what the twelve citizens who were sitting in the jury box would think of HPD's techniques for handling evidence.

Jacobs, Shaver and Crump—when they got over their initial shock— knew that they could still present a strong case. They ultimately presented 33 witnesses in all. There was a web of physical evidence from which there was no escape for the defense: a fingerprint analyst, a blood-typing chemist, and the stolen property. There was a witness whom the defendant had told "it was easy" to kill an old lady. There was going to be more than enough evidence to secure the conviction, even after the loss of Bobbie Dodd's testimony, even after the tapes, even after the silverware and the statuette. There would be more than enough, that is, unless the jurors had been so shaken in their confidence in the prosecutors' case that they would acquit anyone. And that was certainly possible.

The last piece of evidence that turned up missing was a set of photographs of the autopsy. "They can't locate them over at the medical examiner's office," Jacobs said. That meant that the prosecutors would be unable to show the jury the wounds that Gerald Bodde had inflicted upon Bernice Hartsfield.

By this time, the prosecutors were stoic. They sat at the table and thought about it. Truth is stranger than fiction, the saying goes. And, as they also say, when it rains it pours. I only hope the clerk's office doesn't lose the indictment before the trial is over, Crump thought. But all he could say to Jacobs was, "That's incredible."

*   *   *

The defendant's lawyers did not present any evidence.

Marvin Teague rested his case immediately after Jacobs rested for the prosecution. That was the best defensive strategy, actually. It would allow the defense lawyers to argue, effectively, that the burden of proof was on the State and that a reasonable doubt remained in the case.

For a few minutes, there was a recess.

The lawyers — prosecutors and defenders alike — sat together in the judge's office, waiting for him to prepare the charge. It was a time for relaxation, like the lull that is in the eye of a storm. It was even a moment for companionship between two sets of tired adversaries.

"Can the jury be sent back to the hotel for the time being?" someone asked.

"Yes," responded defense lawyer Donald Rogers. He smiled, and added: "We want them in the best mood possible." A comfortable, contented jury might be more lenient toward the defendant.

"Are those good hotel rooms?" another defense lawyer asked.

"Yeah," said Doug Shaver. "The ones we saw were very good ones. Individual, private ones."

"We were over there reading the paper with Mrs. Black," said George Jacobs. He was joking with Rogers; Mrs. Black was a juror, and the jury had been sequestered in a hotel because of sensational publicity during the trial. Jacobs added, "We also read a few of the stories to Mrs. Tewsky." Mrs. Tewsky, as it happened, had been a subject of some interest to the six male lawyers in the case, because she was a very good-looking woman.

Shaver, with his best effort at a straight face, said: "The jurors thought those flowers we sent them from the prosecution team were a nice touch."

But Marvin Teague was not one to be outdone, even at gallows humor. "Did they like the candy old Bodde sent over?" he asked.

Everyone laughed in spite of himself. None of it was uproariously funny, exactly, but everyone in the room was emotionally drained and physically exhausted. Any kind of comic relief was welcome.

The conversation was typical of the situation in which these two teams of advocates found themselves, for the mark of a good trial lawyer is comradeship outside the courtroom and partisan zeal inside it. To each of the prosecutors, the defense lawyers were professionals. To each of the defense lawyers, the prosecutors were also professionals. They could all enjoy each other's companionship in a moment of relaxation. Then each could go to his respective table in the courtroom and do his best to destroy the opposing side's case.

There was a pause in the conversation, and then one of the defense lawyers said to Jacobs: "Gerald's not as friendly to you, George, as he was at first. I leaned over and told him, 'That man—the prosecutor—wants to kill you.'

"It's taken a long time, but I think he's finally snapped to it that that's what this whole trial is about."

"Give me another legal pad," said the Judge. He had the charge almost prepared.

A few moments later, the lawyers were standing before the jury to deliver their final arguments. The bantering was over. It was the adversary system, in full swing.

* * *

"I think they've proved that a kidnaping occurred," said Donald Rogers to the jury.

"But that doesn't prove a murder."

Rogers told the jurors that there had not even been proof that the property or the car was stolen from Bernice Hartsfield. For all anyone knew, he argued, she could have consented to the defendant's taking it. "It hasn't been disproved," Rogers added, "that Bernice Hartsfield could have loaned the property to Gerald Bodde."

What Rogers was suggesting was that an elderly lady, frugal almost to the point of miserliness, had loaned her bond certificates to a kidnaper and then turned up dead by coincidence. On reflection, that was hardly likely. But it was Rogers' job to look for doubts in the case, and that was what he was doing. No one could rule out the chance that the jury might accept it.

Rogers' strongest argument, which he repeated over and over, was that "it's a circumstantial case." It was circumstantial, of course, because the little girl could not testify. But the State still had the burden of proof. That was the important thing.

"I ask you," Rogers went on, "has the state really proved that Gerald Bodde killed Bernice Hartsfield? And if he did, did they prove he had the specific intent to kill? And third, if he did, did they prove he did it in the course of a robbery?"

Again, Rogers reminded the jurors: "It's a circumstantial case."

The defense lawyers had agreed to divide their argument time among them. And so Rogers was followed by Frank Shepherd, who also argued for an acquittal. "What appalls me," Shepherd said, "is that they ask you to find this defendant guilty not only of murder, but of robbery-murder." Robbery-murder, of course, carried the death penalty, while ordinary murder did not. "It scares me," Shepherd went on, his voice rising. "It scares the hell out of me. On such flimsy evidence, they want you not only to find him guilty, they want you to KILL him."

Shepherd was shouting his words by now.

"The prosecutors may talk to you about cleaning up the community," he said passionately. "But you don't do any good at all talking about convicting a man" — here Shepherd reached his peroration, and also the peak of his volume — "a man who ISN'T GUILTY."

When the defense lawyers were finished, it was the prosecutors' turn.

Assistant District Attorney Doug Shaver had a different view of the case than the defenders. The defense argument, he told the jurors, reminded him of "when I was a little boy, and my daddy would take me fishing. He'd take out a lure and throw it.

"And if it didn't work, he'd throw out another lure. And if that didn't work, he'd throw out another lure. And he'd keep on like that, trying one after the other, just hoping that some fish'd bite at one of those pretty, bright, attractive-colored lures."

The point was obvious. "Don't you see," said Shaver, "That's what the defense is doing here. They want you to bite at anything to get him off the capital murder charge. They even tell you what I think is the most ridiculous statement I've ever heard: that she 'might have loaned it all to him,' including her car, her rings off her fingers, and her nonnegotiable bonds."

George Jacobs ended the arguments.

"They've talked to you about circumstantial evidence," Jacobs said. "Well, circumstantial evidence can be good evidence. It's physical. It's there.

"But as you know," he went on, "we have more than circumstantial evidence here. We have a direct statement out of the defendant's own mouth. 'I've just killed an old lady. And I'll kill Bobbie too.'"

Jacobs started to go over the evidence, chronologically. The lawyer and Mrs. Hartsfield, looking at the bonds. The kidnaping, that same day. Bodde driving the car away, with the little girl, at the time of the murder.

The ransom demands, the attempted pickup, and the admission of the killing to Jean Dodd. And how had the police learned of the killing? "At this point, they still didn't know about the murder. It wasn't until they picked up the little girl, and questioned her, that the police went to Mrs. Hartsfield's house."

And how had that happened, Jacobs asked the jury? Then he answered his own question. They had learned of it because the little girl had been with Gerald Bodde — with the murderer, when he killed Bernice Hartsfield.

Jacobs lined up all the stolen property in the jury's view. The two diamond rings, taken from the dead woman's fingers. The keys, taken out of her pocket. The bonds, a stack of certificates nearly an inch tall, taken from her safe. The pictures of her car. The radio, the clothing —

"He took this pipe and killed her," Jacobs said, lifting the murder weapon for the jurors to see. "You can speculate, you can say, 'Maybe some guy crawled in through the keyhole and killed her, then got out without breaking the locks.' But that's not what happened, and you know it.

"We ask you to bring in a guilty verdict, because it's right. It's what the evidence shows."

It was a few hours later, shortly after five o'clock, that the jury returned with its verdict. The prosecution's evidence had been enough. Gerald Lee Bodde, the verdict said, was guilty—guilty of capital murder.

The penalty hearing lasted three days.

Most of that time was devoted to the hearing of objections by the defense. The evidence itself was short. It consisted of four character witnesses, who testified about Gerald Bodde's propensity toward violence, and of evidence about the defendant's prior criminal record.

Finally, it was time for argument on the question of life or death.

"I've been brought up to believe that no one has the right to take life," said Frank Shepherd. "We've been taking life since the time of Christ. It doesn't work. If we want to deter crime, why do we do executions behind closed doors in Huntsville? Why not do it all at the Astrodome, so everybody can see it?

"The prosecutors," Shepherd went on, "say, 'Wipe him out. Eradicate him.' Then we'll have two murders instead of one.

"And you," — Shepherd looked at the jurors — "you will have participated." If he could make the jury feel guilty about the death penalty, the verdict would be one of life imprisonment.

It was a powerful argument. And Rogers and Teague both drove it home to the jury. "If there's a mistake, you can't change it—if you pull the switch," they told the jurors.

The defense lawyers also worked to humanize their client in the eyes of the jurors—to make them see him as a human being caught in a situation not his fault, and the crime as a tragic mistake. "The only possible conclusion," said Rogers, "is that he isn't very bright. This is a stupid crime." The argument was simplistic, but it might be effective. Everyone who owns a television watches Kojak, where the crooks are all knowledgeable and clever; perhaps the jury would be persuaded to be more understanding of a crook who was not. That was the strategy.

Then it was time for the jury to hear from the other side.

Doug Shaver, for the prosecution, reminded the jury of the crime. "Consider the evidence," he said. "She was hit with a pipe. Over and over again. Fragments went into her brain, fragments of her skull. And her face, all over, was black and blue."

There was plenty of other evidence of violent conduct by Gerald Bodde, Shaver went on. He quoted the defendant: "I can kill the little girl." That was what Gerald Bodde had said: "I'll kill the little girl and send her home in a pine box." At the time of his arrest, Bodde had had his hand on a pistol, Shaver reminded the jurors. It was loaded with five live rounds. The police had caught him before he had had a chance to use it.

George Jacobs, again, closed the argument for the prosecution.

"The defense lawyers," he explained to the jury, "want to put the fault on you." He was referring to Frank Shepherd's argument—that a death sentence would be another murder, in which the jurors would be participants. "They want to make it like it's your responsibility he's here in court," Jacobs went on. "But it's not your fault. It's not mine, or Mr. Shaver's. Gerald Bodde doesn't need to look any farther than himself."

It wasn't possible, he added, to think of two more innocent victims. "An old lady. A little girl." And as for Gerald Lee Bodde, Jacobs said, "there will always be a probability that he'll do it again."

The jury retired in late afternoon. That evening, they were back. They had answered both of the penalty questions "Yes."

That meant that they had sentenced Gerald Lee Bodde to death.

* * *

Why did the Gerald Bodde case end as it did?

Why did the defendant receive the death penalty?

It was certainly one of the strangest cases that any of the six participating lawyers had ever seen. There was the little girl who couldn't testify. There was the disappearing evidence. There were the intricate, technical points that decided what parts of the evidence the jury could or could not hear. Gerald Bodde's trial was an exaggerated version of the evidence problems in every criminal trial before a jury, in which the unexpected is the norm. The jurors hear random bits and pieces of truth through a filter of complicated rules. The rules are supposed to ensure reliability of the evidence, but more often they result only in blindfolding the jury.

The key to the Bodde case was that the evidence was strong enough to filter through to the jury in spite of all the incidents that diluted it.

Actually, a combination of factors led to the ultimate verdict. For one thing, the jury was capable of responding to the evidence. For another, the murder itself was conscienceless and brutal. And as Jacobs pointed out, the victims were both chosen by the defendant because they were helpless. But it was the quirks in the evidence—the accidents that hampered the prosecutors' case, and the way that technical rules affected the testimony—that set Gerald Bodde's trial apart.

Jacobs, Crump and Shaver will undoubtedly each remember, forever, one strange incident that was produced by the complicated, technical rules of evidence.

Crump and Jacobs were never able to persuade Judge Walton to let the child's story be told to the jury. The judge had ruled against that. In fact, the jury never even saw Bobbie Dodd. But Crump and Jacobs did manage to persuade the judge that the jury should not be left completely ignorant of what had happened. The prosecution, they argued, had the right to tell the jurors exactly *why* Bobbie Dodd could not testify. They showed the judge decisions by Texas courts that said so.

Judge Walton, when he was persuaded it was the law, agreed.

And so one of the last witnesses the jury had heard, ironically, had been Assistant District Attorney Doug Shaver, who had explained the little girl's absence from the list of witnesses.

"Do you know Roberta Dodd?" Jacobs had asked his colleague, when Shaver had seated himself in the witness chair.

"Yes," Shaver had replied, with the jury listening. "I last saw her here, in this courtroom. The jury was not present. I myself, and you, Mr. Jacobs, brought her into the courtroom."

The jurors had not known what was going on outside their presence. Until now, they had not been told why the child was not called as a witness. They had known only that they had been kept from the courtroom for several hours. Now, they were learning the reason for the first time, during this testimony from Shaver.

"Was she able to answer any questions?" Jacobs had asked.

"No," Shaver had said. "She covered her eyes."

That was all the jury ever knew. They had seen nothing of the little girl herself. They had not watched while she sat, in frozen fear, and glanced furtively at the defendant. And they never heard Bobbie Dodd's story.

When the final verdict came in, a group of elderly men and women sat in the audience benches in the back of the courtroom. For weeks, throughout the trial, they had been sitting there. They were the friends and relatives of Bernice Hartsfield. Each day, they brought their medicines to the courtroom and took them during the proceedings. Each day, in stoic silence, they watched the trial through their thick eyeglasses.

The United States prides itself on the equality of its justice. But it will be the last country in the world, it seems, to provide equal dignity to its elderly. Faced with poverty and loneliness, old people in America are victims of serious crime at an alarming rate. Many of them become prisoners in their own homes because of the fear of crime. That was part of the tragedy of Bernice Hartsfield's death; the schoolteacher had refused to accept the insularity and helplessness that goes with advancing age. She had rented a room to a young man down on his luck. Now her friends and relatives were sitting through a trial that had lasted three months and that resembled, at times, a game of chess more than an inquiry into the truth of her murder.

They knew the ordeal that Bobbie Dodd had suffered. They had watched the arguments and the technical objections. Each day, they looked at the man with the greasy hair, combed to a point at the front of his head, who had bludgeoned to death their sister, their friend. The man whose cowardice had led him to exploit the two most helpless victims he could find. The man who had killed Bernice Hartsfield.

The jurors had not been permitted to hear everything. But they had heard enough.

And they knew it too.

*   *   *

The trial of Gerald Bodde was extraordinary. But it was to be expected that it would be extraordinary; capital murder cases are nearly always extraordinary.

The trial of Kenneth Brock, for instance, had involved an unusual crime: a murder committed before the very eyes of six police officers. Certainly the Halloween Candy Murder case had been unusual too. And the John Stiles Griffin case had been unusual not just in the nature of the killing, but in the personality and background of the murderer. It was not surprising, therefore, that Gerald Bodde's case was extraordinary too. Among capital cases, the extraordinary is the norm.

And at the time Gerald Bodde was tried, an even more amazing case — one of the most extraordinary capital cases the city had ever seen — was also awaiting resolution in Houston.

It was the case of a bizarre group of men who called themselves "The Brady Bunch." The members of the Brady Bunch participated in at least six brutal, execution-style killings and confessed to them on television. Had it been told in an earlier, more peaceful time in this country's history, the story of the Brady Bunch would scarcely have been believed.*

---

* The following names in this chapter were changed, without alteration of the incidents in which the persons were involved: Mrs. Black, Mrs. Twesky.

Chapter 14

The Brady Bunch, Part I: Suppression of the Evidence

Jack Cato, of the Houston News Service, was the best known police reporter in the city.

He paced back and forth in the office and waited.

Larry Connors of Channel 13 was there too. So were Bob Wolfe of Channel 11 and Rick Hartley of Channel 2. All of them scratched their heads and wondered.

It was going to be a most unusual press conference.

The reporters were here at the Houston Police Homicide Division office for a simple reason—they had been summoned. But it wasn't the police who had asked for them. It was a group of prisoners.

Four prisoners, who wanted to talk to the press—that was what the reporters had heard.

"What's this all about?" one of them asked.

"I don't really know," said another. But he began to explain the rumors he had heard. There was a group of men who had confessed to a string of robberies and murders. It was said that the men were pretty brazen about it. The odd thing was, the members of the gang had asked to talk to the press. It was they who had called this press conference.

While the reporters were discussing this strange development, the police officers in the homicide division stood by and waited. The situation was strange to them too.

For the police department and the district attorney's office, it had been hard to know just what to do when these four prisoners had said they wanted to talk to the press. It was a damned-if-you-do, damned-if-you-don't situation. The publicity might endanger a prosecution. But on the other hand, the American Bar Association's guidelines say that it is proper to let a prisoner be interviewed when he has consented. And this was a situation in which the four men had not just consented, but *demanded* to see the press. You ought not to stop someone who wants to talk to reporters from talking to them.

All across the country, the police officers knew, there had been lawsuits by prisoners denied access to the outside world. The courts had often prodded wardens to allow contact with prisoners. And it usually looked, to the public, like a cover-up if the press was excluded, anyway.

That was why the decision had been made to allow the press conference. That was why the four prisoners were on their way to the homicide office now.

One of the reporters said, "I hear they call themselves 'The Brady Bunch.'"

"The Brady Bunch?" said someone else. "Why the 'Brady Bunch'?"

The explanation for the name was really quite appropriate, it seemed. There was a television show called "The Brady Bunch." The name of this group was a take-off on that. It was rumored that the four men had committed their first robbery-murder on Brady Street. It had been reported in all the papers as the "Brady Street Murder." From that, it was said, the four men had started calling themselves the Brady Bunch. The name stuck.

The Brady Bunch. A group of killers who had given themselves that name, and who wanted to get on television to talk about their crimes. It sounded like news; it might make some footage for six o'clock.

The reporters set up their lights and cameras at one end of the room. And they waited.

*   *   *

Bernardino Sierra was a thin man with a tooth missing in front. He had greasy hair combed in ducktails and a huge, spidery tattoo on the front of his neck.

He was the chief spokesman for the Brady Bunch.

A few seconds ago, the door to the office had opened. The reporters had seen four men, in prison whites, walking languidly into the room while a small army of officers kept them under guard. The four men had been brought across the room. They had given their names: Sierra, Vargas, Ruiz and Fuentes — the Brady Bunch. Now, as they stood blinking at the television cameras, Bernardino Sierra stepped into the limelight. The questioning began almost immediately, with Jack Cato.

Cato: "The Officers and the District Attorney's Office say that you were involved in a ring that was killing people. Is that right?"

Sierra: "Well, that's what I — you could — yeah, that's right."

Cato: "Can you tell us about it?"

Sierra: (Unintelligible)

Connors: "Tell us the best way you can, Mr. Sierra."

Sierra: "Let Richard tell you about it."

Richard Vargas stood beside Bernardino Sierra. His appearance was different from Sierra's, but he was no less threatening. Richard Vargas was a short, stocky man, with a strong build. He had a burr haircut and smoldering eyes.

Now, the newsmen turned to him.

Cato: "What started it? Why did it start, you robbing places?"

Vargas: "No reason at all."

Connors: "What started the killings? Do you know how many you killed?"

Vargas: "Well, one on Almeda — two on Almeda, and one on Brady."

Connors: "Why?"

Vargas: "For no reason."

Cato: "Do you feel bad about it since there was no reason?"

Vargas: "It don't bother me."

The newsmen were incredulous. They had never seen or heard anything quite like this. Here were these four men, nonchalantly saying, with soft, calm voices, that they didn't care about killing. They were having obvious trouble remembering just how many people they had killed. It was going to make better footage than the reporters had anticipated.

The questioning went back to Sierra. The reporters were interviewing these four murderers as though they were visiting dignitaries.

Cato: "You shot somebody over on Middle Street, didn't you, a man that you didn't know?"

Sierra: "I didn't shoot him."

Cato: "Who did?"

Sierra: "I ran over him."

Cato: (surprised) "You ran over him?"

Sierra: (nonchalantly) "Umhum."

Cato: "Why? Why did you pick this man out?"

Sierra: "He was messing with my woman."

Cato: "And what did you do?"

Sierra: "Robbed him."

Cato: "And then what?"

Sierra: "Ran over him."

Cato: "How did you feel about it after you did all this?"

Sierra: "All right."

While Sierra talked, matter-of-factly, about the Middle Street Murder, Houston Detective James A. Pierce was watching. And he thought about the Middle Street case too.

The mangled body of a Latino man had been found in an empty field on Middle Street. It had taken the police department months to identify the body. It had been crushed and deformed to such a point that it was nearly unrecognizable. It had finally been identified through fingerprints.

The autopsy report on the Middle Street Murder had shown a killing of unusual ferocity. The report had listed eight different factors in the cause of death, ranging from "1. fractured skull" to "8. multiple lacerations and abrasions of head, trunk and extremities." In lay terms, the autopsy had come down to this: The victim had been stabbed repeatedly in the head and other places with a large blade. Then he had been dragged by a car. Then he had been run over several times.

In other words, it had been exactly as Sierra was now saying.

When the police had finally identified the victim of the Middle Street Murder, they had been surprised at who he was. It would have seemed, given the nature of the homicide, that he would be an uncommon person —a person with enemies, or at least a person with a police record. But this victim was just an average citizen. He had worked at a bookstore. Yet he had been stabbed, dragged and run over with a car, and now that the Brady Bunch were describing how they had killed him, it sounded as though they were describing how the milkman delivered the milk.

Actually, most of the Brady Bunch cases were execution-style killings. Sierra and Vargas were talking about them freely now, with evident pride, in their soft, polite voices. Somehow, the politeness made the cases all the more frightening.

The press conference was now in high gear. Sierra and Vargas had overcome some of their initial shyness. They were talking naturally and pleasantly, correcting the reporters whenever they had their information wrong. The reporters were loosened up, too. They had started this interview not knowing exactly what they had; and now that they knew, they wanted to find out as much as they could.

Cato: "How about that store owner over on Harrisburg you shot down?"

Sierra: (correcting him) "Navigation Street, you mean?"

Cato: "Navigation, yeah."

Sierra: "Umhum."

Cato: "Did you feel bad about that one afterwards?"

Sierra: "No, I don't feel bad. . . . They can only burn me once, anyway."

Cato: "Why did you call this conference? You don't have to put up with all these questions? Why did you call it?"

And then Jack Cato answered his own question: "You wanted to be in the newspapers and on TV, didn't you?" He said. "Do you feel it will help you, talking to the people out there about what you all did? Do you feel good about it?"

"I don't feel bad about it," Sierra said. "I wanted to say something."

The press conference went on.

The newsmen tried hard to pin down the killings—how many there had been, and where they had been. No one could be sure. At times, it seemed the Brady Bunch members themselves could hardly be sure. But there were at least five that were certain. The original one, on Brady Street. That was one.

Number two was on Navigation Street. Number three was on Almeda Road. Number four was on Middle Street. That was the one where Sierra said he didn't shoot the victim, he "ran over" him.

Number five was in Fort Bend County, Texas, just outside the city limits of Houston. And that, it appeared, was all of them.

Once the murders were sorted out, the next question was — Why? Why had they done it?

Of all the Brady Bunch members, Richard Vargas was the most eloquent in explaining the motive — or lack of it — for the killings. Did he ever feel bad about killing anyone? "No, sir." Did he ever even think about it? "No, sir." If he were out on the streets now, would he do it all again? "I guess so." Why would he do it again? "I guess just for kicks."

Did he enjoy it, the reporters wanted to know? "Yes," Richard Vargas told them, "it was all right." And what had he thought about, when he saw the victims dying, bleeding to death from gunshot wounds and knife wounds? "Well, they was gonna die, that's all," said Vargas pleasantly.

But perhaps the most unusual exchange happened just before the news reporters packed their gear to head back to their stations.

"I got something else to say, man," said Richard Vargas.

"You got something else to say?" Cato answered, turning toward him. "Go ahead, Richard, just tell us."

"Well," Vargas said, "How come they don't want us to tell you about the Murder in the County Jail?"

To the reporters, this was a complete surprise. Besides the five murders they had heard about, there was a sixth one — a Murder in the County Jail.

Vargas began to explain. It seemed the police had not known it was a murder. They had thought the victim died of a heart attack. Vargas had finally told them about it, but they didn't want to make it public because it was — well, it was embarrassing to the police. They hadn't solved the crime or even known about it.

Vargas, now, was going to enjoy embarrassing them.

He explained how he and Sierra had done it. Using a plastic bag, they had suffocated a fellow inmate in order to rob him. It had happened because when the Brady Bunch had first been arrested, the police had not known how violent they were, and they had put them in a community jail tank. Sierra had held the man down by sitting on his chest. Vargas had held the bag over his face.

"Well, the man came in," Vargas said, "and, uh, he was wearing a diamond ring. He started shaking. I started talking to him, you know, and he told me that his wife sent him in here for drunk.

"And later that night we killed him and took his ring."

That was all there was to it. The Murder in the County Jail.

The reporters dismantled their equipment and packed it up. Then they rushed back to their stations to get the Brady Bunch — plus, of course, the Brady Street Murder, the Navigation Street Murder, the Almeda Road

Murder, the Middle Street Murder, the Fort Bend County Murder, and last, but not least, the Murder in the County Jail—on the news at six o'clock.

* * *

The press conference had been held soon after the arrest of the Brady Bunch.

Now, four months later, Assistant District Attorney Stu Stewart flicked off the tape recorder as he finished listening to it one more time.

It was unbelievable, he thought.

And the most unbelievable thing about it was that the press conference would not be admissible before the jury at all, during any of the trials of the Brady Bunch members. The jury could never even be told about it.

Once again, Stewart read the provision of the law that said so. It was article 38.22 of the Texas Code of Criminal Procedure, and there was no way around it. The tapes and videotapes of the press conference could not be used as evidence, because article 38.22 said that if a prisoner was in custody, only a signed, *written* statement was admissible in evidence. An oral confession—even if it was recorded—couldn't be used at all.

Charles Dickens once wrote that "the law is an ass." Here, the law said that a written statement would be admissible, but it allowed the Brady Bunch members to call a press conference before television cameras and tell the whole world how much they enjoyed killing—then keep it hidden from the jury that would decide the case.

Charles Dickens was right.

At least, Stewart reflected, there was a set of admissible confessions. The Houston Police Department, aware of the provisions of article 38.22, had gotten written statements at the same time as the press conference. The statements recited all the warnings required by the Supreme Court's decision in *Miranda v. Arizona*. They were all signed. And these written confessions were completely voluntary; everyone connected with the events, including the television newsmen, could testify to the circumstances.

It was unfortunate, Stewart thought, that there was no way to show the jury the chilling, frightening quality of these murderers that the press conference showed so graphically. The written confessions contained a description of the crimes on paper. They would not give the jury the insights that the press conference did into the kinds of men these Brady Bunch members were.

Still, Stu Stewart was never one to quarrel with the law. Or to try to circumvent it.

Even his opponents held Stu Stewart in high regard. In fact, one might say, especially his opponents—they respected him. "He's stronger than a Mexican plate lunch," said one lawyer who fought against him in court.

"But he doesn't pull any bullshit tricks on you, either. Nothing cheap, no cheap shots.

"He beats you fair and square, or not at all. He's just a good guy."

Stewart was a big man. He radiated strength and solidity. Born in Texas, he had gone to college in Tulsa, Oklahoma, where he combined a starting position on the football team with a high grade average. He came to the District Attorney's office after graduating at South Texas Law School in Houston, and he had been a prosecutor for over seven years when he was assigned to handle the Brady Bunch cases.

Now, as he prepared these extraordinary cases for trial, he knew what the defense would do. The defense lawyers would not be satisfied with exclusion of the press conference. They would try to get the written confessions thrown out of court too. They would say the confessions were coerced and involuntary, and they would claim that their client's rights under the fifth, sixth and fourteenth amendments had been violated.

That was the defense lawyers' job. They would be subject to criticism if they didn't try to get the confessions thrown out.

Stewart turned on the tape recorder again. He heard the voice of the news reporter, Jack Cato, asking the Brady Bunch members something that would be of the utmost importance in the pre-trial hearing concerning the confessions.

Cato: "You've been treated all right? You haven't been hit or mistreated?"

Voices: (all defendants) "No."

Cato: "Do all of you agree on that? You haven't been mistreated?"

Voices: (Unintelligible)

Cato: "Nobody's laid a hand on you, have they?"

Voices: (several responses, of defendants) "No."

Cato: "On you?"

Voices: "No."

Cato: "Let's see, all four of you agree. Nobody's—Okay."

That, Stewart thought, made it pretty clear. The defense lawyers might challenge the confessions. In fact, they were certain to. But in the pre-trial hearings before the judge, the tape recording *would* be admissible. And it showed how spectacularly evident the voluntariness of the confessions really was.

Stewart shut the tape recorder off and began to prepare his case.

* * *

Defense Attorney Stuart Kinard was studying the press conference too. He had a different view of it than the prosecutor.

Stuart Kinard was Vice President of the Texas Criminal Defense Lawyer's Association. He taught an evening course in criminal defense trial practice at a local law school. He was smart, and tough, and a seasoned criminal lawyer.

He had been appointed by the court to represent Bernardino Sierra, the leader of the Brady Bunch.

The case against Sierra, he knew, contained all the elements of a death sentence case. A written confession to five murders. A trail of robberies with eyewitnesses who could identify Kinard's client. Sierra had even been arrested while he was committing a robbery, and the gun he was using was the weapon he had used to commit one of the five murders.

Kinard wanted to save his life. But even that would take a miracle.

"There's no question about it," he thought to himself, " I've got to try to get the written confessions thrown out. Not just the videotape of the press conference—because article 38.22 does seem to exclude that, in any event—but the written confession, too."

Kinard went over the transcript of the press conference with a fine-tooth comb. It would not be admissible before the jury, but it would be seen by the judge during the pre-trial hearings.

It was the key to the case.

And Kinard found several things that seemed promising to the defense.

During the press conference, Sierra had been asked whether he had been promised anything by the officers to get him to confess. Sierra had said, "Yeah, I been promised that my mother was gonna get cut loose."

In fact, Sierra's mother had been arrested along with the Brady Bunch members. She had been in possession of a cache of stolen property. The police had released her immediately after the last of the confessions, because all the Brady Bunch members said that she didn't know the property was stolen.

Kinard read on in the transcript.

It seemed that Sierra had been fairly persistent in naming his mother's arrest as one of the reasons he had confessed. When Jack Cato had asked, "Why did you call this conference?" Sierra had answered, "Well, uh, my mother, you know, like I say, she was gonna be charged with something she didn't do, so, uh, I didn't want her to be in jail no longer."

That would be his theme, Kinard decided.

Sierra wasn't beaten. No one laid a hand on him. He wasn't mistreated in any way. Kinard's defense would be that he was forced to confess in order to free his mother from prison. It was not physical coercion, but it was coercion nonetheless.

It would be a hard argument to make. The police were not outside the bounds of propriety if they arrested Sierra's mother with probable cause, and it seemed they had that, since they found her in possession of the property. And they were not outside the bounds of propriety if they released her when they got information which they believed, which showed them that she hadn't known the property was stolen.

But if Kinard could show that the police had arrested Sierra's mother for the purpose of using her as a hostage, and threatening to hold her without evidence until the Brady Bunch members confessed — if he could do that, the confessions might be considered involuntary. And that would mean they would be thrown out.

The press conference itself, and the ghoulish delight that the Brady Bunch members took in bragging about their exploits, was the prosecution's answer to the defense theory. To counter the press conference, it would be Kinard's job to put on evidence of coercion so powerful that it resulted not only in the written confessions, but in the press conference too.

It seemed far-fetched at first. But it might work.

The lawyers who represented Richard Vargas agreed to let Kinard take the lead in the pre-trial hearings. Vargas didn't have a mother in jail, and he had almost nothing that could be used to dispute the confessions — outside of whatever might splash over from Kinard's attack on them on Sierra's behalf. Fuentes and Ruiz's lawyers, too, were content to let Kinard take the lead.

This defense became known as the "Sierra's Madre" Theory, and it went like this: all of the written confessions, and the press conference with its appearance of voluntariness, were in fact the result of pressure that was applied to *all* the Brady Bunch members, through the fear that Sierra's mother might have to take a bum rap. The four men's voluntary appearance at the press conference was a put-on. It wasn't really voluntary. The Brady Bunch members had turned in an Academy Award performance in front of the television cameras, and they had done it because the police had forced them, psychologically, to do it. Kinard was enough of a wag to refer to his theory as "The Pressure of Sierra's Madre."

* * *

"I think it's incomprehensible," Judge Jefferson said, "that that sort of thing could happen in this country."

Judge Jefferson wasn't talking about the crimes the Brady Bunch had committed. He was talking about the press conference.

As he saw it, the broadcasting of the confessions was an attempt to taint the trial with publicity. Stu Stewart protested; the "Bunch" members had demanded to see reporters, and that was why they had been allowed to see them.

Judge Jefferson didn't see it that way.

The frame of mind that Andrew Jefferson brought to the case was going to matter a great deal. He was the judge of the 208th Criminal District Court of Harris County. And as it happened, the Brady Bunch cases had all been consolidated and assigned to the 208th for pretrial hearings.

Judge Jefferson was an impressive man. He liked to use street slang whenever the King's English was insufficiently expressive, but he had come a long way since his beginnings. As a black man he had graduated from the most prestigious law school in the State—the University of Texas—at a time when black law students were all but unheard of. From there he had become an Assistant United States Attorney. There, his obvious capabilities and his background appealed to many potential employers—both in and out of government. It was not long before he was employed in the office of the general counsel of what is now the Exxon Corporation, and that made him one of the chief legal officers of one of the largest companies in the world.

He had been appointed to his present position about a year before the Brady Bunch cases came to him.

Judge Jefferson's diction and his command of the English language were part of what made him a commanding figure in the political arena. It was said that he was as good a speechmaker as Congresswoman Barbara Jordan, who was a friend of his, in fact.

There was one other noteworthy thing about Judge Jefferson—something that was of particular importance to Kinard and the other Brady Bunch defense lawyers.

The judge had a dislike for some of the policies of the District Attorney's Office that seemed to have blossomed into a personal animosity toward the District Attorney himself. The District Attorney, in turn, had publicly criticized some of the judge's decisions.

Relations between the two men had become so strained that Judge Jefferson, on one occasion, interrupted a public hearing, for which he had summoned the District Attorney to his court, to ask him, on the record: "What is your attitude toward criticism of judicial decisions, Mr. Vance?"

The District Attorney had replied, in so many words, that no public official holding an elective office was immune from criticism. That was legally correct, of course, and the first amendment to the Constitution said so; but it did little to ease the tension between these two powerful men.

It was early January, 1975, when the hearings on the Brady Bunch confessions got under way in Judge Jefferson's court.

"Any opening remarks, Mr. Stewart?" Judge Jefferson asked.

The prosecutor stood up. "We recognize, your honor, that the burden is on us to show that the confessions were voluntary," Stu Stewart began. "We intend to more than shoulder that burden."

He would produce the tapes of the news conference, Stewart went on. He would produce as witnesses the newsmen who were present at the conference, to show how it was conducted and to testify about the demeanor of the Brady Bunch members. He would produce all the police officers who had been present and a number of lay witnesses.

And so the hearing began.

Officer James A. Pierce, who had been present when Sierra signed his written confession, was one of the first to testify.

"Did you ever make any promise, or offer any inducement to them?" Stu Stewart asked.

"No," was Pierce's answer.

As to Kinard's charge that he had used Sierra's mother to get Sierra to confess, Pierce said, "He heard his mother was in jail. He asked to see us, not the other way around. He wanted to tell me his mother had nothing to do with it.

"We told them we couldn't make any promises."

When the Brady Bunch members had asked to go on television, said Pierce, "I called the District Attorney's Office." The decision to allow the newsmen and the prisoners to get together was made personally by the District Attorney, on the ground that if inmates wanted to talk to the press, and you didn't let them, it would create more problems, and violate their rights to a greater extent, than if you kept them incommunicado.

Stuart Kinard's questioning was acute. He wanted to know why Sierra's mother was marked "hold for investigation" on homicide division records instead of burglary and theft records.

"We had information there were other killings besides the ones we knew about," Pierce answered. At the time, there were only two cases—the Navigation Street Murder and the Almeda Road Murder—that the police had solved. "The families of these men had property including guns used," Pierce said. "We didn't know the extent of this thing."

The explanation was plausible. The judge might accept it. But Kinard had some other points to make.

Wasn't it a fact, he asked, that all of the Brady Bunch lawyers had been appointed before the press conference? And none of them were notified that the press conference was going to take place?

And wasn't there a time when not only Sierra's mother, but Joe Ruiz's mother and father were under arrest and in custody?

There was indeed, Pierce replied. But Ruiz's parents, too, had been found in possession of stolen property, and they had been arrested for that offense. It was an arrest on probable cause, and it was not used in any way to elicit the confessions. As far as the lawyers were concerned, the Brady Bunch members had full access to them, had met with them, and had been advised of all their rights. They hadn't wanted to consult their lawyers. They had wanted to get on television and brag about their crimes.

After Pierce, Stewart called a news photographer, Nancy Redding, to the stand. She identified photographs she had taken at the time Sierra and Vargas had made and signed their confessions. The photographs showed them smiling in amusement. One of the pictures showed Richard Vargas, seat-

ed at a desk, looking at something. His face had a look of bemused interest in it. The witness explained that Vargas was looking at a photograph
of one of his victims, which he had asked the police to see.

But the star witness in the case was a tape recorder.

The chilling, calm voices of the Brady Bunch members wafted through
the courtroom. Judge Jefferson listened intently. He heard Sierra talking
about the Middle Street Murder, telling reporters he hadn't shot the man
but had "run over" him. He heard Vargas tell how much he enjoyed the
killings and how he "guessed" he would do it again. And he heard the
astounding revelation of the Murder in the County Jail, which the police,
far from forcing the Brady Bunch to confess, had wanted to keep confidential.

Judge Jefferson heard the entire press conference.

Finally, Stu Stewart rested his case. He had put on nearly two dozen
witnesses; it had taken seventeen days. The evidence that the confessions
were voluntary, he thought, was overwhelming.

*   *   *

During most of the hearing, the four members of the Brady Bunch —
Sierra, Vargas, Ruiz and Fuentes — sat in the empty jury box.

That seemed the most appropriate place to put them. The hearing had
started with them at counsel table with their lawyers, but that had not
worked out at all. They had spent a great deal of the time talking among
themselves and laughing.

There had been one point in the hearings when Judge Jefferson had said
something about holding Stu Stewart in contempt and putting him in jail.
That had been the high point of the trial for the Brady Bunch, who had been
unable to restrain their glee. They were laughing at a system in which the
judge presumed them innocent after they had confessed to six sadistic murders on television, but threatened to put their prosecutor in jail.

Now, it was time for the Brady Bunch themselves to testify.

One by one, each of them claimed that he had confessed because of the
fear that his own mother would be arrested by the Houston police.

"But your mother wasn't in jail," Stewart said to Richard Vargas. "How
did they make you confess?"

"They told me they'd go arrest her," Vargas answered.

To Fuentes, Stewart said, incredulously, "Your mother was in Mata-
moros, Mexico. How did they make you confess?"

"They told me they'd find her," Fuentes replied.

It was too much for Judge Jefferson to believe, the prosecutor decided.
The Sierra's Madre Theory just required too much imagination for anyone
to swallow it. It required one to believe that the arrest of Sierra's mother,
on probable cause, had led to a series of events that culminated in the press

conference, at which the four men, in spite of their low intelligence, fooled everyone into thinking they were acting voluntarily when in fact they were not.

*   *   *

It was only a short time later that Judge Jefferson made his decision public.

"... the court finds that the state has failed to meet its burden to prove by a preponderance of the evidence that the said confessions were voluntary," the judge's order read. And with those words, he threw out the written confessions of Sierra and Ruiz.

Two days later, he entered another order, throwing out the confessions of Vargas and Fuentes.

The four men had confessed on television, put it in writing and signed it, and said they were never mistreated by the police—and yet there it was. None of it could be used in court against them. Judge Jefferson had accepted the defendants' theory. And there was nothing that Stu Stewart could do about it.

Within a matter of months, before any of the Brady Bunch cases was settled by trial, Judge Jefferson resigned to enter private practice.

And he went into partnership with two of the lawyers who had represented Brady Bunch members.

There was no impropriety in this, of course. The judge had a right to resign, and he had a right to form a partnership with whomever he chose. But there were some people who thought that his new practice explained why the judge thought the way he did. He simply was more in tune with defense lawyers than with lawyers for the state. It wasn't an attempt to question the judge's motives, just an inference that he tended to be defense-minded.

But that was only one view of it. Judge Jefferson was fiercely independent, and he had never been suspected of personal favoritism. That was a real achievement in a courthouse full of elected judges. He explained his decision in a written order: the evidence and the law required him to do what he did. The state just hadn't carried its burden of proof. The possibility of coercion hadn't been overcome, and the police and prosecutors had committed a gross impropriety by not calling the defense lawyers before they held the press conference. The judge had appointed skilled defense lawyers, ones whom he respected, because this was a serious case; and it was for similar reasons that he had ended up in practice with them.

For Stuart Kinard, the confession hearings were an amazing success. It had looked like an impossible argument for the defense, at first. Now, his "impossible" task of defending Bernardino Sierra had moved a little closer to accomplishment because he had shown that the Sierra's Madre Theory was credible, after all. Of course, the prosecution could still proceed to try the Brady Bunch members, using the evidence they had left—eyewitnesses, circumstantial evidence, and the like—but the confessions, the most damning evidence, were out of the picture.

Stu Stewart, the prosecutor, had a different perspective.

"That was the strangest hearing I've ever seen," he said, when it was over. And he added: "Or that I ever hope to be a part of."

But every trial lawyer is used to adverse decisions. And so Stu Stewart, now, got ready to try his case against the members of the Brady Bunch. The first of the cases to reach a jury was the one against Richard Vargas. And as it happened, the suppression of the confessions was only the beginning of the courtroom battle over Richard Vargas' life.

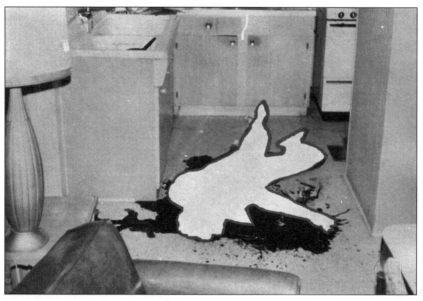

The Brady Bunch. This bizarre group took its name from the fact that one of its first robbery-murders was this brutal killing at an address on Houston's Brady Street.

The Brady Bunch. The members of the group demanded to meet with news reporters. From left to right, Richard Vargas, Joe Ruiz, Bernardino Sierra and Angel Fuentes meet the press (Photograph courtesy Houston Post).

The Brady Bunch. Bernardino Sierra, shortly after the giving of his confession concerning the Fort Bend County Murder. This was two days after the press conference. Detective Chuck Lofland has just said something funny, causing Detective Terry Pierce (standing) and Sierra to laugh. (Photograph courtesy Nancy Redding).

The Brady Bunch. When he confessed to Fort Bend County authorities, Richard Vargas wanted to see police photographs of his victim. Here he studies those pictures, with a newspaper containing front page coverage of the press conference in front of him. (Photograph courtesy Nancy Redding).

The Brady Bunch. Homicide scene photograph of the Middle Street Murder. The victim, an ordinary citizen who worked at a bookstore, was stabbed in the head, chest and extremities with a large blade, then run over and dragged with a car.

The Brady Bunch. Homicide scene photograph of the Almeda Road Murder. The victim, who had completed the requirements for a college degree in pharmacy and was awarded his diploma post-humously, worked as a night manager of a grocery store to put himself through. He was forced to lie here, behind the cash register, and was shot in the back of the head.

The Brady Bunch. One of the robbery victims in the Navigation Street Murder re-enacts the crime by showing the position in which he was forced to lie.

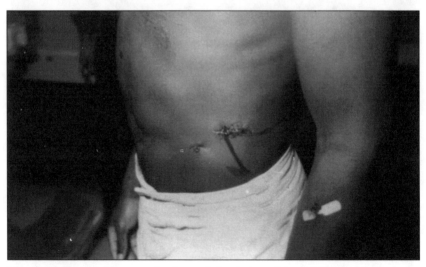

The Brady Bunch. The wounds of one of the victims of the stabbing inside the county jail. Sierra smuggled in a pair of scissors and attempted to kill two other inmates with them. This episode followed Sierra's escape from jail (he was apprehended without violence) and the incident in which Sierra and Vargas successfully killed an inmate to steal his ring.

Chapter 15

The Brady Bunch, Part II: The Trial of Richard Vargas

"I been nervous a long time," the prisoner said. He stared down at the floor.

The psychologist looked at him. "Have you gotten any medicine for it?" he asked. "Or any treatment?"

"No," said the prisoner indifferently.

The man was trying to be as unresponsive to the questions as possible, the psychologist noticed. In fact, he was acting out a classic example of what psychologists call "passive-aggressive" behavior. Inside, he was smoldering with hostility. Outwardly, he expressed that hostility by ignoring the interviewer.

He told the psychologist his name was Richard Vargas. And he added that he was a member of the "Brady Bunch."

The psychologist tried again. For him, the purpose of the interview was fairly simple; he had some straightforward questions that had to be answered. Was Richard Vargas rational? Would he be able to communicate with his attorneys and assist them in his defense? The law said that before any individual could be tried for a crime, he had to be mentally competent.

It was the psychologist's job to find that out.

The prisoner was only minimally cooperative, and he expressed his aggression by grunting, staring or saying "I don't know." But that was a mode of behavior the psychologist knew only too well, and he knew of standard methods for dealing with it and getting the information he needed. And so in many respects, the process was routine.

But in another way, it was anything but routine.

The interview was taking place on the ninth floor of Houston's Jefferson Davis Hospital. That was where the maximum security wing of the hospital was located. And the subject of the evaluation, Richard Vargas, was charged with multiple counts of capital murder.

The first step in a psychological interview is to take a history. That was hard to do, given this subject's lack of cooperation, but it could be done with patience and repetition of questions. And so, slowly, the psychologist began to learn something about the unusual human being who sat before him.

Richard Vargas was born May 30, 1951, in Brownsville, Texas—deep in the fertile Rio Grande Valley, just across the border from Mexico. Reports on the number of his brothers and sisters varied, but it was clear there were a lot of them. His mother had said that there were seventeen children in all. Richard Vargas, when he was asked about it, said that he "wouldn't try" to figure out where he ranked in age among them.

The prisoner's work history was sporadic and unstable. He had been employed mainly as an unskilled laborer. That, in turn, was tied to his lack of success in school; for although Richard Vargas had made it through the elementary grades, he had progressed only into the first year of junior high school. In 1965, the psychologist learned, Richard Vargas had earned his first institutional commitment—to the State Reform School in Gatesville, Texas. That marked the end of his formal education.

That may also have been when drugs became a regular part of Richard Vargas' life. The psychologist learned that this prisoner had used LSD, amphetamines and barbiturates on a regular basis. But the drug Richard Vargas used most frequently, he said, was alcohol. Becoming intoxicated was an everyday occurrence for him.

As the history progressed, in spite of Richard Vargas' hostile resistance to the interview, the portrait of a killer emerged. Bit by bit, the doors to the information the psychologist needed began to open. The keys to the doors were sometimes under the surface—not just in the prisoner's answers themselves, but in his behavior too.

Now, the psychologist began to ask direct questions aimed at finding out whether the prisoner perceived the situation he was in. Did the prisoner know what he was charged with? Yes, he did; they were murders and robberies. Did the prisoner understand that he could get the death penalty for the crimes he was charged with? Yes, Richard Vargas said, he understood.

"I don't think about it," he added. "They can only burn me once."

By now, the man's basic mental condition was clear enough to the psychologist. Richard Vargas was sane. He was competent to stand trial. He had a rational understanding of the reality that surrounded him. Hostile, aggressive, even cynical—but rational.

Still, the interview wasn't enough by itself.

Because of the seriousness of the charges, the psychologist knew that further examination would be appropriate—just to make sure. And so he turned to the diagnostic techniques of modern psychology. By testing the prisoner with ink blots, drawings and carefully prepared questions, he hoped to get an inside view of Richard Vargas' brain.

*   *   *

The Bender Gestalt Test is used to determine the presence, or absence, of physical brain damage.

It was the first of a battery of tests that the psychologist administered to Richard Vargas.

The Bender Gestalt Test is deceptively simple. All it consists of is a sheet of paper with diagrams on it. At the top of the page is a circle and a diamond, with a row of twelve dots beneath them; the rest of the sheet is a complex pattern of dots and squiggles. The test subject is given this sheet, together with a blank sheet and a pencil, and he is asked to copy it.

A subject with brain damage produces a characteristically distorted pattern. That was what the tester had to look for.

The psychologist waited while Richard Vargas copied the Bender Gestalt pattern. Then he looked at the results.

The prisoner's drawings were sloppy and crooked, and there were blanks that were attributable to his laziness and lack of cooperation. But the spatial relationships of the dots and squiggles on the copied sheet was generally faithful to the original Bender Gestalt Test pattern. That was the important thing. It meant that there was no organic damage to Richard Vargas' brain.

And so the Bender Gestalt Test told the psychologist that Richard Vargas' brain was normal—at least physically.

Now, the next test.

The psychologist showed Richard Vargas a sprawling, discolored ink blot with a series of white spaces in the interior. It was the first "plate" in the famous Rorschach, or "ink-blot," test.

The first plate in the Rorschach test is sometimes called "the bat," because that is the most popular description of this symmetrical smear. The psychologist got Richard Vargas to give a "free-association" description of the "animal" he saw in the blot. Then he asked about the details of the figure that Richard Vargas said he saw.

Then, one by one, the psychologist repeated the process for each of the other plates in the Rorschach series. There were ten in all.

The Rorschach test is one of the most widely used tests in all of psychology. It is simple to administer and it is marvelously versatile. It is capable of detecting both psychoses and neuroses, as well as a wide variety of other personality imbalances.

If the subject gives wildly unconventional descriptions of the imaginary anatomy he sees in a particular blot, for instance, it may lead to a diagnosis of schizophrenia. If he responds with explanations that indicate fear or disgust, it may be an indication that the schizophrenia is of the paranoid type. The emotional content of the response, the number and type of details that the subject perceives, and the part of the blot that is described—all of these are windows into the personality of the subject, for a psychologist skilled in the art.

And so it was in Richard Vargas' case.

The psychologist found no evidence of delusions or hallucinations. There was no interference with the prisoner's rational thought processes. The prisoner was not suffering from any known psychosis or neurosis. And that, in itself, was significant.

The results of the ink blot test, in other words, were consistent with the psychologist's conclusions from the interview.

That left one more major area to be tested: It was necessary to know something about the prisoner's level of intelligence.

Using a technique called the "Ammons Q. T. Test," the psychologist soon had an evaluation. Richard Vargas' responses indicated an I.Q. of 75. But that score did not take account of the language barrier. Since Richard Vargas' primary language was Spanish, the true value would be slightly higher. The psychologist estimated Richard Vargas' true I.Q. to be between 80 and 90.

Again, the findings showed no abnormality. Richard Vargas had a level of intelligence that was only slightly below the average of the adult population in the United States.

Now the psychologist's test results were complete.

They showed something that was really quite startling. The prisoner was normal, in most respects.

He was of normal intelligence. There was no brain damage. And he had no delusions or interference with his rational processes. The psychologist's report was simple: Richard Vargas was sane and competent to stand trial.

But that, of course, left the biggest question unanswered.

Why was this man a killer?

The textbooks call it "antisocial personality." This label, the textbooks say, "is reserved for individuals who are basically unsocialized and whose behavior pattern brings them repeatedly into conflict with society. . . . They are grossly selfish, callous, irresponsible, impulsive, and unable to feel guilt or learn from experience or punishment."

That description fit Richard Vargas perfectly.

But the label, "antisocial personality," is not a very useful label.

At different times during the history of psychiatry, people with what is now called "antisocial personality" have been called "psychopaths," "sociopaths," or other names. The psychiatric profession has changed the name of this particular personality disorder repeatedly, every few years. And the changes are really quite important, because they are an indication that the psychiatrists do not know very much about this condition. Every few years, they change their collective mind about what "antisocial personality" (or whatever it is called) really means.

It is also a fact that the psychiatric profession is utterly unable to agree on the causes, the nature and the treatment of an antisocial personality. Little, if any, treatment is possible.

In Richard Vargas' case, it was like saying that he was a criminal because he had a personality that was suited to his being a criminal. That was the best that experts on the human mind could do.

The psychologist finished dictating his report. He flicked the tape recorder off.

* * *

At the courthouse, Assistant District Attorneys Stu Stewart and David Crump studied the evidence against Richard Vargas.

The evidence included the reports of the psychiatrists and psychologists who had examined him.

Usually, the psychologist is viewed as a witness for the defense. He is an expert on the issues of insanity and mental incompetence. His normal function is to give evidence on whether the defendant can "tell right from wrong," has a "mental disease or defect," has "capacity to conform his conduct to the law," or whatever other language is used to express the test for insanity. The prosecution, too, sometimes uses psychologists, but it is almost always in answer to a claim of insanity or incompetence that has been raised by the defense.

But the trial of Richard Vargas was going to be different.

When it comes to the death penalty, a psychiatrist or psychologist can give information that is useful on matters unrelated to sanity or mental competence. A psychiatrist or psychologist can give evidence that relates to the basic issue of the appropriateness of capital punishment.

In a capital case in Texas, the jury has to answer a question about the defendant's tendency toward violence in the future. This is a subject on which the psychologist's expert knowledge can be revealing. And in this case, there would be a defense psychologist—a defense expert—and so it would be proper for the prosecution too.

As they prepared for trial, Stewart and Crump decided to introduce psychological testimony in the trial of Richard Vargas, in answer to the defense evidence. It had been done in a few cases before. It had never been done in Houston.

Prediction of future violence, they knew, was difficult even for experts in the field. It was particularly difficult in marginal cases. But with a clear case—a strong case, someone like Richard Vargas—the psychologist might be able to say something that the jury could hang its hat on.

It was decided that Stewart would handle the case during the first trial, the trial on Richard Vargas' guilt or innocence. He would prove the elements of the offense. He would put on the evidence that would secure a conviction for capital murder.

The second trial—the penalty hearing—would be handled by David Crump.

And in the penalty hearing, the prosecution would present a picture of the personality of the killer, a psychological portrait.

That meant that the prosecutors' preparation for the penalty hearing would be unusual. It would require knowledge about the techniques of psychiatry and psychology that were used to evaluate Richard Vargas. That would require, in turn, an understanding of the Bender Gestalt Test, the Rorschach Technique, and the Ammons intelligence test—the tools that the psychologist had used.

These were technical concepts. Their use was generally confined to practitioners in white coats who inhabited the realm of ideas about the human mind.

But in the trial of Richard Vargas, they were about to become weapons in a battle over life and death.

*   *   *

The trial of Richard Vargas was in its second week when Stu Stewart rested the case for the prosecution.

The evidence of the defendant's guilt was overwhelming.

Stu Stewart had presented a total of nearly two dozen witnesses. Three of them were eyewitnesses to the killing itself. Their testimony showed a murder that was strikingly devoid of any reason or justification.

The four members of the Brady Bunch had stopped at a grocery store during a pleasant summer evening. Bernardino Sierra and Richard Vargas had gone inside. They had made everyone in the store—patrons and manager alike—lie face down, on the floor.

Vargas had sat on the counter, the witnesses said. He leaned over it and pointed his gun downward, into the area behind the cash register. That was where the store manager was lying.

And in that position, Vargas had fired his .22 pistol twice.

"Did he ever change expression, the expression on his face?" Stewart had asked one of the witnesses.

"No," was the witness' answer.

There had been no need for the killing. The manager had not resisted; in fact he had not moved at all after lying down. The autopsy pictures showed the jury where the gunshot entry wounds were; they were squarely in the back of the manager's head.

The only plausible explanation was that Richard Vargas had killed the man for amusement.

Houston Police Officer R. A. Noskrent had been the first investigator on the scene. He described the victim. In life, Ashokkumar Patel had weighed only 120 pounds. He was a tiny man, just over five feet tall. As it happened, he was a citizen of India, from the state of Madras, going to school in the United States and working his way through by managing this grocery store.

Now, a year and a half later, Noskrent was visibly shaken by the effort of testifying about the murder.

He had arrived as Patel was dying. In court, he told the jury he had heard the victim chanting in his native tongue as the officer wrapped his exploded head in a towel and waited for an ambulance.

"What did he appear to be saying?" Stewart asked.

"It appeared to me he was praying," Officer Noskrent said slowly.

* * *

Victor Blaine is one of the best criminal lawyers in Harris County.

He is also one of the most straightforward and honest.

The two attributes do not always go together. In fact, it takes a real effort to combine them. The criminal law is a cesspool of injustice, and the frustrations of practicing it day in and day out can soften any man or woman to the easy temptations it presents. And that leads to dishonesty, to the opposing evils of selling out a client or suborning him to perjury.

Vic Blaine and his partner Bob Carroll were well known and respected at the courthouse. They represented their clients within the boundaries of the law. But they did it vigorously, and they always gave those to whom their duty was owing a skillful defense.

Now Blaine and Carroll were applying their talents to the defense of Richard Vargas.

Blaine—with his curly, salt-and-pepper hair and his accent that told of his youth in Mississippi—had an excellent record in capital cases. Since the capital murder statute had been enacted in Texas, he and Carroll had defended three cases—and saved their client from the death penalty each time.

In this case, though, Blaine and Carroll were going to have a difficult time of it. The evidence was strong, the crime was brutal, and the defendant—the defendant would be seen by a jury, after all the evidence was in, as a person who ought to be subject to the death penalty. It would take a vigorous defense to prevent that from happening.

Blaine and Carroll decided to make an issue of the witnesses' identification of the killer. The witnesses were mistaken—that was their defense. The two defense lawyers presented a witness who had seen the killing and who had not been called to the witness stand by the prosecutors. The witness said he was not sure whether it was Richard Vargas who had pulled the trigger in the grocery store that night. He was unable to identify the killer at all. He said it "could have been" Richard Vargas, or it "could have been" someone else; he just didn't know.

It was good defensive strategy, even though the testimony was not highly credible. The prosecution had the burden of proof, and that burden was to show the defendant guilty beyond a reasonable doubt. As a practical matter, jurors demand much higher proof in a death penalty case. Could this testimony create the doubt Blaine and Carroll needed to acquit Richard Vargas?

It was possible.

But as with every strategic decision, this one had some risks associated with it.

The robbery-murder of Ashokkumar Patel was not the only crime Richard Vargas had committed on that summer evening. He had committed a series of ten robberies, plus a murder and an attempted murder in addition to the crime he was now on trial for. Up to this point in the trial, Texas law had prevented the prosecutors from telling the jury about those other crimes.

But the rule against "extraneous offenses" in Texas has some important exceptions. And one of them says that if the defense challenges the identification of the suspect by the witnesses, the prosecution can put evidence before the jury concerning all other similar crimes committed by the defendant.

And so it was that Blaine and Carroll's calculated risk opened the lid to a Pandora's box for the defense. With witness after witness, Stewart traced the path the Brady Bunch — Vargas and Sierra together — had followed on that day in March. Stewart called an associate of the Brady Bunch who had turned State's evidence after Vargas and Sierra had threatened to kill him; there was no question of his being mistaken in his identification. The license number of the car was traced to a friend of Vargas'.

Stewart even showed that Vargas was wearing a disguise at the time of his arrest.

Blaine and Carroll had made a decision that had much to recommend it when they raised the issue of mistaken identity. It was just that it had backfired on them.

The jury returned a verdict saying that Richard Vargas was guilty as charged.

* * *

It was three days later, when the penalty hearing was well under way, that the State called its expert witness.

"What, if anything, did you observe about the way in which Richard Vargas regarded the future or its consequences?" David Crump asked.

"He doesn't care much for the future or its consequences," the psychologist answered, "especially as compared to what he wants at the immediate moment."

"Did he appear to have a high regard, or a low regard, for the fate of other human beings, including himself?"

"A low regard," the psychologist answered.

It had taken the jury a little over an hour to find Richard Vargas guilty of capital murder. But as is usually the case with a death penalty trial, that was only the beginning of the battle.

Blaine and Carroll had offered the testimony of Richard Vargas' mother. Pleading with the jury for his life, Mrs. Cruz Vargas had looked down at her feet and said, "my son is sick." And they had offered the testimony of a college administrator who had known the Vargas family for several years. "I'd take a chance on him," this witness said to the jury, earnestly. "I think his prospects are good." The college administrator had training as a psychologist and sounded like an expert.

Now, the jury was hearing the State's psychologist. This was the key witness. And his opinion of Richard Vargas was different.

The testimony was strong, and the jury was listening to it closely. The psychologist described Richard Vargas as impulsive, hedonistic, sensation-seeking. He described Vargas' passive-aggressive behavior during the interview. Such an individual would probably not cooperate to any greater degree with a psychiatrist who was trying to treat him, and there was no real "cure" for the antisocial personality anyway. The psychologist added that Richard Vargas was perfectly sane, and capable of conforming to the law if he chose to do so, but his attitude of contempt toward the law prevented him from it.

"The best indicator of future conduct is past conduct," the witness said near the end of the examination. There would be "a high probability," he added, that Richard Vargas would commit violent crimes in the future if he got the chance.

Both sides rested the case. The evidence was closed.

* * *

Testimony from a psychologist at a death penalty hearing is unusual today. In a later case called *Smith v. Estelle*, the United States Supreme Court held that it was unconstitutional to use it. The Court said that the psychologist's interview of the defendant violated the defendant's rights under the Fifth Amendment to remain silent.

But there is an exception. If the defendant offers his own psychologist, who has interviewed the defendant himself, then he waives his Fifth Amendment privilege. The expert witness offered by Vargas's lawyers perhaps waived the right, in his case. We can never know with certainty.

Today, knowing about the *Smith* case, most defense lawyers would hesitate about calling a defense psychiatrist. They consider carefully the possibility that the waiver of the right to remain silent will allow psychological testimony from the prosecution. But Vic Blaine did not have the *Smith* opinion because it had not been decided yet. Would that have made a difference? It seems doubtful. But again, we can never know.

* * *

The courtroom filled with spectators.

The front row was occupied by lawyers. The rear was crowded with news reporters.

The prosecutors' argument to the jury was about to begin.

Crump and Stewart had agreed to split their argument time, with Crump opening and Stewart closing. In between would come the arguments of Blaine and Carroll for the defense.

Crump's argument was concerned with evaluating the facts of the case. But it was also concerned with another issue: the death penalty itself.

"Why is this a death penalty case?" he said to the jury.

"Well, in law school I learned several basic purposes of sentencing. I'd like to talk to you about them.

"For one thing, those purposes include *justice.* Justice to society. And justice to the victims. Justice to people like Mr. and Mrs. Ashokkumar Patel.

"Another purpose is *rehabilitation* of the offender to return to society —if that is feasible.

"Another purpose—the third purpose—is *protection.* Protection of society, victims, witnesses and everyone else from the offender.

"The fourth purpose is to have a penalty that will make other people stop and perhaps not commit crimes. In other words, *deterrence.*"

Here the prosecutor paused, then said: "Let's look at those things.

"First, a society that loses its ability to do justice," he said, "soon loses everything."

"Every society has to have some way of securing justice in a murder case. Justice that is equal to the crime."

The jury was listening, Crump saw. He went on.

"In primitive societies, it's done by one's kinsmen and tribesmen. They go out and avenge their slain relative.

"Today, we don't do that. But it's clear that sometimes people in our society still take the law in their own hands. If we are to have a government of laws, we should keep the function of administering justice in the place where it belongs—with the jury. People will do that so long as, and only so long as, they are confident the jury will do its duty."

Crump talked about Ashokkumar Patel. The victim had been in his final year at Texas Southern University. He had been studying pharmacy. He had been awarded his pharmacy degree—posthumously. He had left a wife, who happened to have been pregnant at the time; he now had a son. A son whose father Richard Vargas had murdered.

Justice demanded the death penalty in this case.

The next thing to discuss was rehabilitation.

"Rehabilitation?" Crump went on. "That's proper in many cases; maybe in most. But there comes a point where the chance for that is slim—remote —in this case impossible.

"This man's character is so hopeless, this man's crime is so deliberate, unnecessary, inexcusable, monstrous, that if we dream about rehabilitation, all we're doing is saying, 'Let's ship him off to somebody else and let them take care of him.'"

At this point, the prosecutor reminded the jurors of the testimony of the psychologist.

And then he moved on to another reason for capital punishment in this case.

"Basically," he said, "we need protection from this kind of homicidal, violent killer. That's the third consideration.

"We can't just foist him off on somebody else. Violent crime—from rapes through fist fights through robberies through maiming, mayhem and murder are a danger to people inside prisons. Prisoners in the prison system are entitled to be considered as people, too.

"Think about it. What's the major reason you wouldn't want to be locked in a prison today? I bet high on the list is the fact that there are people like Richard Vargas inside there too.

"You could never be sure of your plain old, physical, personal safety if you were locked up together with him."

This was the strongest point, Crump thought. Protection. People might debate whether capital punishment was just. They might debate the deterrent value of it. But this factor—protection—was an absolute. There was no other way to prevent this unbelievably dangerous man from killing again.

And so the prosecutor hammered the protection argument home.

"There's no way to build a prison that complies with our laws that will ensure safety for inmates, guards, wardens, case workers, librarians, doctors, teachers and everybody else that's in the environment. There's no way to keep this man from getting access to spoons, mattress covers, and any one of a thousand other things that can be used in violence. How will he shave? Eat? Sleep? Bathe? Or do any of a hundred other daily chores that will bring him in touch with free world persons?

"And I don't have to tell you that just because a man is in prison for a term, is no guarantee that he won't come into contact with people on the outside."

Richard Vargas, of course, was the man who had committed the Murder in the County Jail, plus at least five others in the free world. And bragged about it on television.

But the jury didn't know any of that, because it wasn't admissible in evidence. Crump just had to hope they had heard enough.

The prosecutor moved on to the subject of deterrence.

"Finally," he said, "there was a great judge who once wrote, 'the law must keep its promises.' People who break the law ought to know that definite consequences come from it.

"If you commit a robbery, you know, you've already committed an offense for which you can get life imprisonment. Why not kill everybody in a robbery? . . . In this state, that kind of murder carries the death penalty. Now, by itself, that won't stop crime. It won't stop every robbery-murder, by any means. But we can't just throw up our hands.

"If it will prevent any one robber from killing any one innocent person lying on the floor groveling and begging for his life, it's justified."

The remainder of the argument consisted of a summary of the evidence. Crump tried to show the jury that the answers to the two questions they would have to answer was "Yes." The killing was obviously deliberate. And all the evidence—from the crime itself to the psychologist's description of the killer's personality—made it clear that Richard Vargas was likely to commit future crimes of violence.

The argument lasted about thirty minutes. For a jury argument in a capital case, that was not very long. But Crump felt mentally drained when he finished and sat down.

Now it was Blaine and Carroll's turn.

* * *

Bob Carroll's argument emphasized that the burden of proof was on the State. "I don't think I'd want to have somebody spend two hours with you and decide you should get the death penalty," he said, referring to the psychologist.

"There is a man who is dead. But that doesn't answer the question. Each of you told us you'd require them to prove their case to you.

"Ask yourself: have they proved it to you? What they've given you is like tossing you a life preserver.

"I think he should get life imprisonment. If he goes to the penitentiary and goes to school, I think he'll get educated.

"Life's a heck of a good thing."

Victor Blaine took up that theme, too.

"Where the death penalty is still invoked, that is where the crime rate is highest," he said. "People are going to have a low regard for life if we take life.

"The only question is—if you don't burn him, would he do it again?

"The psychologist said he 'probably' would," Blaine said emphatically. "He can't prove it to you beyond a reasonable doubt."

The final argument—the last of the four—was Stu Stewart's.

"You have a fact situation that cries out for the death penalty," the prosecutor said, his voice shaking. "What else can you do in this case?"

"I asked all of you, could you give the death penalty in a proper case? Your answers were unequivocal that you could.

"Our system is based on evidence and responsibilities."

* * *

The jury was out until late afternoon.

The courtroom was still full when they returned.

Judge Peter Solito read the verdict. First, the deliberation question.

The jury's answer was "Yes."

The answer to the second question, the violence question, was also "Yes."

"The defendant will rise and face the jury," the judge said. And he assessed the sentence of Richard Vargas at death.

Stu Stewart was outside the courtroom. Victor Blaine walked with Richard Vargas back to his cell. And Bob Carroll shook David Crump's hand. He refused to listen to any condolences. "If you can't drop one, you've got no business trying it," he said.

* * *

It was several days later when Crump tried to reconstruct what had happened.

What were the reasons that Richard Vargas had been sentenced to death?

The answer lay in the evidence.

The jury in the Vargas trial was attentive, intelligent and strong-willed. They were able to follow the court's instructions in the case, and decide it as the law required. But of course, there was another side to that coin; the defense lawyers had had a hand in selecting the jury too. They knew that they had selected a jury that would find against the state if the prosecutors failed to carry the burden. The answer was that the evidence made the life-or-death difference.

The case showed, once again, how quirks of fate could govern the availability of the evidence. The confessions that were suppressed: that had started the process with the state being put at a disadvantage. But the eyewitnesses to the crime had been convincing and sure. They had made the case for the prosecution.

The raising of the identity issue by the defense may have been another factor. For Vic Blaine and Bob Carroll, that had been a tactical decision, and a reasonable one. But it had meant, under the rules of evidence, that the prosecution had been able to give the jury a glimpse at the rest of Richard Vargas — other robberies, another murder, another attempted murder.

The murder in the county jail — that had not been admissible. But the jury had heard enough that was.

Then there was the penalty-hearing evidence. The testimony of the psychologist—and his insights into the mind of a sociopathic killer—that added the last convincing touch to what was already a strong case.

Many factors go into the decision of a criminal case. The composition of the jury, the decisions of the judge, even the personalities of the lawyers—all these can influence the outcome of a trial.

But it was the evidence, and the evidence alone, that made the life-or-death difference in the trial of Richard Vargas.

*   *   *

Richard Vargas was the first of the Brady Bunch to be tried before a jury.

After Vargas had been sentenced, Stewart began to concentrate on the cases against other Brady Bunch members.

Angel Fuentes was one of the Bunch. But he was a hanger-on, and his involvement in the violent activities of the Brady Bunch was peripheral. In Fuentes' case, Stu Stewart was satisfied to ask for a sentence of fifteen years. Joe Ruiz, the third man, was more deeply involved than Fuentes—but still not as culpable as Vargas or Sierra. Ruiz was convicted of capital murder and given a sentence of life imprisonment.

That left Bernardino Sierra. Sierra, the leader of the group; Sierra, the pathological killer. Sierra, whose case was to become a paradox, because he would never be convicted before a jury of any of the six murders he had committed.

Chapter 16

The Brady Bunch, Part III:
The Navigation Street Murder

The judge's bench in the 209th District Court is low. It bears little resemblance to the towering masses that dominate Houston's more traditional courtrooms.

A judge sitting at this bench sits only a few inches off the floor. He is almost at eye level, in fact, with a person standing in front of him.

Judge Frank Price sat at the bench of the 209th and looked at the prisoner who faced him just a few feet away. The man was slender, with greasy hair. He had a tooth missing in front and a sprawling tattoo on his neck.

"You are Bernardino Sierra?" the judge asked, in the tone of voice of a man reciting a familiar ritual.

The prisoner looked briefly at the two lawyers at his side, the lawyers who had saved his life. Then he looked back at the judge.

"Yes," he said.

"Is that your true name?" the judge went on.

"Yes," said the prisoner.

"You're here in court with your attorneys, Mr. Stuart Kinard and Mr. Terry Gaiser," the judge said. "You're charged by indictment in cause number 214,983 with the offense of murder. How do you plead, guilty or not guilty?"

The judge spoke quietly and politely. There was none of the strident adversity that accompanies a contested jury trial. In fact, no jury was present. The courtroom was nearly deserted.

"Guilty," Bernardino Sierra said softly, in answer to the question.

The outcome of this proceeding had been agreed upon in advance. All that had to be done was the ceremony that the law required for every plea of guilty. It was a ceremony familiar to any criminal lawyer—the completion of a plea bargain. Bernardino Sierra was pleading guilty for a lesser sentence than he might otherwise get.

But this was no ordinary plea bargain.

It was the Plea Bargain of the Century.

Why was it happening? Why wasn't a case of this magnitude being decided by the adversary processes of trial? The answer to that question lay buried in a history that spanned Bernardino Sierra's life, his commission of the Navigation Street Murder, and a death penalty trial that failed to produce a verdict. It was a long history, and one that was both fascinating and repugnant.

*   *   *

It had seemed, at one time, that there was no one in Houston who was a better candidate for capital punishment than Bernardino Sierra.

The four capital murder indictments pending against Sierra were only the tip of the iceberg. He also had one other murder case — for non-capital murder — pending against him, as well as too many robbery indictments to count.

He had even killed inside the county jail. He had participated with Richard Vargas in the incident resulting in the suffocation of an inmate to steal his diamond ring. But Sierra had taken up where Richard Vargas left off. On another occasion, again inside the county jail, Sierra had gotten a pair of scissors smuggled to him — and he had tried to kill two more inmates, stabbing them over a dozen times.

He had escaped from the county jail at least once. And he had arranged with other members of the Brady Bunch to try to kill the witnesses against them.

Who was this man, who was pleading guilty to three murders?

Where had he come from, and why had he done what he had done?

Bernardino Sierra was born March 16, 1947, in the city of San Marcos — on the plains of central Texas, a beautiful, lush country with rolling hills and the best ranching land in the world. When he was a child, his father and mother separated. His mother, who raised thirteen children in addition to Bernardino, moved often from place to place.

Bernardino Sierra finished school through the seventh grade. He was put in a class for slow learners and failed the second grade. There was no question he had difficulty in school, but it was hard to see why — since psychological testing showed that he had an intelligence comparable to the average in the adult population, in the 95 to 105 range.

He was raised primarily by his stepfather — a man with a reputation for large alcohol intake and a bad temper. At an early age in his teens, young Sierra quit school to go to work in a restaurant. During his childhood and early youth, he was abused by his father, who was often angry and drunk at the same time.

It was not long before Bernardino Sierra patterned himself on his father's habits. He had tried drugs of different kinds, but his drug of choice was alcohol. "A case of beer," he once said, "goes down easy." When he was evaluated psychologically, he gave a history of arson and cruelty to animals as a child.

Young Bernardino married at the age of seventeen. He worked successfully for a time. He even had two children, and was able to support them and his wife. His criminal history began in 1970, at the age of 23, when he was convicted of burglary. He was released on probation, without imprisonment. But a year later, he committed another crime, and his probation was revoked.

He spent three years in the Texas Department of Criminal Justice. He was released, then, on parole.

He came to Houston, got a job as a forklift operator, and stayed out of trouble for only a few months before he was arrested and charged with a string of capital murders and robberies.

A psychiatrist who examined him found him "nonchalant, almost proud of his current situation, almost proud of the publicity he has received."

There was nothing wrong with Bernardino Sierra's mental abilities. He was perfectly sane, perfectly rational. And yet the psychiatrist reported that he "seems to have no remorse, whatsoever, about the recent episode."

The psychiatrist's report concluded with a summary of his findings about Bernardino Sierra. It said, "Impression: Antisocial personality, manifested by violent acting-out, marked negativism, extremely poor impulse control, manipulativeness, passive-aggressiveness and destructiveness."

That was Bernardino Sierra.

And so a quarter-century of development lay behind the guilty plea that was taking place in the 209th. It was the development of a personality that could kill, sadistically, without conscience or remorse. That was part of the history behind the plea bargain.

But there was another history, a shorter one, that was equally important. It was the series of legal maneuvers that had led the prosecutor to recommend a life sentence, rather than death, for Bernardino Sierra. It was a history of difficulties for the prosecution—strange quirks in the law, strange quirks in the rules of evidence—that made it possible for Sierra to escape the ultimate penalty of death.

*   *   *

The history began before the trial date of Bernardino Sierra.

In his office, Stu Stewart sighed—and looked, once more, at his file.

Four indictments for capital murder. And every one of them, Stewart knew, would present problems for the prosecution. The suppression of the confessions by Judge Jefferson had been an omen. It had signalled how the rest of the case might go.

This case, Stewart knew, was going to be different from the case against Richard Vargas.

The trial of Richard Vargas had involved powerful, and positive, eyewitness testimony. There had been a number of people inside the store who had been able to see what happened, and one of them was close enough to see the killer's fingers tighten when he pulled the trigger. The cases against Bernardino Sierra, although there were a lot of them, did not involve any such powerful evidence.

To Stewart, it was frustrating. He knew that the availability of evidence was controlled by chance; but still, it was frustrating.

As it happened, the strongest case against Sierra that the prosecution had was a capital murder committed in the course of a robbery of a small grocery store called the Crescent Food Market. Sierra had shot and killed a customer, execution style. He had also shot, and critically wounded, a store employee.

It was called the Navigation Street Murder, because the Crescent Food Market was located on Navigation Street.

There were plenty of other Brady Bunch cases, but each one of them had problems for the prosecution insofar as convicting Sierra was concerned. Four of the murders—the Brady Street Murder, the Middle Street Murder, the Fort Bend County Murder, and the Murder in the County Jail—had very little evidence other than the confessions to prove them. For all practical purposes, Judge Jefferson had thrown those cases out when he had ordered the confessions suppressed.

The fifth case, the Almeda Road Murder, was a strong case—but that was the one Richard Vargas had committed. It was the murder of Ashokkumar Patel. Sierra had participated in the robbery on Almeda Road, and so he might be guilty of the murder as a co-conspirator in the robbery; but Stu Stewart concluded that it would be inappropriate to ask a jury to sentence him to death when he had not personally participated in the killing.

That left the Navigation Street Murder as the logical one for the prosecution to focus on.

The trouble with the Navigation Street Murder, though, was that no one had actually seen Sierra pull the trigger there. Everyone in the store had been lying face down. The witnesses had all been located where they could not see the murder itself. Several of them could identify Sierra, Vargas and Ruiz as the robbers, but the evidence that could put Sierra behind the murder weapon—the evidence that might get him the sentence Stewart felt he deserved—was all circumstantial.

There was a time, Assistant District Attorney Stu Stewart says now, "when I didn't know what to do.

"I got ballistics tests run on the gun Sierra was arrested with. It was the same type of gun used in the Navigation Street Murder. But the bullet was too deformed from colliding with the victim's body. It went clear through it, from side to side. And an identification of the gun wasn't possible.

"All the eyewitnesses were on the floor and none of them saw anything.

"No one saw it but Sierra, Vargas and Ruiz. And I couldn't exactly put them on the witness stand."

At least, Stewart could show that Sierra was the only one carrying the kind of gun that had been used in the murder. That was some evidence. But he faced the prospect of going to trial with no proof of the murder itself that would stand up in a court of law.

Finally, Assistant District Attorney Stu Stewart went to the books for help. He re-read the Texas criminal code.

And he found a provision that seemed to fit the case perfectly.

It was a new law, just recently passed by the Texas legislature. It said, in essence, that if a person entered into a conspiracy with any other person, he would be guilty of any crimes that he "should have anticipated" his co-conspirators would commit.

As Stewart re-read these words, it dawned upon him: here was a way to prove his case. It was clear that Bernardino Sierra had entered into a conspiracy. He had formed a tacit agreement with the other members of the Brady Bunch—a conspiracy to commit robberies. And from the whole picture, it was clear that that murder was a result that "should have been anticipated" by all the members of the Brady Bunch.

Generally, to be a principal in someone else's crime, a person had to share the intent to commit it. That was what could not be shown in Sierra's case, with reference to the Navigation Street Murder. But this new provision said that in a conspiracy situation, the defendant could be guilty of a crime that "should have been anticipated," even if he had no intent to commit it at all.

And so, irony was piled upon irony. Sierra had, of course, admitted in his written confession that he had pulled the trigger in the Navigation Street Murder. He had even bragged about it in a press conference which he himself had called. The case had been assigned, then, to Judge Jefferson, and he had decided to suppress the confession; and that had left the prosecution unable to prove his act of murder directly.

Now, however, there *was* a way to prove Sierra guilty. Not as a murderer in his own right, which he was, but as a conspirator in the robbery which produced the murder he himself had committed.

"Sometimes the law makes sense," Stewart said. "Sometimes it doesn't. And sometimes it makes sense in spite of itself."

Of course, whenever the law "makes sense in spite of itself," it begins to look like nothing more than a game of words.

So it was in Bernardino Sierra's case.

Sierra had pulled the trigger, but the evidence to prove he had pulled the trigger had been thrown out, and therefore he could not be guilty of pulling the trigger. But he could be guilty of conspiring with the person who pulled the trigger, or in other words, with himself. The long and the short of it was that Sierra could be proved guilty as a principal in a murder which he himself had committed.

* * *

This conspiracy theory was Stu Stewart's key to the whole case.

The jury began to get a view of it, finally, when the trial of Bernardino Sierra was in its fourth week.

When the prosecution began to put in its conspiracy evidence, Stewart's first maneuver was an unusual one. He offered into evidence a large map of the city of Houston. And he held in his hand a set of little red flags, each of them glued to a pin.

He explained to the judge what he intended to do. Each one of the red flags would represent the site of a murder or robbery committed by Bernardino Sierra, together with the Brady Bunch, on one particular summer day.

That was the day of the Navigation Street Murder.

By showing that Sierra had repeatedly committed robberies together with his companions, Stewart knew, he could legally prove that a conspiracy to commit robbery existed. For the Navigation Street Murder had not been the only crime the Brady Bunch had committed that day. They had started in the morning, and they had pulled one "job" after another until the wee hours of the following morning. Of course, Stuart Kinard—as Sierra's chief defense lawyer—did not accept the conspiracy theory. He argued strenuously to the judge that it did not apply in a capital murder case. And at the first mention of an offense other than the Navigation Street Murder, he stood up and objected that his client was not being given a fair trial.

"It would show an extraneous offense, your honor," he said.

Stewart, as prosecutor, had anticipated this objection. He was well aware that the Texas law usually excluded from the jury's consideration evidence about crimes other than the one for which the defendant was on trial. But he thought he had a right, under the law, to show the jury this particular crime spree, since it happened all in one day. It was a continuous event.

"It goes to show that Bernardino Sierra was involved in a conspiracy with Richard Vargas and Joe Ruiz," he argued to Judge Price. "That's the whole issue in the case."

Since the prosecution could not produce an eyewitness to the actual shooting, Stewart said, the conspiracy provision came into play.

"It also goes to show that murder was a result they all could have anticipated," Stewart said. "That's what the law requires us to show. And the fact that they committed all these robberies, plus shooting three people, goes to show that."

Judge Price pondered the issue for some time.

There was no precedent for what Stu Stewart was trying to do. There could not be, because the conspiracy provision had just been passed recently by the Texas legislature, and no one knew exactly what it meant. It was a pure judgment call. And Judge Price knew the penalty if he guessed wrong: the Court of Criminal Appeals of Texas might reverse the conviction and require a retrial of the case.

But the judge was persuaded by the prosecutor's argument.

"I'm going to let the evidence in," he said. "The objection is overruled."

Stu Stewart looked at his list of witnesses. If he was going to be allowed to present them all, it would be a very long trial.

Aided by Assistant District Attorney Vic Driscoll, he set up his huge map on an easel and had it received into evidence. And he stuck the first red flag into it, near the center of the city of Houston.

＊ ＊ ＊

"Is that where your store is located?" Stewart asked the man from the U-Tote-M Store.

"Yes," the robbery victim replied.

Upon getting this answer, the prosecutor walked between the jury box and the judge's bench, glancing at the witness. He reached toward the big city map and put another red flag near the center of the city. The witness nodded.

There had been a parade of witnesses to the activities of the Brady Bunch that day, and the map was already becoming congested with little red flags. The map was probably the most powerful piece of evidence Stewart had.

The first crime of the day had been the robbery of a "Stop-N-Go" store —a small grocery chain. Stewart had produced witnesses from the store who told how Vargas and Sierra had come into the store and robbed it.

That was the first flag on the map.

The second flag marked the location of a fast food store called Shipley's Do-Nut Stand. Again, Stewart had called the victim to the stand to identify Sierra and tell about the robbery.

The third flag was the robbery of a small pinball-and-pool establishment called the Fun Arcade, near the center of Houston. The fourth was the Navigation Street Murder itself.

The fifth flag marked the site of the Almeda Road Murder—the crime in which Richard Vargas, in Sierra's company, had flushed away the life of the little Indian immigrant, Ashokkumar Patel.

Still, the Brady Bunch had not been finished after that murder. And now, neither was Stu Stewart.

The sixth flag in the map was a "Seven-Eleven" grocery store. The seventh was another "Stop-N-Go." The eighth was a U-Tote-M store, another small grocery chain.

The ninth stop for the Brady Bunch—and the ninth flag for Stu Stewart—was a second location of Shipley's Do-Nut Stand. Apparently, the Bunch did not mind hitting the same store chain twice, as long as it was at different locations.

And then Bernardino Sierra had made the last stop alone.

He had gone into a restaurant, called the Early Roberts Cafe, and he had stuck a gun under the manager's face. As it happened, Houston Police

Officer George Rojas was in the cafe having breakfast in the wee hours of the morning. He hadn't quite believed what he was seeing.

Rojas had stepped up from his chair, stuck his own gun in the robber's back, and told him to "Freeze."

And so now, as Stewart stood in the courtroom and pushed the tenth and last pin in the map, he marked the location of the Early Roberts Cafe. That was where the robberies had ended.

Of course, the real issue was the Navigation Street Murder. And Stewart called witness after witness to talk about it.

The Navigation Street Murder was an uncommonly sadistic and unnecessary killing. Sierra, Vargas and Ruiz had walked into the Crescent Food Market and ordered everyone to lie on the floor. And Sierra had shot one of the employees in the chest.

Then, as Sierra was leaving, he shot an elderly patron in the left side of the body, for no real reason. The bullet burst both of the man's lungs as well as his aorta, and it exited just under the armpit on the opposite side of his body. The man was named Joseph Picinich, and he was called "Papa Joe." He was just a few days from his sixtieth birthday. He died almost immediately.

Papa Joe had lived in the neighborhood, just four blocks from the Crescent Food Market, and he had come here that night to buy some cigarettes. As Sierra had finished killing him, he had walked out of the store, got in the car with the others, and drove away—to commit, next, the robbery that took the life of Ashokkumar Patel.

Stewart could not tell the jury about the Brady Street Murder, the Fort Bend County Murder, the Middle Street Murder, or the Murder in the County Jail—because none of those were admissible in evidence. They hadn't happened on the same day, and so they weren't as relevant as the ones that were part of this particular crime spree. But by the time Stewart rested the case, the jury knew a great deal about the Navigation Street Murder. And the map with the little red flags looked like the map of a battlefield.

The defendant offered no testimony.

When it came time to instruct the jury, Judge Price again considered whether Stu Stewart's conspiracy theory was right. Stuart Kinard and his co-counsel Terry Gaiser, for the defense, objected to it with all the force they could muster; and Kinard got his objections into the record as grounds for his appeal. But the judge ultimately accepted the prosecutor's reasoning.

He instructed the jury that they should find Bernardino Sierra guilty if they believed, beyond a reasonable doubt, that the death of Joseph Picinich was an event that should have been anticipated as a result of the robberies.

The jurors had heard more than enough evidence to answer that question. They remained in the deliberation room less than 25 minutes before finding Bernardino Sierra guilty of capital murder.

Chapter 17

The Brady Bunch, Part IV:
Bernardino Sierra's Plea Bargain

Before the jury returned its "guilty" verdict against Bernardino Sierra, Stu Stewart's map and little red flags had been the focus of everyone's attention.

But now the trial on the guilt-innocence question was over.

The penalty hearing was under way.

And in the penalty hearing, the focus of everyone's attention was on the witnesses Stuart Kinard began to call for the defense.

"We call Dr. Bowers to the stand," said Kinard, as he began to put on the evidence he hoped would save Bernardino Sierra's life.

Stu Stewart waited. He had no idea, of course, what the witness was going to testify to. The fifth amendment protected not only the defendant himself, but the defendant's case as well, from prosecution discovery. Kinard, like any good defense lawyer, had not tipped his hand to the State.

"Will you tell the court and the jury your name?" Kinard asked.

"William Bowers," the witness answered.

"And what is your business or profession?" asked the defense lawyer.

"I am a statistician," was the answer.

Almost immediately, Stewart recognized what the witness was going to say. Kinard was not going to focus on Bernardino Sierra personally. He was going to mount a frontal assault on the death penalty itself.

The statistical profession is deeply divided on the capital punishment issue. Many statisticians believe the evidence indicates that the death penalty is not a deterrent to crime. Others believe that the statistical evidence shows that it is an effective deterrent.

It was not difficult to guess which camp this witness was in, since he had been called by Stuart Kinard.

The defense lawyer drew out the witness' scholarly background. It was impressive: degrees, professional societies, and the like. Then Kinard reached the crucial point.

"Is the death penalty an effective deterrent to the crime of murder?" he asked.

"We object, your honor," said Stu Stewart. The jury was not allowed to consider whether the legislature should have passed the death penalty statute, he argued to the judge. The jury was not even allowed to consider whether the death penalty was proper. All they were required to do was to answer two factual issues—deliberation and violence—that pertained to the individual on trial, Bernardino Sierra.

"That's sustained," said Judge Price.

"Dr. Bowers, you will have to step down," said Kinard. " I'm sorry." The witness left the courtroom, unable to testify.

But most of the story of Dr. Bowers' testimony had unfolded while the jury was in the courtroom, listening to every word. Whether the evidence was admissible or not, Kinard had gotten part of his message across.

"The defense calls Mr. Don Reid," said Stuart Kinard.

Stu Stewart recognized this name. Don Reid was editor of the Huntsville *Item*. The *Item* was the principal newspaper in Huntsville, Texas, the town where the Texas electric chair was located. Don Reid had witnessed, personally, over a hundred executions. He was a well-known writer on the subject of capital punishment.

It was a pretty good guess that he, too, like Dr. Bowers, was not going to testify about Bernardino Sierra. He was there to do what he was famous for—to attack the basic idea of capital punishment.

"Your honor, I would ask that the testimony of this witness be taken first outside the presence of the jury," Stewart said. He explained that it seemed clear Don Reid's testimony was not going to be admissible.

"Well, let's see what he gets into," said Judge Price, overruling Stewart's request.

Kinard asked about Reid's profession, his background, and his experience. Then he began to ask the witness about his beliefs concerning capital punishment.

"Objection, your honor," said the prosecutor.

"That will be sustained," said Judge Price, once again.

The witness was excused. But again, part of the message had come across, inevitably, to the jurors, who heard what was going on.

The testimony of the third defense witness was nothing short of amazing, even though it, too, was inadmissible.

"State your name for the court and jury, please," said Stuart Kinard, when the man was seated in the witness chair.

"Edgar Smith," replied the witness.

Edgar Smith, it developed, was a businessman from San Diego, California. He was Chairman of the City's Bicentennial Commission. He was obviously a solid citizen, successful and respectable.

Kinard asked him about his background.

"I was on death row, myself, in the State of New Jersey," the witness said.

At one time, Edgar Smith had been convicted of a capital crime and sentenced to death. He had spent time on death row for the offense. He had won a new trial, and in that new trial he had again been convicted and sentenced—this time, to a term of imprisonment. He had served a part of his sentence and had been paroled.

From there, he had gone on to make a success of his life. Now he was testifying on Bernardino Sierra's behalf. The point was already obvious before Kinard went into the issue of capital punishment. Stewart again objected, and again his objection was sustained. But again, the jury had heard most of what Kinard wanted it to.

Defense witness number four was Bernardino Sierra, Jr. This was the son of the defendant on trial.

He was there mainly to "humanize" the defendant in the eyes of the jury. Here was a young boy, the message went; and he needed his daddy at home. Kinard had prepared the child carefully for what he was about to say.

"Do you know this man?" Kinard asked, indicating the defendant.

"Yes," Bernardino Sierra, Jr. replied. "He is my father."

"Do you know who these people are?" Kinard asked, indicating the jury.

The child looked at the twelve people. "Yes," he said.

"Do you know what they are here to decide?"

"Yes. They are here to decide whether my fathers lives or dies."

Kinard was asking his questions slowly, letting the answers sink in. Finally, he asked: "Do you have anything you want to say to them?"

"Yes," answered the child. "that I love my father, and I miss him—very much."

It had nothing to do with the issues in the trial. And at the time, Stu Stewart was prohibited from calling the relatives of any of Sierra's murder victims to testify that they missed their loved ones, even though a change in the law now allows that kind of "victim impact" evidence. The defense attorneys would have objected that the victims' evidence would divert the jury from what they were supposed to be considering. But that was precisely the purpose for which the testimony of Bernardino Sierra, Jr. had been offered.

And Kinard was not finished yet.

Defense witness number five was Bernardino Sierra's mother. She testified that the defendant's stepfather was an alcoholic who beat him regularly and mistreated him in other ways and that Bernardino Sierra himself was a heavy drinker.

The sixth, and final, witness was named Dr. Richard Jones.

"And what is your occupation?" Kinard asked.

"I'm a clinical psychologist," Dr. Jones replied.

Stewart began to take notes. This witness was obviously going to testify on an important point: the probability of future violence on Bernardino Sierra's part.

"Do you recall how many tests you administered to Bernardino Sierra?" Kinard asked.

"I administered the Wechsler Adult; the Bender Gestalt Test; the drawing test of Howstret, the person drawing test; and the Rorschach technique — it's commonly called the ink blot test," the witness answered. He also named several other diagnostic tests he had used.

Kinard asked what the findings had been.

"My primary impression," the psychologist answered, "was that of alcoholism. Habitual drinking; type, severe. The second diagnostic impression was that of personality disorder, antisocial type.

"The third diagnosis was that of borderline mental retardation."

This "third diagnosis," Stewart knew, was in direct conflict with the findings of the State's psychiatrists and psychologists, who found Sierra to be of average or above-average intelligence.

And there were more conflicts as the witness' opinion emerged more clearly. Bernardino Sierra did, he acknowledged, have an anti-social personality. But he was only "moderately" antisocial, and that was not the primary reason for his violent acts. The primary reason was alcoholism. That, plus the beatings and mistreatment Sierra's mother claimed he had received as a child. So Dr. Richard Jones concluded.

Now Kinard was ready to drive his point home. "First of all, I would like to ask you if you are aware of the prison commissary selling alcohol?"

Everyone smiled.

"It is my understanding that one cannot," replied the psychologist, with mock gravity.

Kinard next asked whether Bernardino Sierra would be likely to commit acts of violence inside a prison, where alcohol was not sold.

"Well, as I understand, either circumstance would involve a structured environment, an alcohol-free environment," Dr. Jones said.

"I wouldn't predict anti-social behavior under those circumstances."

Bernardino Sierra would be an ordinary, docile, nonviolent member of the prison population, in other words.

Stu Stewart gagged in disbelief and consternation.

The psychologist was saying this, of course, about a man who had suffocated one person inside a jail and tried to kill two others by stabbing them with a pair of scissors. But the judge's rulings meant that the jury could not be told about those incidents. The psychologist's opinion was going to be all the jury would hear, and Stewart would be deprived, by the rules of evidence, of the means to show it for what it was. That was the way the rules sometimes worked.

* * *

There was, at least, one thing Stewart might be able to do to combat this testimony from the defense.

He could call a psychologist who had examined Bernardino Sierra on the State's behalf, a man named Jerome Brown.

"We would call Dr. Brown," he said.

Stuart Kinard was on his feet immediately. He objected to the testimony of the state's psychologist being heard by the jury at all. This interview of Bernardino Sierra had been "done without his consent, and without counsel being present." Therefore, said Kinard, Dr. Brown's testimony would be like the repetition of an inadmissible confession. It would violate the fifth and sixth amendments to the Constitution of the United States, as well as article 38.22 of the Texas Code of Criminal Procedure.

Kinard made his objection without the jury being present.

In his chambers, Judge Price told the lawyers that he was persuaded by Stuart Kinard's argument. "They took him over there for the psychological evaluation, and it wasn't voluntary," said Judge Price. "Besides, it wasn't an interview about the death penalty. It was to determine his competence to stand trial and his sanity."

It was likely that the fifth amendment would be violated if Dr. Brown testified to the results of his evaluation, the judge concluded.

"I think I'm going to keep it out," he said.

That was the end of the prosecution's ability to counter the defense. Bernardino Sierra had, of course, consented to the interview by his own psychologist, Dr. Jones, so it was admissible. But the prosecution could not counter that testimony with its own psychologist because of the judge's ruling. And the prosecution also could not disprove the defense psychologist by showing the defendant's conduct inside the prison.

Worse yet from the prosecution's standpoint, Kinard had succeeded in preventing the jury from knowing that these items of adverse evidence even existed. And by offering his own evidence before the jury, evidence about the deterrent value of the death penalty, which Judge Price had ruled inadmissible, he had forced Stewart to object in the presence of the jury. To the average juror, it must have looked as though Stewart, the prosecutor, was suppressing evidence— while Kinard, for the defense, wanted only to bring out all the facts.

* * *

Inside the jury room, the twelve people who had been brought together by the battle over Bernardino Sierra's life became divided. Almost immediately, there were two irreconcilable camps.

The first ballot produced nine slips of paper that answered both of the penalty questions "Yes." That was nine votes for the death penalty.

The other three votes were for life imprisonment.

For three days, these two warring factions glared at each other, sweated, and argued. The numbers on each side shifted from time to time. But they were still not able to agree.

And so the verdict was—nothing.

It was a hung jury.

After the trial was over, and the jury had been excused, both the prosecution and the defense interviewed individual jurors. Their efforts gave a unique picture of the jury's deliberations.

The three "No" jurors, who favored life imprisonment from the start, had offered their reasons to the rest of the jury. The prosecution, they said, had not shown any "pattern" of violence. The prosecution's evidence had shown the jury "only thirteen hours," and not Sierra's "entire past life." There might be "some good" in the defendant, these jurors said, and this one "spree" was only "a small part of his life."

Inside prison, the "No" jurors argued, Sierra would be "treated"—by both psychiatrists and psychologists—for all his ills, including his antisocial personality and his alcoholism. Prison would be an endless, structured, alcohol-free environment where Sierra could do no harm.

The "No" jurors also argued that Stewart had "suppressed" evidence. He had done this by objecting to the statistician's testimony. And the "No" jurors maintained, vigorously, that the State, through prosecutor Stewart, had "shirked" the burden of proof. "The State didn't present psychiatric testimony to refute Dr. Jones' testimony," they said. Of course, none of the jurors knew that Stewart had tried to present a psychologist, only to be prevented by Kinard's objection.

The jurors voting for the death penalty saw the case in a different light. What sort of person would do what Sierra had done? What sort of person would be released from his first prison sentence and then embark, within a matter of days, on a spree like this?

How many people did Bernardino Sierra have to rob? How many did he have to kill, before he could be stopped? Didn't that show he was dangerous?

No, it didn't, said the "No" jurors.

Sierra had a low I.Q. Dr. Jones had said so. "Could he have actually been the leader in such a state of mind?" the "No" jurors asked. With Sierra so handicapped, these jurors concluded, "Vargas must have been the leader."

The "Yes" jurors thought that argument was unpersuasive. After all, it didn't take a college degree to rob a store and shoot somebody.

The "No" jurors had an answer for that.

Sierra did the actual killing, but Vargas had influenced him. Vargas was the "real" killer. He was the one "responsible."

The first day of jury deliberations was a Thursday. It was occupied by discussion that seesawed back and forth.

On Friday, the second day, another vote was taken.

There had been a shift. Now, instead of nine to three for death, the jurors were divided evenly — six for life, and six for death.

On the third day, Saturday, the jurors discussed again an issue that had worried them throughout their deliberations.

The question they had to answer asked whether there was a "probability" that Sierra would be violent in the future. What did the word "probability" mean? If one wasn't sure, did that destroy the "probability?" How much of a "probability" did it take? And how could somebody prove "beyond a reasonable doubt" that a "probability" existed?

The jurors had read the question over and over. They had analyzed its sentence structure; they had dissected its words.

And they found, now, that they had gotten themselves thoroughly confused as to what the question meant.

In Saturday's vote, the balance finally tipped in favor of life imprisonment. The "No" jurors now numbered seven, the "Yes" jurors five.

The "No" jurors, and their arguments, made a fascinating study of the reasoning process of a criminal jury.

Here is a portrait of those jurors, with a brief sketch of each one, taken from Stu Stewart's investigation:

Voting No from the Beginning — Arnold White, a young man who felt a personal identification with Bernardino Sierra. White had himself had problems with a father who died of alcoholism. He broke down on two occasions and emotionally stated that he might have run with a gang, too, as Sierra had, if he had not had the luck to find a job upon leaving college. White repeatedly stated he believed Sierra would be thoroughly rehabilitated. He said, "Who can he harm in Jail?" and even asked, "Did we hear of any killings while Sierra was being held for trial?"

There had been one, the Murder in the County Jail, but Arnold White never knew about it — because the court had decided it was inadmissible in evidence. So was the incident in which Sierra had stabbed two other inmates with smuggled scissors.

Voting No from the Beginning — Betsy Bagdikian, who also had an alcoholic father who "gets mean when he drinks." This juror said she, herself, could have done "the same thing under similar circumstances." Showing emotional sympathy with Sierra's mother, Bagdikian maintained that "without alcohol, he would be a different man. His antisocial personality could be treated in a liquor-free environment." And she asked, "How many people has he hurt while he's been in jail?"

Voting No from the Beginning—Andrea DeCarlo, who broke down, emotionally, on several occasions and said, "If I believe for a moment that without alcohol he can be rehabilitated, how can I kill him?" She argued that Sierra's murders were only short term, and did not describe his "general adjustment in life."

The judge's rulings had prevented Stu Stewart from telling Ms. DeCarlo any more about Sierra's "general adjustment in life"—which included a number of other murders and a frightening psychological portrait, in addition to the escape attempt, the murder and two attempted murders inside the county jail.

Voting Yes, Changed to No—Phyllis Nardone. Another juror described Ms. Nardone as possessing a "remarkably dull mentality," and in any event she gave little argument to explain her change in vote.

Voting Yes, Changed to No—Edward Pennington. Pennington had difficulty with the terms "reasonable doubt" and "probability." Finally, he came to the conclusion that there was reasonable doubt as to the probability of anyone committing crimes of violence inside a prison.

Voting Yes, Changed to No—Marie Gessler, who had the same difficulties as Edward Pennington with the words used in the question and who felt that Sierra's "low intellect" made his "degree of guilt" such that he did not deserve a sentence of death.

Voting Yes, Changed to No—Janet Albedeck, who changed her vote in the last five minutes of deliberations. This juror apparently voted "No" in an attempt to resolve the case and prevent the necessity of a retrial. She said, "It would be a shame if all our time here had been for naught. And the man might be re-tried as effectively next time." She added, "Something is better than nothing."

What Ms. Albedeck was saying made sense, but it did not persuade the other jurors. They were convinced of Sierra's dangerousness. If this jury was too silly to see it, he should be re-tried—before another jury, which hopefully would be more sensible. This was a strange group, and the pressure of deliberations was affecting them. One juror, a grown woman, had sent a request through the bailiff for her Teddy Bear. It was brought to her.

At last, a note came out from the jury. It informed Judge Price that there was a hopeless deadlock.

Reluctantly, the judge declared a mistrial and excused the jurors.

The mistrial meant that the entire trial had been a waste of time. The conviction—the guilty verdict—was wiped out too. The case would have to be tried again, from jury selection all the way through the end.

* * *

On Tuesday, July 6, the lawyers for the prosecution and the defense met in Judge Price's chambers.

This was the day set for the retrial.

Judge Price had set the case for trial, and he had been prepared to set his other cases aside. But it was clear to everyone that he was concerned about the time, the expenditure, and—above all—the uncertainty, that a re-trial would involve.

He had a point. The two defense lawyers were being paid by the government, at a minimum rate of $250 a day. That was $2500 a week. If there was a four-week jury selection, that alone would mean ten thousand dollars. Many times that amount had already been spent on the services of the defense lawyers, and if the presentation of evidence, jury arguments, punishment hearing and so forth had to be done again, it would boost the fee into the hundred thousand dollar range. Appeal would add tens of thousands of dollars to that.

And if one considered the cost of the courtroom, the salary of the judge, bailiff, court reporter, prosecutors and other personnel that were necessary for the process, that cost would be multiplied several times over.

The trial of Bernardino Sierra was going to cost the State somewhere in the quarter-to-a-half million dollar range, fairly estimated.

Of course, that much expenditure might be justified.

But there was more to it.

The judge had a heavy docket of other cases. Many of them involved accused robbers and murderers who were dangerous, too. A trial that lasted several months would hamper efforts to do justice in those cases.

And there was one other consideration.

"I admitted all the robberies and murders from that same day into evidence last time," said Judge Price. "But we don't really know whether they were admissible or not, because the Texas Court of Criminal Appeals hasn't ruled on the question."

The judge turned to Stu Stewart, and he went on.

"I can just imagine what will happen if you retry Sierra, and the extraneous offenses are admitted," he said. "The Court of Criminal Appeals might reverse the conviction. And then we'll be left with a situation where you have to try him again, for the third time. That might be three or four years down the road."

Everyone knew what a retrial four years later would mean. It would be next to impossible for the state to get all its witnesses together. It might, conceivably, mean that Bernardino Sierra would escape conviction for any of the six murders he had committed.

Judge Price was not forcing Stewart's hand. "He never did that," Stewart said later. "He was just seeing the case from a perspective that was neutral."

Stewart discussed the case privately with Kinard. He knew that the judge was right; he had problems with his case. If the extraneous offenses were taken away, he might even have trouble getting a verdict of guilty. The defendant deserved the most severe sentence that the law allowed, but the rules of evidence stood as a barrier to achieving that objective.

"There's a possibility we could do this," Stu Stewart said to Kinard. "Accept a guilty plea to three of the murder cases, and recommend a life sentence on all three. Then we'd accept a guilty plea on the robbery indictments, and recommend concurrent sentences of fifty years on each."

That would impress even a reckless parole board, Stewart thought. It would assure that Sierra would not soon be free.

"I'd like to talk to my client about it," said Kinard.

* * *

That was the way that the Plea Bargain of the Century came into being.

Judge Price, after he had heard Bernardino Sierra's admission of guilt, received into evidence three sheets of paper that contained stipulations of the facts of the murders.

Those three sheets of paper became the only court records that showed what had happened to a man named "Papa Joe" Picinich on Navigation Street, a man named Jose Cruz Davila on Brady Street, and a man named Gilbert Moreno on Middle Street. They were all that was left of three innocent human beings.

There is an ancient prayer that reads, "God grant me the serenity to accept the things I cannot change, the courage to change the things I can, and the wisdom to know the difference." That prayer could have been written for a prosecutor. It expresses the soul of the prosecutor's dilemma, for the prosecutor can do as much harm, sometimes, by trying to change something he cannot as by failing to fight to change the things he can. And the wisdom to refrain from fighting invariably involves the most painful decision a courtroom lawyer ever has to make. Stu Stewart was feeling the full weight of it now, as he kept his bargain with Bernardino Sierra's lawyers.

"Your honor, the State recommends a sentence of life imprisonment on each of the three murders, and fifty years on each of the robberies," Stu Stewart said.

"On your plea of guilty," said Judge Price to Bernardino Sierra, "I find you guilty.

" I assess your punishment at life imprisonment on each of the murders and fifty years on each of the robberies."

The ceremony was over.

If he wanted to, Bernardino Sierra could take with him to the penitentiary a copy of his press conference. He could take the written confession in which he had admitted his participation in the most conscienceless killings that Houston had seen in some time. And so if anyone doubted that this had, indeed, been the Plea Bargain of the Century, Bernardino Sierra had the proof—for the whole world to see.

There was one final irony in this extraordinary case. It concerned Edgar Smith, the witness who attacked the death penalty on Bernardino Sierra's behalf—the man who had spent over a dozen years on New Jersey's death row, then lifted himself by his bootstraps to become a solid citizen and chairman of San Diego's Bicentennial Commission. The irony was that Edgar Smith's "rehabilitation" was incomplete. A few short months after Bernardino Sierra's Plea Bargain, Edgar Smith was arrested, convicted and sentenced to life imprisonment for attempted murder. Edgar Smith took the position that capital punishment was not an effective deterrent to crime. The death penalty had not, indeed, been effective in his case—primarily because it had not been imposed.*

---

* The following names in this chapter were changed, without alteration of the incidents in which the persons were involved: Arnold White, Betsy Bagdikian, Andrea DeCarlo, Phyllis Nardone, Edward Pennington, Marie Gessler, Janet Albedeck.

PART FOUR

Of Barbarism — And Justice

SO FAR, WE have treated these cases as a collection of individual stories. Even that way, they make a fascinating, if disturbing, narrative.

But there is more that we can get from them.

In this section, we shall use these six cases to examine what the death penalty is all about. What are the arguments in favor of society's use of the death penalty? Here, we shall see that the six cases in this book provide evidence to support those arguments. And on the other side, what is the best part of the opponents' case against capital punishment? As a reader, you cannot allow your mind to sit back in an easy chair, because the six cases provide evidence to support the opponents' arguments, too.

Chapter 18

The Dilemma of Capital Punishment

Early in 1977, convicted murderer Gary Gilmore became the first person to be executed in the United States in nearly a decade when his life was ended by a Utah firing squad. Gilmore's spectacular willingness to die led the Supreme Court to say, "This case may be unique in the annals of this Court."

Gilmore's case attracted so much of the attention of the national press —and of Hollywood celebrities—that it almost came to symbolize the issue of capital punishment. But the question remains whether it was the proper case to bring the capital punishment issue into focus. In other words, was there anything unique about Gary Gilmore that bears on the capital punishment dilemma?

The answer to that question is a resounding "No."

Certainly, what Gilmore *did was* not unique. Both of Gilmore's murders could have fit into this book without adding anything drastically different. He killed two innocent strangers in Provo, Utah, one a gas station attendant and one a motel manager, by forcing them to lie on the floor and shooting them in the back of the head. Both of Gilmore's murders were carbon copies of what Richard Vargas did to Ashokkumar Patel in the Almeda Road Murder. And for sheer, execution-style murdering, Gilmore's crimes pale by comparison to Bernardino Sierra's Middle Street Murder or Kenneth Brock's homicide in front of six police officers, not to mention Ronald O'Bryan's cold-blooded elimination of his own son or Gerald Bodde's unbelievably senseless murder of an 81-year-old woman. It is a sad conclusion, but it is impossible to conclude otherwise: Gary Gilmore's crimes, for all their horror, did not qualify him for the death penalty any more than many others.

It has been said, on the other hand, that what was unique about Gilmore was his personality. For one thing, he is sometimes described as having been extraordinary in his manipulative abilities. He seems to have had an uncanny knack for "putting on" his prison keepers, so as to maneuver them into doing what he wanted. But compared to John Stiles Griffin, Gilmore was a novice at it. Griffin was the man who taught motivation classes in prison and convinced his case worker that he "definitely" could lead a clean life, but then embarked on a series of murders that made Gilmore's crimes seem almost pleasant by comparison. And for sheer straight-faced mendacity, neither Gilmore nor Griffin could match the Halloween Candy Murderer, Ronald Clark O'Bryan.

Gilmore is sometimes said to be unique in his death wish. But his suicidal urge was no more reckless than that of the members of the Brady Bunch, who proudly confessed on television and repeated, over and over, "They can only burn me once." Gilmore was not unusual in this regard. Death row is filled with men who do not care whether they live or die, because they do not care whether anyone lives or dies.

What, then, was unique about Gary Gilmore?

One Hollywood celebrity announced that he wanted to telephone Gilmore to keep him from becoming depressed on death row. The question arises whether this major entertainer wanted to call the families of Gilmore's victims; most of America did not know their names. You could read *Time* and *Newsweek* that week without learning them, but you would find out a great deal about the murderer. And on NBC's Saturday Night Live, a troupe of comedians sang: "Let's give Gary Gilmore what he wants for Christmas."

"Cut Rona Barrett!" shouted the ABC newsman who circled over the Utah penitentiary in a helicopter during Gilmore's execution. Speaking into his microphone, the reporter added that from his vantage point, he could make a gripping television broadcast for the network's "Good Morning America" Show. The reference to Hollywood gossip reporter Rona Barrett sums up what was unusual about Gilmore.

It was sheer Hollywood hype.

And when all is said and done, the public debate over Gilmore's case had very little to do with capital punishment.

Unfortunately, that is frequently the problem with the debate about capital punishment today. Much of what is said is nothing but Hollywood hype. Those who favor the use of the death penalty and those who oppose it shout slogans at each other across a void, and neither side faces the issues that the other raises. In fact, neither side ever examines its own arguments to see whether they hold water.

Is the death penalty morally acceptable? Given the imperfections of our system of justice, can we tolerate the risk of using it? If we abolish it, will it lead to increased numbers of murders of innocent people? Will abolition cause Americans to lose faith in their system—and perhaps take the law into their own hands? Can justice be done without the death penalty?

Will there be a public reaction against the use of capital punishment a few years hence? If so, will it be of sufficient strength to induce a repeal of current death penalty laws?

No one really knows the answers to any of those questions. And the debate about capital punishment today is not likely to produce the answers.

Each person must struggle to find them for himself or herself. Not only can we not afford to leave the issue to the experts; we have to realize that, insofar as the death penalty is concerned, there *are* no experts. That is why it is important that each citizen equip himself with sufficient knowledge to turn aside the sophistries with which he is assaulted daily from both sides. And that, in turn, requires that each citizen know something about the cases—the kind of cases that are subject to the death penalty. That knowledge is hard to come by, because stories about people like Gary Gilmore on the one hand, or reasoning that fails to come to grips with the issues on the other, account for most of what is available. That is why we have written this book.

*   *   *

This book tells the stories of six men who were accused of capital murder. Five of the six were convicted by juries, and one pled guilty.

The question might legitimately be asked: How representative are these cases? Can they be taken as showing something that is useful to know about capital punishment?

The Houston cases of the same time period, taken as a whole, showed roughly the same proportion of convictions, hung juries, life sentences and death sentences as the cases in this book. And while these cases are sensational, there was at least one other Houston case that happened about the same time—the trial of Ignacio Cuevas, for two murders during an eleven-day escape attempt at the Walls Prison Unit in Huntsville—that received more national publicity than all the ones in this book combined. In short, we believe that the cases in this book are representative. That is an unpleasant conclusion, because the cases are nightmarish. The point is that an examination would show that all of Houston's capital cases are nightmarish.

Furthermore, the rate of convictions and the ratio of life or death sentences does not change dramatically when the statistics are taken from the entire State of Texas. Evidently, there are enough Kenneth Brocks, John Stiles Griffins, Ronald O'Bryans, Gerald Boddes, Richard Vargases and Bernardino Sierras to account for all the capital cases in the state.

For that matter, it seems likely that there are enough people who are willing to commit these sorts of crimes to go around in every state of the union, from Maine to California. And so in most respects, we think that the cases in this book are a fair sample—and taken as a whole, they provide a good map of the Road to Death Row. They certainly have more to do with what capital punishment is all about than did the publicity surrounding Gary Gilmore's case.

Of course, it is not enough to map the Road to Death Row and leave it at that. Some people think that the Road ought to be maintained or expanded, and there are others who believe that it should be torn down completely. What, then, is the case for capital punishment? And what are the best of the abolitionists' arguments?

Chapter 19

The Best of the Abolitionist Argument

Representative Craig Washington is an impressive speechmaker. And for him, attacking the death penalty was the most important task of the legislative session. He put all he had into it.

The legislature had before it a bill that would re-enact the death penalty in Texas. The bill was the Texas capital murder law. As Washington wound up his argument, there were cheers from people on both sides of the capital punishment question—cheers for the eloquence with which this high-profile legislator had presented his views against capital punishment.

If death was a deterrent, Washington said, why not do it in public? Why not, indeed, at the State Capitol? Washington suggested amending the proposed bill so as to require the legislators themselves to vote on every capital case—and then to witness the execution. He predicted that there would "never be a majority of this House with the moral conviction to stand eye to eye with a convicted felon and watch him fry on the floor of the House."

What Washington was saying, really, was the simplest and most basic of the objections to capital punishment. It was that capital punishment is unacceptable on moral grounds.

Soon after Washington made his modest proposal, State Senator Jim Wallace proposed an amendment that would have required executions to be carried out by "smiting" the convict with "instruments of iron, wood or stone." The amendment was based upon Biblical scripture, from the Book of Numbers. Wallace was doing the same thing as Washington: through satire, he was trying to say that the death penalty was morally unacceptable. His amendment was immediately voted down.

Then the Texas House listened in silence while Representative Mickey Leland quoted a telling phrase from the Bible: "And God spoke these words, saying, thou shalt not kill." It was the same message, but taken from another source.

And ACLU spokesman Wayne Oaks summed up all these arguments of the opponents by saying of the death penalty, "It's barbaric. It's unconstitutional. It's inconsistent with contemporary standards of decency and morality." Oaks added that in his opinion the problem of violent crime had nothing to do with the death penalty, but was caused instead by "sloppy and inadequate law enforcement."

These arguments did not prevail. The supporters of the death penalty were the ones who had the votes. In spite of an attempted filibuster by opponents in the House, a spokesman for the governor's office predicted that the new law would pass "going away." And so it did.

But the echoes of those arguments can still be heard today. And they are still disturbing. How do the supporters of the death penalty answer the claim that it is "immoral?" What do they say when capital punishment is called "barbaric?"

Two years later, a test case reached the United States Supreme Court —a test case involving the Texas capital murder law. And it provided a partial answer to the "barbarism" claim. When the Court heard from lawyers in argument, Justice Lewis Powell asked the attorney for the condemned man, Anthony Amsterdam, whether he could think of any crime meriting the death penalty. Amsterdam said no. He was opposed to capital punishment under any circumstances, on principle.

Mr. Justice Powell then asked whether the commandant of Buchenwald might have deserved capital punishment.

Amsterdam paused and thought about that one. Then he said, "My instinctive reaction is to say yes." But, he added, he was opposed to capital punishment on principle, on the ground it was unconstitutional, and therefore he was bound to say no.

Mr. Justice Powell persisted. "Suppose a terrorist destroys New York City with a hydrogen bomb?"

The answer was still no, Amsterdam replied. It was his position that such crimes could be prevented by "police methods" rather than fear of punishment.

Within a few months of Amsterdam's statement, a terrorist placed a bomb in the baggage area of New York's Laguardia Airport. The resulting explosion killed eleven people, and if Amsterdam knew of "police methods" that could have prevented it, he failed to divulge them to the New York City Police Department in time. But in any event, the Supreme Court did not accept Amsterdam's argument. Justice Potter Stewart explained the reason: it is much easier to view the death penalty as immoral or barbaric in a purely academic discussion than it is when one is confronted with a crime so gross, so heinous, so brutal that anything short of the death penalty seems an inadequate response. Perhaps the basic human yearning for justice is itself "barbaric." But even if that is so, the morality of the death penalty ought to be decided by a citizenry aware of the kind of cases to which it applies.

They are cases such as the ones in this book.

Is it, then, barbaric or immoral to use capital punishment in Richard Vargas' case, or Gerald Bodde's, or Bernardino Sierra's, or Ronald O'Bryan's? Every person has to decide that question for himself.

* * *

Another of the arguments against capital punishment is that the chance of executing an innocent person is unacceptably high.

"You have to live with this verdict," Bob Carroll argued to the jury that sentenced Richard Vargas. "You can't change the verdict you render."

"It scares the hell out of me," said Frank Shepherd to the jury that sentenced Gerald Bodde. "If you make a mistake, you can't change it—if you pull the switch."

What are the chances of a mistake?

In the cases in this book, there are two examples of people who were falsely suspected of capital crimes. One was Walter Hixson, who was actually arrested in the wake of his wife's murder—a murder of which he was innocent, a murder that had been committed by John Stiles Griffin. The other was William Hudspeth, the man whom Ronald O'Bryan falsely identified as the man who had given him the poisoned Pixy Stix. But the significant thing is that the falsity of the evidence in both instances was detected immediately; Hixson was released in a matter of hours, and Hudspeth was never arrested. It is inconceivable that either of these men could have been indicted, tried, convicted and falsely sentenced to death before a jury.

But, opponents of the death penalty argue, can one *guarantee* that a death sentence for one falsely convicted can *never* occur?

Supporters of the death penalty, if they are honest, have to answer that question no. It is as though they were asked, each time they boarded an airliner, whether they could guarantee absolutely that it was safe. It is quite clear today that capital punishment can miscarry, just as an aircraft may crash.

The 1999 case of Anthony Porter in Chicago is a shocking example. After sixteen years on death row for a double murder, during which Porter came within two days of execution, prosecutors arranged for his release because a journalism professor and his students demonstrated that he almost certainly was innocent. "I don't think I can give you an answer," said a prosecutor, asked how it could happen. "I've never seen anything like this."

But a few years earlier, there had been a similar event, also in Chicago. Rolando Cruz was released after 10 years on Chicago's death row. Instead, the states' attorney charged somebody else: the prosecution team. Three prosecutors and four detectives now face conspiracy charges for improprieties in the Cruz case, carrying up to five years in prison. In all, there have been thirteen men released from Illinois's death row since 1987 because of doubts about their guilt.

Then, in the year 2000, Illinois Governor George Ryan took action. He imposed a moratorium on all executions in the state. He explained, "I cannot support a system which, in its administration, has proven to be so fraught with error and has come so close to the ultimate nightmare, the state's taking of innocent life."

And death penalty opponents immediately claimed that the same problems exist in other states—they just haven't been discovered. The only differences, they say, are the dedication of Illinois lawyers and journalists and a state law providing for DNA testing in death cases. Death penalty supporters, on the other hand, see no reason to suppose that lawyer dedication or DNA testing is confined to Illinois; still, they cannot rule out the possibility of execution of an innocent person.

And it isn't just the purely innocent who can make these kinds of claims. There also is the odd-sounding concept called "actual innocence of the death penalty." A defendant can be guilty of heinous crimes, including murder, but not be liable for capital punishment. In such a case, a death sentence also is wrongful. For example, a drifter named Henry Lee Lucas confessed to scores of murders, and he was convicted in Texas and sentenced to die for the homicide of an unidentified woman known only as "Orange Socks" because that was all her body was wearing. Later, the headlines screamed, "Lucas may die for wrong crime!" Governor George W. Bush ultimately commuted Lucas's sentence, even though he remained incarcerated in other cases, because the evidence showed that it was improbable—not impossible but highly improbable—that Lucas was even in Texas on that day.

And what about Kenneth Brock? What if his claim of accident was true, if the gun did, in fact, go off by accident? It seems unlikely, and the jury found that there was no reasonable possibility of it—but could it be true? If so, Kenneth Brock, who was sentenced to death, could claim that he was not guilty of capital murder, but only of "plain murder." And he could claim "actual innocence of the death penalty."

And so, it is fair for capital punishment opponents to emphasize the danger of execution of an innocent person.

Of course, it also seems fair to turn the question on its head. Can opponents of capital punishment guarantee that their own position has not *already* cost the lives of some innocent human beings? Just to ask the question is to answer it; the answer is "of course not." In fact, it is clear that failure to impose the death penalty has cost some innocent lives, as we shall see in the next chapter. But the focus is rarely on *that* kind of innocent lives, just as Hollywood's focus was on Gary Gilmore rather than on his victims. The innocent person killed in a murder is out of sight and out of mind—like the victims of a mass disaster, an earthquake or a flood, in a remote village with a foreign name on the other side of the globe.

This book shows what a capital trial is like. The lawyers for the defendant are charged with the responsibility of finding any argument—irrespective of whether they think the argument is reasonable, themselves—that would acquit their client or prevent a sentence of death. The jurors are instructed, over and over again, that they are to make their findings based upon the reasonable doubt standard. Supporters of the death penalty accept these protections as valid, but opponents do not consider them sufficient in a life-or-death case—and therein lies the difference between the two positions.

* * *

Another argument advanced by opponents of capital punishment is that it will lead to an increase, rather than a decrease, in murders. "Where the death penalty is still invoked, that is where the crime rate is highest," says Victor Blaine. "People are going to have a low regard for life if we take life."

There is some evidence that violence begets other violence. It is true, for example, that a child who watches violent behavior on television will sometimes imitate it. Social psychologists say that impressionable people can be induced to commit violent acts by "modelling" their behavior after other behavior they have seen. Could the same result follow from the death penalty? Could people be induced to commit acts of violence by "modelling" their behavior on an execution?

When Gary Gilmore was executed, the press wanted to be present, and a newsman brought suit against the Utah prison authorities seeking the right to film the execution for television broadcast. The court refused to grant this request, partly on the basis of testimony from a psychologist who said that there was a danger that impressionable people might see the execution, model their own behavior on it, and go out and shoot someone themselves. Perhaps, then, there is something to the argument. At least from this one case, there is expert testimony that says that the death penalty, if it were to be televised, could lead to other killing.

Of course, that does not really answer the question. The psychologist *also* said that if the execution were not televised, and only printed accounts of it were to reach the public, the danger of modelling would be much less significant. A person does not ordinarily model his behavior on a violent example unless that conduct is shown graphically and in detail—the way a television program is shown. Violent people, to the extent that they learn their conduct through modelling, learn it from acts they see—through being abused as children, through fighting, through watching television. At least, that is the position of those who favor capital punishment; their opponents disagree.

* * *

Opponents of the death penalty also argue that capital punishment is discriminatory, arbitrary and capricious. They point out that blacks, poor people and persons of low intellect are disproportionately represented on death row. "In Nazi Germany, Hitler tried to kill off all the people he thought were inferior," says Bob Carroll. He adds, "Maybe we should line up all the minority groups and kill them. All the people that have only a fourth grade education. I don't like the death penalty because I don't think it's fair."

And Adrian Burk told the jury that sentenced Kenneth Brock that the death penalty was "unfair from this standpoint, that you don't see any rich people getting the electric chair."

It is undeniably true that blacks, poor people and persons of low intellect are disproportionately represented in the ranks of those sentenced to die.* For instance, at the beginning of the year after the last of the trials in this book, there were 57 persons on death row in Texas, and of those 57, 29 were white, 21 black and 7 Spanish surnamed. But it has to be remembered that the vast majority of capital crimes occur in cities, where black and Chicano populations are greater. For instance, the statistics are not out of line with the population of the city of Houston, which then was close to a fifty-fifty split between Anglo and non-Anglo peoples. When that fact is taken into account, the disproportion decreases—although it does not disappear.

The supporters of capital punishment look at another aspect of the matter. They point out that minority groups are disproportionately represented in nearly all crime statistics, not just in the death penalty. The relevant question, they say, is this: if a person is accused of capital murder, will his life depend upon whether he is black or white?

The answer to that question, from the statistics, appears to be no. In Texas, 56 percent of black defendants tried for capital murder were sentenced to death during the first two years that the present law was in operation. During that same period, 58 percent of Caucasian defendants tried for that crime were sentenced to death. Although the difference is not statistically significant, the figures are paradoxical. They show that, if anything, a black man accused of capital murder has a slightly better chance than a white!

In modern cases, opponents have virtually stopped arguing that there is discrimination based on the *defendant's* race. The argument simply isn't sus-

---

* This issue provides an example of one respect in which the cases in this book are not representative. All the defendants in this book were Anglos—except for the Brady Bunch, who were Latinos.

tainable. Instead, they have argued that the discrimination is based on the *victim's* race. They cite statistics purporting to show that when an African-American kills a white victim, he is more likely to receive the death penalty than if the victim is black. In a recent case, called *McCleskey v. Kemp*, the Supreme Court rejected this argument. It is extremely difficult, through statistics, to reflect the differences in individual cases; for example, the black-and-white killings were more likely to be stranger-upon-stranger killings than those of black victims.

The supporters and opponents will continue, undoubtedly, to place emphasis on different figures. Opponents will point out that there are more blacks on death row than their proportion of the population, and they also continue to argue that a defendant is more likely to be sentenced to death if the victim is white. Supporters will rely upon the data that show that a black man and a white man have virtually identical chances of escaping the death penalty once charged. Once again, the reader might well consider the cases in this book. When a crime such as Bernardino Sierra's, or Gerald Bodde's, or John Stiles Griffin's, comes before a jury, does the race of the defendant affect the outcome?

* * *

Opponents also argue another kind of discrimination. Sometimes the worst murderers escape capital punishment, while those who are guilty but less blameworthy receive the death penalty. Is it fair, for example, that Richard Vargas received the death penalty while his co-participant, Bernardino Sierra, did not? Is Kenneth Brock's death sentence appropriate for a single killing, when John Stiles Griffin got life for his multiple, frightening crimes? Opponents say that comparisons like these show an arbitrariness in the imposition of the death penalty that human institutions will never be able to correct.

It is true that the worst killers sometimes avoid their just deserts. This book shows examples. Supporters of the death penalty must come to grips with this criticism. But they can respond by pointing out that our system is designed —not accidentally, but deliberately designed—to err on the side of caution. In other words, there is a high burden for the imposition of capital punishment (just as opponents would want there to be), and this burden is precisely the reason why the most blameworthy defendants sometimes escape it.

Also, the law is clearer today than it was in Sierra's or Griffin's time. If their cases were tried today, there would be no question that all of their related acts of violence would be admissible in evidence—including Sierra's multiple acts while in jail. Clarity in the law, which comes with time, tends to reduce the disparities, although it never will eliminate them.

* * *

Opponents also use what might seem an odd argument: the money that it costs to carry out capital punishment. The dollars we spend on it, as opposed to life imprisonment.

In other words, they argue that the enormous cost of providing counsel for both the state and the defendant in a death penalty case, plus the cost of lawyers in the long series of later appeals, stays and habeas corpus proceedings, is so high that it is unjustified.

There are several ways to look at this argument. The victim's rights group Justice for All argues that it is factually incorrect — that life imprisonment actually costs more. It's harder to compute these costs than one might think. Justice for All says that when a conservative inflation rate, geriatric care, security costs and the mathematical value of losses to violence compared to risk, and other costs all are included, the death penalty costs less than an equivalent case of life without parole.

Another possible response is, it shouldn't matter what the cost is. Let justice be done. There even is a Latin phrase for it: "Fiat justitia, ruat coelum (Let justice be done though the heavens may fall)." This argument has a certain appeal, but we don't, and we can't, apply it literally. We have to put law enforcement resources where they will do the most good; we can't afford to waste them.

Again, the opponents have a point, but so do supporters, and it depends on how you look at it.

* * *

There have been dozens of other arguments offered against the death penalty. But these are the main ones — that capital punishment is immoral, that it risks execution of innocent persons, that it cheapens human life and that it is arbitrary and discriminatory. Still, the debate does not end there. The supporters have a case to make in favor of capital punishment, and the opponents, as might be expected, have an answer to each point.

Chapter 20

The Case for Capital Punishment

Supreme Court Justice Lewis Powell was one of the most outspoken of the nine justices during arguments on the constitutionality of the death penalty. As the government's lawyer, Solicitor General Robert Bork, spoke in favor of capital punishment, Justice Powell asked him about deterrence of murder.

"While I recognize that deterrence may not be the controlling factor here," the Justice said, "I invite your attention to the report of the FBI." Justice Powell then summarized what the report had to say: that murder had increased 42 percent in one 5-year period. "It is fairly obvious," he went on, "that we need some way to deter this slaughter of Americans. I say 'slaughter' because that word was used in describing the American death toll during our involvement in Vietnam. Comparing the records of Vietnam and the FBI's figures, it appears that, on an annual basis, more Americans are murdered in this country than were killed in Vietnam."

The Solicitor General agreed. It could not rationally be maintained, he said, that capital punishment was not a deterrent. "Respectable academic authority can be cited on this point," he said, "but I think common sense is sufficient to tell us that if we raise the cost and risk of certain conduct, the incidence of that conduct decreases." The Supreme Court would be taking an awesome responsibility, Bork went on, if it were to outlaw capital punishment. That, he said, would condemn thousands of potential murder victims in order to save a few hundred guilty people.

This exchange was significant. It led to the ultimate acceptance by the Supreme Court of the deterrence argument. For some crimes, wrote Justice Potter Stewart, "the death penalty is undoubtedly a significant deterrent." And the acceptance of this argument, in turn, was part of the reason for the Supreme Court's ruling upholding the death penalty.

But the deterrence issue is far from resolved. There is still vigorous debate, and vast difference of opinion, on the question whether the death penalty has any deterrent effect at all.

Could some future Ronald O'Bryan be deterred from a murder for money by the cold calculus of capital punishment? And what of a Bernardino Sierra—is there any possibility that he, or someone else in his position, may be prevented from murder by the death penalty? What of Kenneth Brock, who considered strategy before killing his hostage? The ordinary passion killing, of course, would not be stopped by capital punishment. But supporters point out that the death penalty does not apply to passion killings; it applies only to intentional and deliberate killings of types that are most likely to be deterred by it. They are crimes like O'Bryan's, or Sierra's, or Brock's.

The Texas Capital Murder statute, for instance, is typical of those of other states, in that it covers just a few kinds of murders. They are murders of peace officers, murders of prison employees, murders during violent felonies, murders by escaped convicts, multiple murders, murders of children, and murders for hire. Even in these instances, the death penalty is inapplicable unless the murder was deliberate and the killer can be proved to be likely to repeat his crime. Supporters contend that these are the instances in which the deterrent value of the death penalty is highest—and most necessary.

Opponents of capital punishment see the matter differently. They answer that there is no scientific proof that the death penalty is a deterrent. And they point out that there will probably *never* be any such proof either way. The usual way of examining the deterrent effect of the death penalty has been to compare crime statistics from states that have capital punishment to those that do not. But the results, by definition, are inconclusive. "The inescapable flaw," writes death penalty opponent Charles L. Black, "is that social conditions in any state are not constant through time, and that social conditions are not the same in any two states. If an effect were observed (and the observed effects, one way or another, are not large) then one could not at all tell whether any of this effect is attributable to the presence or absence of capital punishment."

But scientists have tried anyway, and the results they have produced are interesting.

For example, in 1975 a statistician named Isaac Ehrlich published the results of his study on American murder rates and capital punishment. His results did not amount to scientific proof of the deterrent value of the death penalty, but they are fascinating nevertheless. Ehrlich used a sophisticated technique called multiple regression analysis, which produced a prediction that capital punishment would deter some murders. Since the multiple regression technique gives quantitative results, Ehrlich was even able to put a figure on the number of murders that an execution would deter: He predicted that the first execution would prevent eight homicides. The prediction is not scientifically exact, and Ehrlich is the first to admit it; for one thing, the deterrent effect could easily be miscalculated because of other variations—what scientists call "noise"—in the statistics. For another, the prediction can never be tested, for the simple reason that it will never be possible to identify and count all of the murders that are deterred by capital punishment.

Ehrlich's work was criticized by an army of statisticians and sociologists. One of its weaknesses was that Ehrlich's data included no recent executions, because the Supreme Court had stayed them all for over a decade and had struck down all existing capital punishment statutes.

In 1985, a statistician named Layson updated Ehrlich's work and found a significant deterrent effect. Again, critics noted deficiencies in the study.

There is one type of evidence, however, that strongly supports the deterrence argument. This evidence comes from the individual stories or confessions of robbers and kidnappers who have expressly explained that they refrained from killing their victims because of the death penalty. Over the years, we cannot know precisely how many such cases there have been, but there have been many. This kind of data sometimes is dismissed as "mere anecdotal" evidence, but surely it shows the existence of a deterrent effect in some kinds of cases.

And so the deterrence argument remains, thus—and science will probably never resolve it. This is not an issue for computers. This is an issue, like many other issues of law or government, that has to be resolved by each citizen. The supporters of capital punishment, agreeing with Solicitor General Bork, say that the evidence today is sufficient; but opponents demand more concrete proof, while at the same time pointing out that it is impossible to obtain.

*   *   *

There is one effect of capital punishment that is clear and absolute, and that is that capital punishment prevents future crimes by the same killer.

To Detective Carolyn Stephenson, this is one of the most important considerations. "How can they say it's not a deterrent?" she asks. "It deters that particular person from doing again what he's already been convicted of doing." Technically, this is not deterrence, but rather prevention of murder by the same person, or what punishment philosophy calls "incapacitation." But the murders it stops are equivalent to those stopped by deterrence.

There can be no question that this is an urgent consideration. The cases described in this book provide an illustration of the reason. John Stiles Griffin, for example, escaped from custody and killed three women. Whether he would have killed his five Galveston victims had he had the time, or the police officer who arrested him in Port Arthur, is a matter of conjecture. But it is beyond conjecture that he is a dangerous man even inside a prison. The ease with which he smuggled escape implements and manufactured weapons in a solitary cell in the county jail is proof enough of that.

And in addition to John Stiles Griffin, there are the members of the Brady Bunch. Inside the county jail, Richard Vargas and Bernardino Sierra suffocated a fellow inmate; Richard Vargas attempted suicide by setting his cell on fire; Bernardino Sierra escaped from the county jail on one occasion, but was recaptured; and Sierra also attempted the murders of two other inmates with a pair of smuggled scissors. These men too are dangerous inside or outside of prison.

All told, the six men described in this book accounted for nineteen known murders or attempted murders. An astounding six of those—four murders and two attempts—were committed while the killers were confined in prison or during escapes from custody. It is certainly fair to ask, as George Jacobs asked the jury that tried Gerald Bodde, whether there will someday be other killings.

And these six cases are not unique. Murders or assaults by inmates upon inmates are commonplace in prisons. Perhaps there are methods that could be used to reduce the incidence of such assaults, and certainly well-run prisons, such as the Texas Department of Criminal Justice, have fewer than others. Can they be eliminated?

The opponents of capital punishment think so. "Who can he hurt in prison?" was the question the jurors in Bernardino Sierra's trial asked themselves. And one of Ronald O'Bryan's character witnesses put it this way: "If a man has been incarcerated, it is the state's job to rehabilitate him, not to take a life."

To death penalty supporters, that last remark betrays a lack of understanding of the problem. A prison cannot "rehabilitate" men like the six men described in this book. Opponents of capital punishment frequently conceptualize rehabilitation as a simple process—as though it involved a simple medicine that could be poured into a killer's head to make him refrain permanently from his conduct. But the fact is that there is no clear "cure" for the antisocial personality, and that is the affliction from which most capital murderers suffer.

The poster boy for the incapacitation argument is Kenneth McDuff, who started to rape, torture, kidnap and murder in his teens. In 1972, he had been on death row for six years for one of his early killings, but that was the year that the Supreme Court abolished all existing death penalties. Four years later, McDuff was eligible for parole, and he blended into the prison population until an overcrowded system released him in 1989.

McDuff then embarked on an orgy of killing. Colleen Reed was only one of the "new" victims, but her memorial service was unique: an army of police officers attended, led by an honor guard of uniformed officers. They fought back tears as the names of fourteen known McDuff victims were read, and Reed's sister put fourteen white roses into a vase.

McDuff often dug graves beforehand and selected victims at random. He kidnapped and raped them, then killed them in savage ways after, as he put it, he had "used them up." He usually boasted afterward, and he made sure that he could revisit each grave, locating all of them close to landmarks. His bragging ultimately was his undoing, as he was convicted on the testimony of acquaintances.

McDuff finally died by lethal execution on November 17, 1998. His case makes the incapacitation factor clear: if he had been executed the first time, his many later victims still would be alive.

Anthony Amsterdam suggests that the answer is "life imprisonment in solitary confinement and without benefit of parole." And perhaps that would be an improvement on today's "life" sentences.

But to supporters of capital punishment, the idea that a prisoner will not be dangerous because he is in solitary confinement is equally unrealistic. Day after day, year after year, the prisoner has to be kept securely, but human contact can not be eliminated entirely, and the necessities of hygiene can not be withheld, nor can dozens of other items that are potential weapons. Death penalty proponents are also skeptical about whether withholding of parole will really be done. The state Supreme Court in California, Professor Amsterdam's own home state, has already acted in at least one case to strike down restrictions on granting parole to a prisoner — on the ground that restrictions of this type are unconstitutional. And besides, if a prisoner could be kept under all these conditions, what is to be gained by it? Would not the regimen that the State would thus impose upon the prisoner be more cruel than death itself?

*   *   *

Capital punishment also involves a question of justice.

When the Texas capital murder law was tested in the United States Supreme Court, the matter of justice was a primary concern.

The case that the Supreme Court had before it was called *The State of Texas versus Jurek*. Jerry Lane Jurek had been indicted for kidnapping and attempting to rape a ten-year old girl, whom he strangled and threw in a river after she refused his sexual advances. Jurek had ignored the child's pleas for mercy, which were heard by several witnesses as he drove through the little town of Cuero, Texas. He was ultimately convicted of capital murder and sentenced to death. As Texas Attorney General John Hill argued to the Supreme Court that Jurek's sentence should be affirmed, he emphasized the brutal and callous nature of the murder.

"Do you mean to tell me," Hill asked the justices incredulously, "that the people have no means of taking care of such a crime?"

What Hill was saying — and the justices later agreed — was that sometimes the death penalty is the only sentence that can do justice to the case.

What sorts of crimes are there that require capital punishment for justice to be done? In Houston, the best example may be Elmer Wayne Henley — who participated in the abduction and murder of over two dozen adolescent boys. Many of the victims were homosexually raped and tortured, and the tortures included mutilation of their genitals while they were still alive, handcuffed to a board. Henley was sentenced to six consecutive terms of ninety-nine years. He was exempt from the death penalty because of a ruling of the Supreme Court.

There are dozens of other cases. There is Charles Tuller, the self-styled revolutionary who hijacked an airplane in Houston in an effort to promote "radical politics of change." He killed three innocent human beings in two different incidents. He too was exempt from the death penalty, and he was given a lengthy sentence of imprisonment. Then there was the case of Henry Jarrette, who was serving penitentiary sentences for two stabbing murders. He escaped, and within two days of his escape, he had kidnapped and raped a 16-year-old boy and robbed and murdered a 16-year-old boy. He told the arresting officer that he regretted being unable to kill him too. But all that could ultimately be done was to return Henry Jarrette to the prison from which he had escaped.

There is something more than deterrence involved in these cases. There is the question of justice.

Today, the cases continue to come — in the form of murders and trials such as those involved in this book. Can justice be done in a case such as Richard Vargas' without capital punishment? Can we as a society ask men like Officer Noskrent to serve in his job, and to see the exploded head of Ashokkumar Patel in the course of that job, and then do less than justice in the case? How can an enormous crime such as Ronald O'Bryan's be dealt with by anything short of capital punishment, if justice is to be done? Or the crime of a Kenneth Brock, who executed a hostage in front of six police officers to gain a momentary advantage in his escape plans? Or the crime of a Bernardino Sierra, who bragged about his six killings on television?

Again, the opposition sees these questions differently.

The opponents of capital punishment do not regard the concern for justice as a valid argument. A death sentence cannot be based on the notion that the defendant has earned it, says Victor Blaine. "That's revenge," he maintains. And Frank Shepherd says that when a murderer is executed, there are "two murders instead of one." Justice, it appears, is a false issue in the eyes of the opponents — who regard the death penalty as "atavistic butchery that has run its course."

And so, apparently, it comes down to a simple but insoluble dilemma — the dilemma, that is, that one man's justice is another man's barbarism.

PART FIVE

What Happened to Them?

WE STILL ARE NOT finished telling you the stories of these six cases.

It is one thing to hear the verdict of a jury. Obviously, that is an important event. But it is another thing to see what actually happens to each defendant after years of appeals and petitions for habeas corpus.

And so we are going to take you inside the prison system, now. We shall examine the lives of those two defendants who were sentenced to life imprisonment. And we shall visit death row, to look at the hours and days of the condemned men. We shall track their court proceedings, follow the death watch, and recount the execution protocol.

The ultimate fates of the four condemned defendants may not be what you expect.

Chapter 21

"A Model Prisoner"

Kenneth Brock's last meal, in the terse language of prison records, was ... "a large double-meat cheeseburger with mustard and [a] Dr. Pepper."

You might think this was an unusual last meal. As Houston Chronicle writer Ken Hoffman put it, if he were facing his final walk, he would indulge in a "world class pig-out." "I might even go back for seconds. On everything." They'd have to give him "a prison suit with Sans-a-belt slacks."

And so, you might imagine that coq au vin or at least a heavy Porterhouse steak would be a more common order from Death Row than Brock's final request.

But if you thought so, you would be wrong. "In the early days, when we resumed executions in the '80's, the most requested meal was T-bone steak," says David Nunnelee, the prison's former public information officer. "But lately the top request has been for cheeseburgers and french fries. They eat the meal in their holding cell around four p.m."

Apparently, condemned inmates are like the rest of us: They crave that which is comforting and familiar, especially when they've been deprived of the power to choose. And so, cheeseburgers rule.

There's a limit to how long a last meal can last, because executions are set for six p.m. It's all-you-can-eat. But the menu can't be too exotic, because it's got to be available from the prison kitchen.

The biggest last meal in history was eaten in 1994 by Richard Beavers. He asked for six pieces of french toast with syrup, jelly and butter; six barbecued spare ribs; six pieces of "well-burned" bacon; four scrambled eggs; five "well cooked" sausage patties; french fries with catsup; three slices of cheese; two pieces of yellow cake with chocolate fudge icing; and four cartons of milk.

He ate it all.

On the other hand, Karla Faye Tucker asked for a banana, a peach and a tossed salad. Tucker had been convicted in 1983 of killing a young couple by hacking them to death with a pickaxe, after a witness recorded her on tape bragging that it was such a sexual experience that she "came" with every stroke. But later, locked away from a smorgasbord drug habit that had made her a walking pharmacy in the free world, Tucker discovered Christianity. Her conversion apparently was sincere, and television evangelists joined the worldwide publicity-rich call for commutation. Governor George W. Bush refused, and Karla Faye Tucker died by lethal injection in 1998.

Curiously, Karla Faye Tucker didn't eat her salad, which sounded more like a Weight Watchers ad than a last meal.

But most prisoners do indulge. "By the time their last meal rolls around," Nunnelee explains, "they've come to terms with their situation and they do eat."

As unimportant as it sounds, the last-meal tradition is uniquely significant for condemned prisoners. It provides them a degree of control. It breaks the monotony and lets them make requests that send prison staff scurrying to comply. To use a touchy-feely word, it empowers them.

And so it is not surprising that last meals tend to be idiosyncratic. This is one of the rituals that make death row residents feel human.

*   *   *

Then there is the odd phenomenon of the so-called "volunteers."

This is one of the strangest control efforts known to that strange place called death row. Volunteers are prisoners who drop their appeals, fire their lawyers, and request — or more often, demand — to be executed. Some volunteers start early, at their trials. They may threaten or badger jurors, express pride in their crimes, or hurl obscenities in court.

The reasons vary. Death row observers attribute some volunteerism to mental illness, some to religious fanaticism. Some volunteers, they say, are influenced by lifelong depression, which death row surely must aggravate. In states like California, where appeals and other legal machinery take longer than anywhere else, one might expect the hope for life to flourish — but instead, volunteers are more prevalent in California than in "faster" states.

The biggest reason for volunteers seems to be the hunger for self-determination. "The legal system is very frightening machinery and very often it toys with you and crushes you," says Richard Dieter, executive director of the Death Penalty Information Center in Washington. "Volunteering is a way of controlling the machinery."

In fact, Dieter adds, a desire for control is often what made these inmates commit their crimes in the first place. "Murder is a rather vicious form of control."

California death row inmate Bill Bradford was a vocal volunteer. "What gets me is the not knowing," he says. "The waiting. I am tired of it." In fact, he got tired before his trial, where he fired his defense lawyers and spectacularly taunted jurors to send him to the gas chamber, hinting that he had left numerous other bodies behind.

But then, five days before his execution, Bradford changed his mind. He disavowed his death wish and started to fight for his life.

And this, unfortunately, is another means of asserting control. The inmate asks for execution, and then switches signals—sending the law's machinery scurrying to appoint counsel who will move for a stay of execution and claim that the sentence is illegal.

After all, death row contains a high percentage of manipulators.

But many volunteers stick with their requests. As of 1998, there had been sixty volunteers executed, or more than 12 percent of total executions. Perhaps there is a macho, I'm-a-man-and-let's-do-it kind of bravado behind this singleness of purpose.

And an even more eye-popping statistic concerns suicides in California. Thirteen California death row inmates have committed suicide. It takes determination to kill yourself on death row, where guards take pains to suppress every possible lethal instrument. But as of 1998, the number of these California death row suicides was more than two-and-one-half times the number of actual executions!

Still, most residents of death row fight their sentences. Most try to stay alive. All of the six inmates featured in this book took advantage of every available appeal.

Including Kenneth Brock.

*   *   *

Brock was a student in the Wyndham School District during most of the last years of his life.

Wyndham is an unusual school district in many ways. First, its constituency is the Texas Department of Criminal Justice. All of its students are prisoners.

Second, it has fewer disciplinary problems than some free-world institutions, because there are solid means of enforcement. Unruly students simply find that their education is curtailed. And the prison system also is unique in the encyclopedic variety of courses it offers, through and including college degree programs.

Convicted murderer Kenneth Brock took commendable advantage of the opportunities the Wyndham School District had to offer. He completed his high school education, all "from inside." And then he started college, completing more than a year's worth of course credit while awaiting execution.

During his ten years on death row, Kenneth Brock never lost a single good-time credit that was available to him. Prison officials never took any administrative action against him. Brock's crime was that of a reckless youth, under the influence of heroin, but on the inside, drug-free, he successfully entered and completed the TDCJ Drug Offenders Program. His inmate classification was 1A, which is the highest status available for inmates under sentence of death.

To use a trite but accurate phrase, Kenneth Brock was a model prisoner.

* * *

One of the ironic consequences of the death penalty is that it sometimes is enforced against deserving but less heinous killers such as Kenneth Brock, while some of the worst killers, those who seem most to have earned it, escape from the clutches of capital punishment.

Always and forever, this ironic result will hold true. The reason is that our system is set up to minimize wrongful convictions. We try to err on the side of leniency. Our belief is, "Better that a hundred guilty persons go free, than that one who is innocent be convicted." The bias of the system, then, is that a certain number of less blameworthy (but still deserving) murderers inevitably will be executed, while some of the most vicious are not. This result is inevitable in a cautious system.

And so today, years after Kenneth Brock's death, John Stiles Griffin resides in the Middleton unit of the Texas Department of Criminal Justice, in Abilene.

John Stiles Griffin's classification is S3-C. That is a good classification, equivalent to trustee status, and the "3" indicates the absence of gang affiliations. It seems that Griffin still institutionalizes well.

His custody status is "Minimum In." Translation: Inside the walls, Griffin requires the lowest level of security, but he always stays "in." Maybe the prison system finally has gotten it right: Griffin is not supposed to be allowed outside the walls.

He first became eligible for parole review in 1980, almost twenty years ago, and only a few short years after his last victims were buried. He comes up for parole again on October 1, 1999, just before the new millennium. And every three years after that, John Stiles Griffin will be "card-reviewed," at least: without a live hearing, parole officials will consider his paperwork.

He is unlikely to be released in the near future. State policy strongly disfavors parole of capital murderers, including those sentenced to life. But repeated parole dates usually are an outrage to victim survivors, meaning that they may never reach closure.

Griffin's transfer record shows another feature that is curious. Through 1993, he had numerous medical transfers. Manipulative prisoners typically obtain repeated medical reassignments as a means of controlling their environments. The publicly available transfer records do not reveal whether this is true of Griffin, or whether he really needed chronic medical care.

In any event, John Stiles Griffin lives on, many years after Louise Ponder and Patricia Hixson—and for that matter, Kenneth Brock—have gone to their graves.

Chapter 22

Appeals, Petitions, and Stays

What happens before an execution? What was Kenneth Brock's last day like?

Nobody really yells, "Dead man walking." That happens in the movies.

Instead, the condemned inmate arrives by van at the death house, inside the Walls Unit. It's a fifteen minute drive from the Ellis Unit, where death row actually is located. The transfer usually occurs on the day of the scheduled execution, although at Brock's time, it was done the day before.

The van backs up to the death house door. Officers lock two sets of chain-link gates behind it. The inmate, wearing leg shackles and a belly chain tethered to his cuffs, exits the rear of the van, where five guards immediately surround him. Together, they march into the death house holding area.

A row of six cells and a shower stall, looking like a small but immaculately clean county jail, greets them.

The inmate kneels on a chair cushion. The guards remove all of his irons. But "unless there's a stay, he'll never be shackled again," explains prison spokesman Larry Fitzgerald.

The inmate is ushered into the next-to-last cell, distant from the death chamber itself. The most striking thing about this place is how ordinary, for a prison, it looks, with off-white walls and soothing beige bars.

Kenneth Brock arrived at this holdover cell at 2:55 p.m. on June 18, 1986, the next-to-last day of his life. "His mood," says the execution watch, "is cooperative."

The Walls Unit warden meets briefly with every incoming inmate. Some of his questions are informal, designed to verify the condemned man's coherence to express his last wishes. The others are formal, from a checklist. For example, the warden had Kenneth Brock respond to this multiple-choice question:

> I am ... advised that the services of an attorney can be provided free of charge to prepare a simple will .... I have indicated my desires by initiating one of the following:

A. *The disposition of my estate is complex and could not be appropriately handled by a simple will[;] therefore I have made my own arrangements. [Few inmates choose this option* _____

B. *Disposition of my worldly possessions is covered by an existing will* _____

C. *Services of an attorney [are] requested to assist me in preparation of a simple will.* _____

D. *I do not desire a will.* _____

Brock checked the last space. He had no will and did not want one.

Some last requests are perplexing. The execution watch records that Brock was told he had 22¢ in his inmate trust fund. He asked that it be used to buy "1 Moon Pie and a 2¢ stamp." The records add that this request "was granted."

The chaplain, or the inmate's own selected spiritual adviser, visits next. "The chaplain has one of the hardest duties in the whole system," says public information officer Larry Fitzgerald. "He's got to help the inmate, assuming he's willing, to put his spiritual house in order."

In a short time, the inmate will look through the windows of the death chamber and see the survivors of his victims. They will hear his last words. The daunting responsibility of the chaplain includes "preparing the killer for this confrontation with the loved ones of his victims, during the last minutes of his life," as Fitzgerald puts it.

The inmate may choose either prison whites or work-release jeans-and-blue-shirt as the last clothing he will wear. Brock, like the majority, opted for jeans. He saw a steady stream of visitors: a sister, a brother-in-law, a friend; six more sisters; and his mother.

The inmate is provided a telephone. Brock used it to talk briefly with his attorney, Ms. Carolyn Garcia, at 2:55 p.m. He read newspapers and wrote letters.

During Brock's era, it all ended just before sunrise. Today, the execution protocol takes place shortly after 6 p.m. on the designated day. The warden says something simple to the inmate, such as "It's time. Will you please come with me?"

After witnessing nearly a hundred executions, Larry Fitzgerald cannot recall any in which the inmate has struggled or resisted. Most are resigned.

The last entry in Kenneth Brock's execution watch is, "Appears calm and composed."

*   *   *

Brock's execution was preceded by a vigorous battle over his life or death, just as most executions are.

Kenneth Brock's battle was different, though, because he had an unusual ally.

One of the advocates for Brock's life was none other than George Jacobs, the prosecutor who had asked for Brock's death sentence. Jacobs wrote a forceful letter:

> Texas State Board of Pardons & Paroles
> P.O. Box 13401
> Austin, Texas 78711-3401 . . .
> Members of the Board:
>
> I am writing you this letter to ask you to recommend to the Governor of the State of Texas to grant a pardon to Kenneth Brock from the death penalty assessed for him by a jury in the 178th District Court of Harris County, Texas. . . . I was the lead prosecutor in that case and I asked the jury to assess the death penalty to Mr. Brock. In the years that have passed since that verdict, I have followed Mr. Brock's progress in the Texas Department of Criminal Justice and have monitored his behavior with the prison officials. Now that the execution date for Mr. Brock is drawing near, I feel that I must speak out and make this request on behalf of Mr. Brock in view of his exemplary record for the ten (10) years that he has been confined on death row. . . .
>
> Because the crime for which he was committed was the only act of violence that Mr. Brock was convicted of, and because of his sincere rehabilitative efforts, I do not believe that it would serve any worthwhile purpose to the State of Texas to execute Kenneth Brock. . . .
>
> Please spare Kenneth Brock's life and commute his sentence to life imprisonment which will be in this case justice for all concerned. I am,
>
> Very truly yours,
> George O. Jacobs

Jacob's letter also contained an account of Brock's exemplary prison record: his persistent educational accomplishments, drug rehabilitation, and freedom from any disciplinary proceedings.

Why? How did Jacobs arrive at this stunningly different position, after successfully seeking a death sentence?

The answer is complex. Jacobs had always felt concern about the evidence of Brock's guilt. "The testimony about his eyes, how they were wide when the gun went off, was consistent with an accident." Then there was the pistol itself, a flimsy Saturday Night Special. The defendant was drugged out, surrounded, and stumbling backward. A finding of accident would not have exonerated Brock, because he still would have been guilty of murder. But if the jury had had a reasonable doubt about the possibility of accident, the correct verdict would have been murder instead of capital murder, and Kenneth Brock would not have been sentenced to die.

This possibility weighed on Jacob's mind at the end of Brock's life.

How, then, could Jacobs have asked Brock's jury, in the first place, for the verdict he did? Some assistant district attorneys were critical of his letter, on the ground that "if Jacobs felt that way, he shouldn't have tried the case." But there is a time-honored tradition behind the principle that the prosecutor should present the case rather than judge it. If guilt truly is questionable, or if doubts are apparent, then the prosecutor certainly should move to dismiss; but if reasonable people can disagree, perhaps the prosecutor performs his duty best by entrusting the matter to the court and jurors, rather than imposing his own opinion. And if he disagrees with the result in the end, the prosecutor should advocate clemency—just as Jacobs did.

This is a debate with a long history, probably destined to go on forever. People disagree about exactly where an ethical prosecutor should draw the line.

And, of course, Jacobs wasn't relying only on the crime-scene evidence. He also knew about Brock's spotless record during the last ten years.

But there was another factor at work, too. George Jacobs no longer supports the death penalty.

Perhaps this change is a result of the Brock case. Perhaps it comes from Jacobs's own life experiences: He left the district attorney's office in the late 1970's, and since then, he has defended citizens accused of crime. He has had his own share of personal tragedy. And recently he became an ordained minister.

Jacobs once was a death penalty prosecutor, and a capable and successful one at that. But today, he is a death penalty opponent.

*   *   *

Will Gray was the attorney who represented Kenneth Brock at the end, along with Carolyn Garcia. Gray and Garcia's efforts to save Brock was a labor of love. A commitment to a cause they believed in.

But like most labors of love, this one carried some unfair burdens.

Truly an attorney for the damned, Will Gray took on the neverending task of representing death row inmates, too many of them to count, in repeated cycles of appeals and petitions for habeas corpus. Much of his work was free, as he fought to overturn their sentences, or at least to keep them alive as long as possible.

In the meantime, Gray's principles drove him practically to the poorhouse.

Will Gray was known best by his nickname: "The Old Gray Fox." He built his reputation as an appellate lawyer, although he was an excellent defender at trial, too. Tall and thin, with neat but flowing gray hair and a gray goatee, Will Gray looked like a professor, staring out through thick glasses. He was studious. And serious.

But Will Gray's smile, too, was quick. He often was amused by the ironic results of the legal process, the humdrum injustices and accidental corrections, and he loved the intricacy of it all.

*   *   *

Will Gray and Carolyn Garcia saw to it that Kenneth Brock's case was well presented, to a parade of trial and appellate courts.

First, there was Brock's automatic appeal. The case went directly to the Court of Criminal Appeals, which is Texas's highest court for criminal cases (the Texas Supreme Court hears civil cases only). Brock had been on death row for several years when Texas's highest court affirmed his death sentence.

Then, there was a petition to the United States Supreme Court. Denied, in a one-sentence order.

Then, Gray and Garcia started all over again, in the original trial court, the 178th District Court. Judge Walton, by now, had died, and there was a new presiding judge. Gray and Garcia filed a petition for habeas corpus.

It was denied. They appealed again. Unsuccessfully. And they petitioned the United States Supreme Court. Again, unsuccessfully.

Next, they shifted to the federal courts. These courts can hear petitions for habeas corpus when state court avenues have been exhausted. Brock's first federal habeas proceeding was in the United States District Court for the Southern District of Texas. Petition denied. Then, an appeal to the United States Court of Appeals for the Fifth Circuit. Denial affirmed. And again, a petition to the United States Supreme Court. Denied.

Sometimes there are repeated loops through both the state and federal systems. It was not unusual, in Brock's day, for a death sentence to be reviewed by fifty to a hundred different judges.

*   *   *

But perhaps the most arcane aspect of death row practice is the stays of execution.

When Gray and Garcia filed a petition or an appeal, that didn't keep the death sentence from being carried out. A stay, in other words, is not automatic. The prisoner's attorney simultaneously must file a separate motion requesting a stay, supported by facts and legal arguments that show a chance of success on the petition or appeal.

And for these two lawyers, the death row practice was a chaotic blur. "At one point, Will and I represented about thirty death row inmates," says Carolyn Garcia. "And when you work on just one of these cases, that's all you can concentrate on. With thirty, we had trouble just keeping track of all the execution dates."

As the processes are repeated, stays become more difficult to obtain. A day arrives when the trial court denies the motion. And then there is a hasty appeal. As the end nears, the process becomes increasingly desperate. Motions for stay become "emergency" motions.

And then, there comes a day when the last available court denies the last available motion for stay.

That process still was ongoing, still in the hands of Gray and Garcia, when Kenneth Brock made his last transfer from Ellis to the Walls Unit.

Chapter 23

Life and Death on Death Row

Kenneth Brock is not the only defendant featured in this book, of course.

What happened to Gerald Lee Bodde, the kidnapper who killed his landlady? And what happened to Richard Vargas, the multiple murderer of Brady Bunch fame?

There is surprisingly little information about either Bodde or Vargas in the public affairs files at TDCJ. But the information that does exist is ironic.

Public affairs furnishes a stark sheet of paper headed, "Deaths Other Than Executions." The mere fact that an inmate died on death row does not mean that he was executed. Exhaustion of appeals and habeas will have taken ten to twenty years in the typical case, before the execution becomes a real possibility.

And so, many inmates die on death row of natural causes. And that is what happened to Bodde and Vargas: They both died on the inside, while waiting. While they were warehoused for extermination.

Statistically, it makes sense: In ten to twenty years, a certain percentage of any given population will die. Death row tends to attract undisciplined, unhealthy individuals whose life expectancies already are shorter than average. In some states, such as California (which has the most inmates on death row but nearly the fewest executions), deaths by natural causes far exceed those by carried-out sentences.

TDCJ's deaths other than executions are typical of death rows nationwide. The entries in the records are stark and short: "682,—Turner, Joseph, 07/06/86. Suicide—hung himself." "955, Nelson, Peter, 10/05/92. Cerebral hemorrhage."

Or, "725, Andrews, Maurice, 04/05/95. Stabbed in the temple by inmate Arnold, Jemarr, #987, while on the rec. yard."

Public information officer Larry Fitzgerald is a wizard at supplying these facts, and visiting journalists often are surprised by the openness of his office. More information than this, certainly, exists somewhere in the bowels of TDCJ's electronics. But the easily obtainable facts in the public files are limited to these kinds of brief entries, at least for non-execution deaths.

Here are the entries for Bodde and Vargas. "535, Vargas, Richard, 05/12/81. Heart attack." And, "543, Bodde, Gerald, 07/03/87. Heart attack."

That is all that the front-office file contains about these two human beings. Or about the numerous lives that they ended or ruined. Two entries of "heart attack."

To me, it is ironic. I worked on the capital trials of two vicious killers. But when people ask about the outcomes, the answer is, "Both of them died on death row of natural causes while waiting for their appeals to run out."

And the consequences are more far-reaching than that. The people of this state could have spent the literally millions of dollars that they devoted to these two cases in other ways—on crime detection, alcoholism prevention, and education—and they would have achieved the same penological results for Bodde and Vargas. To the victims, these two heart attacks meant an odd incompleteness: neither killer's sentence was carried out.

Even more ironically, delays of ten to twenty years may mean that we do not really have a death penalty, or at least, not an effective one.

From the standpoint of the offender, this kind of "maybe someday" enforcement destroys the immediacy and predictability of consequences. Capital murderers are reckless people in the first place, and they probably are even less inclined to think about the seriousness of capital punishment if they can rely on the "actuarial" defense—if they can tell themselves, "There's a good chance I'll die before then anyway."

We cannot know whether a death penalty without extended delays would be a deterrent.

In fact, one condemned killer named Clarence Lackey tried a truly novel argument in one of his many habeas petitions. He claimed that keeping him alive, under sentence of death, was unconstitutional. It was "cruel and unusual punishment." His lawyers fulminated that if we are going to have the death penalty in America, "We have to do it right." They pointed out that English common law, from which the Eighth Amendment to our Constitution was derived, required "swift" executions, within a matter of months, to avoid exactly this kind of cruelty.

Lackey's lawyers sounded, for all the world, like prosecutors: A long delay, they said, "undermines the deterrent intent." And although the real prosecutors dismissed Lackey's argument as "remarkable," and it ultimately proved unsuccessful, it won him a temporary stay of execution. The Supreme Court ordered hearings to determine whether state courts were responsible for his delay.

What tended to become forgotten in these debates about Lackey's sentence was the shortened life of Toni Kumpf. She was a young lady whom Lackey had abducted, raped and murdered, almost twenty years earlier.

To victims' survivors, the result of such delays is that closure never comes. Every thought of the crime or offender is a pain that is impossible to describe, and every stay, appeal, reset, denial or petition means a mental reenactment of the horror.

* * *

Even if not much remains in the records about Bodde and Vargas, there is one thing that is clear. Their lives on death row were excruciatingly boring.

Texas prison cells are not air-conditioned. Nobody in the entire system enjoys swimming pools, tennis courts or jogging tracks, and certainly no one on death row has these things. Recreation facilities are limited and inexpensive, and even the small expenditures for this purpose do not come from tax dollars. They are financed by sales from the prison commissary. Inmates do not have televisions in individual death row cells. They share with numerous others (no premium cable), and correctional officers control the channels.

By state law, inmates are required to work, and most inmates want to. But on death row, security limits the work even of work-capable inmates. As for non-work capable inmates, they are assigned to "Death Row Segregation," where every aspect of the inmate's existence, from property to meals to correspondence, is subject to the state's Death Row Plan.

For instance, a Level III inmate taking a shower may possess nothing but "state-issued soap, towel, [and] shower slides," or flip-flops. "A razor," the Death Row Plan adds, "will be issued to a Level III offender [only] after he enters the shower." This simple process, in other words, is controlled, supervised and enforced with commands at every step.

The Death Row Procedures Manual is even more detailed. There are ten different rules, spread over two pages, regarding "Feeding of Lock-Up Wings." And there are other dense, confusing procedures for haircuts, for telephone calls, and for what euphemistically is called "Management of Inmates Who Throw Projectiles." Full-body or strip searches precede every movement. Discipline consists of deprivation: An offending inmate may be transferred to Segregation, and within that classification, misbehavior is punished by Level III confinement.

If you're on death row, precise conditions vary, but you may be locked down an average of more than twenty-three hours a day. During the other short periods, you "exercise" if you want to, under guard and alone or in small groups, in a confined, sunless gymnasium. "Ad seg," or administrative segregation for disciplinary infractions, reduces your exercise time, and solitary means lockdown all the time, twenty-four-seven, for up to fifteen days, with nothing but "essentials" such as soap and toothpaste. Some "super seg" cells in TDCJ have shower heads and drains, so that the inmate need never leave even for cleanliness reasons. The water is turned on only for a brief period each day, as a deterrent to inmates who might otherwise amuse themselves by stuffing the drain to flood the block.

For some types of infractions, you can be sentenced to the dreaded "food loaf" treatment: Your meals are stiff cakelike chunks containing all your nutritional requirements in one blended mass. Or you may have to wear a hospital-style paper gown, unnatural and uncomfortable. In some locations, you will be subjected to constant noise. Screams and yells by nearby inmates echo through your world of unmuffled steel and concrete, so that you have to shout to be understood from a few feet away. But even with these conditions, a few inmates seek segregation by deliberate misbehavior so that they can dramatize their rebellion, obtain protection or isolation from other prisoners, or just change their surroundings for a while.

Perhaps these circumstances explain the docile cooperation of inmates during the execution protocol. Resistance not only is futile—of course, it's futile, when you're shackled and surrounded by five officers—but it also has been drummed out of you by a system of behavior therapy that works. Even with the "better" conditions of institutionalized inmates, one day is like the next.

It is a life of constant waiting, punctuated by commands that enforce stultifying, rigid procedures.

* * *

In 1996, the United States Congress passed the Antiterrorism and Effective Death Penalty Act.

This new law abolishes the freewheeling, endless habeas loop that once made delays interminable. A condemned prisoner has the right to present his arguments only one time to a federal trial court, together with appeals from that court's ruling. A second habeas petition requires extraordinary conditions, such as facts or law that are so new and surprising that a diligent lawyer couldn't have known about them at the time of the first one.

At the same time, many states have shortened their procedures. For example, an inmate's direct appeal traditionally has been followed by a habeas proceeding in the original state trial court, after which there inevitably was a second appeal loop in the state courts, involving closely similar facts and issues. Some states now require the inmate's lawyer to file his habeas corpus petition soon after the death sentence. That way, both the sentence and the habeas ruling can be appealed at the same time. This simple change means that the state appellate court sees all fifty-two cards in the deck at one time, and it also cuts unnecessary years of waiting.

But a state can't use these laws as a shortcut. There is a catch.

The new federal law requires the states to comply with certain standards before they can take advantage of its benefits. The most important standards concern the competency of trial counsel. States must appoint fully competent, experienced and ethical lawyers to represent death penalty defendants.

The idea sounds good. But will it work?

The federal Act is an effort to ensure that the initial trial is the main event, and that its fairness is safeguarded. And after that, the hope is that fewer appellate reviews will be needed. Supporters of the federal Act argue that it will result in better trials, with better defenses, and presumably, fewer death sentences. And then, supporters foresee a shorter series of post-conviction petitions and appeals, which will take on the order of five to six years — rather than fifteen to twenty.

Opponents, of course, are more pessimistic. They express doubts that lawyers or trials truly will improve. And they see the new federal law as a restriction of opportunities for federal judges to find blemishes on state trials. It is as a rush to judgment, they say: a hurry-up response to blood-thirsty public demands for quicker death.

* * *

From all of this, one might get the impression that the death penalty is ineffective. Morally indefensible. And irrelevant to justice.

But then, one should consider the case of Ronald Clark O'Bryan.

The Halloween Candy Murderer has one of the thickest files in the entire TDCJ public affairs office. Perhaps this is fitting. O'Bryan, the man who killed his eight-year-old son with cyanide-laced candy, could be a poster boy for support of capital punishment.

But on the other hand, almost everything that needed to be said about O'Bryan had already been said by the time he was sentenced. If ever there could be a crime that qualified for the death penalty, this one did. And the proof of guilt was convincing.

O'Bryan's lawyer, during his many appeals and habeas corpus petitions, was Will Gray. One of the unsung heroes of this tragic story, Gray had also represented Kenneth Brock. He made sure that the Candy Man received every stay, appeal and petition that the law allowed.

The most extensive federal appeal of O'Bryan's case was heard in 1983. O'Bryan consistently had maintained his innocence. But Will Gray decided that conceding the crime forthrightly was the best strategy. The best way to argue, credibly, that his client had been denied a fair trial was not to challenge the evidence of guilt.

"Petitioner was convicted of capital murder," Gray's brief began. "[T]he jury [found] that on October 31, 1974, he intentionally caused the death of his eight-year-old son by poisoning him with cyanide in order to collect life insurance proceeds."

No challenge to the sufficiency of the evidence. No protestations of innocence. No beating about the bush. And this was probably skillful lawyering, risky as it sounded.

Because the point was, after that, Gray's brief could be aimed entirely at saving the Candy Man's life. There were eleven different constitutional arguments. Point II, for example, was that the death penalty statute "violates the Eighth and Fourteenth Amendments to the Constitution of the United States . . . because it contains no provisions for directing . . . the jury's consideration of mitigating circumstances." Point IV said that the death penalty statute "permits the jury to make a determination . . . by an arbitrary and discriminatory answer . . . that requires no empirical facts or evidence, . . ."

And so on.

But of course, Gray's most serious issue was placed in Point I, strategically. It was based on a Supreme Court case called *Witherspoon v. Illinois*. The *Witherspoon* decision sounds simple enough: A trial judge can't excuse a juror who has a negative attitude toward capital punishment merely for that reason. The excluded juror must absolutely refuse to follow the law, or absolutely refuse to consider the death penalty.

It sounds simple. But with real people, applying the *Witherspoon* case is anything but simple.

Gray's brief talked about three excluded jurors, and it quoted extensively from the examination of one named Steffins:

> The Court: Well, can you conceive of a set of circumstances where you feel in your own mind that the death penalty would be a proper punishment?
>
> A. I believe in my own mind, as I say, it would have to be—I don't know if you call it circumstantial evidence or what type of evidence, but it would have to be actual—I think physical— physical witness.

[What was that?]

> The Court: Let me see if I understand. What you are saying [is] that before you could ever impose the death penalty, you would have to actually witness the crime yourself?
>
> A. Not myself, witnesses in the actual physical witnesses, I think . . . . This is what I'm trying to say and believe this is the way I feel. . . .
>
> The Court: All right. Now, I don't understand that. I'm not following exactly what you're saying.

A. Well, I just—apparently, I just couldn't vote for it with facts even if there were facts of witnesses, I would probably—"...

A. Well, like I say, I still have the mixed feelings there that I don't really think I could make a proper judgment, being a borderline thinker on the subject. I just won't—a decision that I don't know that I could make. Let's put it that way.". . .

The examination of this one juror, on this one subject, splashed over an incredible thirty-seven pages of transcript. At the end, the trial judge had decided to exclude this self-described "borderline thinker." The trial judge simply believed that the man's answers added up to, "I can't do it."

But it was not Will Gray's job to agree. And the absoluteness of the *Witherspoon* decision gave him something to work with, even if the trial judge had struggled heroically to apply it to the real world. It was an excellent brief. If Gray's work were to be paid for by a commercial business at today's market rates, a reasonable free might, conceivably, exceed a hundred thousand dollars.

"Steffins's examination clearly demonstrated that his exclusion for cause cannot stand," Gray wrote. "At no time did he state unequivocally that he could not vote for capital punishment regardless of the evidence."

And therefore, Ronald Clark O'Bryan's conviction and death sentence were unconstitutional, Gray argued. Illegal. He should be granted a writ of habeas corpus. The state should be required to release him, or to wipe out the result and give him a new trial.

*　*　*

I, David Crump, represented the Texas District and County Attorney's Association in O'Bryan's case. My role was to support the death sentence.

I respect my co-author and friend, George Jacobs, but I don't agree with him. I believe that there are some cases in which justice simply cannot be done without capital punishment. I also accept the prevention argument: The death penalty prevents more murders by convicted killers who are warehoused for life. And there also is the deterrence argument. If the execution of a small percentage of guilty inmates can deter the murders of other, innocent people, then I believe that it is not only bad policy, but ethically wrong, to take the easier way.

In all honesty, I must accept that there is the chance that an innocent person will be sentenced to death. This is especially so if one includes murderers, like Kenneth Brock with his accident defense, who claim to be guilty of murder but not to be liable for the death penalty. And I recognize many of the other arguments against capital punishment. Cautiously, and without wanting it to sound like the only claim to the high ground,

I have concluded on balance that the death penalty is a morally proper response to the worst kinds of crimes.

Today, I am the Newell H. Blakely Professor of Law at the University of Houston. I am fortunate enough to hold one of the best endowed chairs in legal education in the country. But I am unusual among law school professors in my position on capital punishment. As a result, I have represented the majority of the states, from Alabama to Washington, in the United States Supreme Court.

I have a beautiful wife and four children. I play baseball (not softball!) a couple of times a week, and I'm a guitarist in a country-rock band, which is called "The BarFlies," because it's composed of four lawyers. But one holdover from my days as an assistant district attorney is that when I think of underprivileged, oppressed members of our society, I do not think about Ronald Clark O'Bryan or Kenneth Brock. I think about Timothy Marc O'Bryan, the Candy Man's murdered son.

I tried to make my brief in O'Bryan's case as restrained, as quiet, and frankly as bloodless as I could. For example, I argued that the trial judge had properly excluded the juror, Steffins, who called himself a "borderline thinker":

> It is natural for potential jurors to equivocate initially, if in fact they are *Witherspoon*-disqualified. [T]hese are jurors whose state of mind requires them to vote in violation of the law and evidence. Their equivocation stems from the natural difficulty of articulating this inability to conform to the law .... [A] juror is properly disqualified if the total examination makes unmistakably clear [that he cannot consider capital punishment]. If initial equivocation meant that [people] who would automatically vote [against] the law and evidence were nevertheless required to be seated on juries, rational capital sentencing would be impossible.

Appeals in death penalty cases always deal with technical issues like these — and maybe they sound boring. It is a paradox. This is a battle about life or death, but only rarely does it concentrate on guilt, innocence, life or death. Instead, it is full of debates about procedural matters, arguing ethereal points of law, the way that medievalists argued over the number of angels that could dance on the head of a pin.

The Fifth Circuit's decision came a few months later, and it was a cliffhanger. One judge agreed with Will Gray. But by a two to one vote, the court rejected O'Bryan's appeal.

* * *

O'Bryan's ex-wife, Daynene, was not sympathetic.

"He made his bed, and now he is having to lie in it," she told reporters. "No, I have no pity for him."

She said she believed in capital punishment. And she added, "I think all these stays are a bunch of malarkey, not just in this case but in all such cases."

Still, O'Bryan seemed to have plenty of friends.

For example, he invited 18-year-old Kim Manganaro to watch him die. But first, he showed good manners: He asked Kim's mother for permission. "I'm old enough to decide for myself, but he asked my mother anyway," Manganaro said. "That's like Ron. Very polite."

She had become O'Bryan's friend after exchanging letters with him. Then she came to visit him on death row. She described him as sensitive and caring, "the type of friend everybody would like to have." O'Bryan repaid her trust by selecting her as one of five personal witnesses to his execution.

The Candy Man arrived at the Walls Unit from Ellis at 6:30 a.m. on March 30, 1984. He was heavyset and wide of girth, and predictably, his supper order was heavy too: "T-Bone steak (medium well to well done), french fries and catsup, whole kernel corn, sweet peas, lettuce & tomato salad with egg and french dressing, iced tea (sweet), saltines, ice cream, Boston cream pie, and rolls."

Outside the prison gates, death penalty protesters carried candles in the darkness. In a carnival-like atmosphere, death penalty supporters tossed Pixy Stix at members of Amnesty International as they heckled them.

"The death penalty doesn't do anything to help the victims. It's a placebo," said one protester, who wore religious vestments.

College students carried signs with sayings such as "Justice Rules!" and "Kill the Worst First." And one teenager, decked out in a rubbery skull mask with yellow teeth, told reporters she wanted O'Bryan to die because "he ruined Halloween for everyone."

In what was now his third federal suit for habeas corpus, O'Bryan's lawyers sought an eve-of-execution stay. By now, he was reduced to arguing that the *Witherspoon* case, upon which he had based his earlier arguments, "is at best ill defined, and at worst, undefined." The court denied the stay in a six page opinion, describing the parade of petitions, motions and appeals previously decided against O'Bryan.

The Candy Man was meticulous enough to write his last words ahead of time. In neat, firm, flowing black handwriting, he again insisted on his innocence. This is what O'Bryan wrote:

> "What is about to transpire in a few moments is wrong! However, we as human beings do make mistakes and errors. This execution is one of those wrongs. Yet it doesn't mean our whole system of justice is wrong.

"Therefore, I would forgive *all* who have taken part in any way in my death. Also, to anyone I have offended in any way during my 39 years, I pray and ask your forgiveness, just as I forgive anyone whose [sic] offended me in anyway. And, I pray and ask God's forgiveness for all of us respectively as human beings.

"To my loved ones, I extended [sic] my undieing [sic] love. To those close to me, know in your hearts I love you one and all. God Bless you all and may God's best blessings be always yours.

"Ronald C. O'Bryan

"P.S. During my time here, I have been treated well."

* * *

Fully a hundred and thirty-two media representatives signed in with the TDCJ public affairs office for the Halloween Candy Murder's execution. They ranged from the local Huntsville Item to the Donahue Show.

Still, almost everything that needed saying had been said years earlier.

Almost everything. The lethal injection was begun at 12:40 a.m., and Ronald Clark O'Bryan was pronounced dead at 12:48 a.m. on March 31, 1984.

Chapter 24

The Execution Protocol

I ran into Victor Blaine on a downtown street a few months ago.

Twenty-plus years after the Vargas trial, Vic looked the same. Maybe a little bit more gray. But he wasn't a criminal defense lawyer any more.

"I just don't want to do it," he explained. His decision was based on a combination of unpleasantries: collecting fees from clients who had difficulty affording them, the company a criminal lawyer keeps, and the way a lawyer feels when a predator does it again. Nowadays, Vic says, he represents victims in personal injury cases.

"That's too bad." I remember being disappointed. Vic Blaine combines skill with self-discipline and class, and we need ethical defense lawyers as much as we need good prosecutors, if not more.

Marvin Teague went on to get himself elected to the Court of Criminal Appeals. It was odd to think of this nerdy, crewcut scholar conducting a political campaign, until you saw Judge Teague in action. His smile was gregarious and he enjoyed interacting with new people.

Until his death a few years ago, Teague was a real force on the Court. He tilted slightly toward the defense side, but he had too much affection for the law to distort it. He also put out a newsletter for criminal lawyers, and it was always a pleasure to read. I remember one essay about how a lawyer could most effectively present what Teague elegantly called "the wee-wee defense." This defense arises when a client gets caught inside the building at 2 a.m., perhaps standing beside the opened cash register with gloves on, and he explains that he's not a burglar—he just needed to visit the bathroom. Characteristically, Teague's article bristled with useful case citations and points of law.

But of all the lawyers in this book, Carolyn Garcia may have had the most interesting odyssey.

She got into defending death row convicts because she shared offices with Will Gray. "Will stuck me with a bunch of them. He talked a federal judge into appointing me. But the appointment didn't mean much, because they didn't pay you. It was all for free." And so, while Garcia represented as many as thirty inmates at a time who faced the ultimate penalty, she had to "make a living on top of that." But she couldn't quit, she says, because "Will was so committed. I couldn't watch him killing himself by trying to do it all."

Most lawyers who immerse themselves in defending these cases are movement people, and they do it because of deep philosophical opposition to capital punishment. But not Carolyn Garcia. "There are some murders," she says flatly, "where the death penalty is the only route." Why, then, did she do it? "Because no one else would. No one would step up to the plate except Will Gray."

Garcia and Gray worked hard to raise consciousness while they plugged the gap as best they could. They helped to start programs. Several big firms took one case each. And finally, in the late 1980's, Carolyn Garcia gave up what she calls "the ultimate pro bono project."

Soon after that, Governor Ann Richards appointed Judge Carolyn Clause Garcia to the bench. To a civil district court. Garcia's practice had always emphasized civil cases, unlike her pro bono efforts. The city named a street after her: Judge Carolyn Clause Garcia Circle. And then, at the end of her term, Garcia went back out into practice again. Today, she does a mixture of civil litigation, criminal defense, and alternate dispute resolution such as mediation.

Her friend and co-counsel Will Gray died in 1999. Recently, I asked Carolyn Garcia whether she would do it all over again. She hesitated. Then, deliberately, she answered, "No. Not voluntarily." But then, after another pause, she added, "Of course, there's always a case that comes along that's so moving, that you've got to get involved."

As for the prosecutors, Stu Stewart went into practice with David Gibson, one of the Brady Bunch defense lawyers. And then, Mike Hinton left the district attorney's office, too. It was the end of an era. Today, Stewart lives on a boat in Galveston Bay and practices criminal defense with Hinton, who is as colorful as ever.

Stuart Kinard met a tough prosecutor named Jeanette, nicknamed "Killer" for her prowess with juries. They fell in love, got married and moved to Austin, every Texan's heaven. Together, they built a practice defending citizens accused of crime, and Stuart wrote a book about how to get drunk drivers off. A while ago, I got a newspaper clipping from Jeanette reporting that Stuart had won a prize for owning the ugliest pickup in the state. It quoted Stuart as saying that he saw it on the street and tracked the owner down to buy it from him. "That's how ugly it was," Jeanette explained.

And, of course, Stuart still remembers Bernardino Sierra, one of his best clients.

* * *

Bernardino Sierra's residence today is the Eastham Unit in Lovelady, Texas. He's in Dorm 11, bunk 007.

His classification is S3-B1, closely similar to Griffin's S3-C. His custody status is "Minimum in." Like Griffin, Sierra has the lowest security classification inside the unit, but he is not allowed outside the walls. His work assignment is "SSI—Orderly." The prison medical service is a big operation, and it depends on inmate help.

Unlike Griffin, Sierra has had ten times in solitary. Prison spokesman Larry Fitzgerald says that this is "a lot" of trips to solitary, and such a number "may indicate a disciplinary problem." Offenses can range from refusing a haircut to assault, and the underlying records are confidential, so it is difficult to tell the reasons for the ten solitaries. But this is the same Bernardino Sierra who killed an inmate a few hours after his arrest, and who committed other violent acts while awaiting his trial.

And there is another way in which Sierra differs from Griffin. His offense of conviction is labeled "murder" instead of capital murder. The difference may turn out to be significant. Parole restrictions on convicted capital murderers do not directly apply to Sierra, because of the plea bargain that Stuart Kinard engineered.

Sierra's next parole date is July 1, 2000. That is more than twenty-five years after the murder of Ashok Patel.

And for that matter, it is many years after the death of Kenneth Brock.

* * *

Brock died at the Walls Unit of the Texas Department of Criminal Justice.

The order for his execution required it to be carried out at any time "before the hour of sunrise" on June 19, 1986.

The execution protocol has changed since then. Today, executions are scheduled for six p.m. In Brock's day, the prison kept exact-to-the-minute records of the time, each day, when the sun rose, because if a stay or other delay prevented the execution from being completed before this instant, the order no longer authorized it.

And so, the prison practice was to perform the task in the wee hours of the morning. The warden came for Kenneth Brock just a few minutes after midnight. The execution watch reports that Brock was "dozing." The warden's exact words are lost to history, but usually, he says something simple, like, "It's time. Please come with me."

A sergeant unlocked Brock's cell. Unshackled, wearing jeans, a blue work shirt and prison flip-flops, he walked twenty-five feet on the concrete floor to the death chamber. He complied with instructions to boost himself onto the gurney and lie on his back.

The death chamber is faced with brick, neatly painted in a quiet sky-blue color. The gurney is white, sitting on a massive steel pedestal. Except for the yellow leather straps that crisscross it, the gurney looks innocuous, even with its two arm extensions. Some people have remarked that, disconcertingly, the execution bed looks like a cross.

A tie-down team of five officers immediately fastened the straps on Kenneth Brock. His head rested on the west end of the gurney, beneath a directional microphone. His feet fit into a circular hole at the other end. It is important for the tie-down team to complete this unpleasant, invasive task as quickly as possible, and the tie-down officers actually practice their assignments beforehand, to develop speed and coordination.

Next, from behind the north wall, where there is a one-way mirror, a member of the execution team steps through the door. He inserts a needle, connected to an intravenous tube, into each of the inmate's arms, just below the elbow. A neutral saline solution begins to flow into the man's veins.

The chaplain stands at the east side, usually placing his hand on the inmate's right leg. The warden stands near the prisoner's head. Once the IV is established, the warden turns toward the south wall. There, behind heavy beige curtains, are two soundproof glass-fronted booths. One is for the witnesses designated by the inmate, as many as five, and the other is for victim survivors and public witnesses.

The warden signals that all is ready.

*   *   *

By now, the victim's survivors already have entered the main prison unit through the front doors. At the warden's signal, they walk through a long glass-bordered corridor, usually used for non-contact visits, and then briefly, they traverse a concrete walk bordered by joyous pansies and zinnias. They enter the chamber through a different door than the one used by the condemned man.

Next, a few minutes later, corrections officers escort the inmate's witnesses to the other glass booth along the same pathway. Usually, the two groups, the inmate's witnesses and the victim survivors, never even see each other.

Inmates sometimes make personal requests, occasionally strange ones, about this last confrontation. Characteristically, one of the most exacting came from Ronald Clark O'Bryan. The Candy Man's execution watch contains a lined page with his careful handwriting:

Request, 3/30/84, Shortly Before Midnight

Dear Warden Pursby:

Please during the execution (if it is carried out) have Miss Kim Manganaro, Rev. Jimmy Jones & Chaplin Perry Barnes stand up front, as close as possible, so that we might maintain constant eye contact during the procedure.

Thank you, Ronald Clark O'Bryan

Kenneth Brock's execution watch contain no such unusual requests. The only witnesses he selected were a sister and her husband.

When all the witnesses are in place, the warden turns to address the prisoner. "Do you have any last statement that you wish to make?"

* * *

Last words are as unique as the human beings that utter them. But most final statements fall into a few categories.

First, there are the stoic, macho kind. For example, G. W. Green said, "Lock and load. Let's do it, man," just before he died on November 12, 1991.

Warren Bridge, on November 22, 1994, was briefer: "See ya." And Carl Kelly, August 20, 1993, said, "I'm an African warrior, born to breathe and born to die."

Sometimes the bravado also includes belligerence. Edward Ellis, March 3, 1992: "I just want everyone to know I think the prosecutor and Bill Scott are some sorry sons of bitches." And Johnny Frank Garrett, February 11, 1992: "I'd like to thank my family for loving me... The rest of the world can kiss my ass."

Then, there are those who protest the injustice of their executions. Robert Drew, August 2, 1994: "Remember, the death penalty is murder." Johnny Anderson, May 17, 1990: "I still proclaim I am innocent and that's all I have to say."

Leonel Herrera, on May 12, 1993, was more definite about it. "I am innocent. I am innocent, I am innocent. And make no mistake about this: I owe society nothing."

A more unusual kind of last statement is the attempted filibuster. Back when executions were set for a time "before sunrise," Larry Fitzgerald recalls one inmate, Raymond Kinnamon, on December 11, 1994, who attempted to stretch his final words beyond the instant when the daylight broke. But this ingenious prisoner made the mistake of including in his statement the admission that he was acting on advice of counsel. "He almost made it," Fitzgerald adds.

Actually, the prison attempts to limit final statements that exceed a few minutes. The policy is so well known that Kinnamon tried to change his explanation for his lengthy last words. "I'm not trying to delay this. I've just got so many people to thank."

Finally, there are statements of peace, reconciliation or acceptance of responsibility. "Don't feel bad, Mama," said Charles Bass, March 12, 1986. "I deserve this."

Markham Duff-Smith, June 29, 1993: "I am the lowest of sinners."
Harold Barnard, February 2, 1994: "God, please forgive me of my sins."
Richard Wilkerson, August 31, 1993: "I'd just like to say I don't hate
nobody. What I did was wrong. I just hope everybody is satisfied with
what's about to happen."

Jeffrey Barney, April 16, 1986: "I'm sorry for what I did. I deserve it. I
hope Jesus forgives me. I'm a-tingling all over."

And Harold Joe Lane, on October 4, 1995, said, "I have everlasting
peace now and I'm ready."

* * *

If Kenneth Brock had any last words, they are lost to history.

At the end of the inmate's statement, the warden gives another signal.
He may say something like, "We are ready." Or, today, he might remove
his glasses. The officers know what it means.

Behind the one-way glass, a member of the execution team uses a syringe
to insert a massive dose of sodium thiopental into a "Y" that is just below
the saline bag attached to the IV tube. This chemical is a sedative, relax-
ing the inmate, although the dose would be large enough to kill him if the
next two compounds didn't kill him first.

Many states, from North Dakota to Louisiana, use an automated deliv-
ery system. The executioner's only function is to press a button that starts
the machine, which doses the three chemicals in sequence. Texas has opted
for a simpler technology, believing that it lessens the odds of malfunction
and that the role of the executioner remains the same.

Unconsciousness takes only a few seconds. The process resembles general anesthesia, in which a medical patient may be asked to count down from
100 and rarely will make it to 90. Larry Fitzgerald recalls the execution
of an inmate he befriended, a sincere Christian convert named Jonathan
Nobles. The condemned man had arranged a signal with the warden: When
he finished reciting a chapter from I Corinthians, he would start singing.
The song that Nobles chose was Silent Night. "He got as far as 'mother and
child,'" Fitzgerald says, adding that it was one of the more disconcerting
of the nearly 100 executions he has witnessed.

The second chemical is pancuronium bromide. This powerful muscle
relaxant collapses the diaphragm and lungs. It produces an odd sound, a
quick snort or moan, with the outrush of the prisoner's breath.

Then, the third chemical, potassium chloride, stops the heart.

The process takes about seven minutes. The cost per execution for drugs
used is $86.08.

During all of this, the prison physician has remained outside the death
chamber. The Hippocratic oath prevents the physician from participating. His only function is to pronounce the inmate dead.

In Brock's case, that happened at about twenty minutes after midnight.

* * *

This description of an execution watch is typical of the way it happens nationwide.

The details and methods differ, of course. California, for example, allows the inmate to choose between lethal injection and the gas chamber. So do several other states, including Arizona, where one inmate recently opted for the gas chamber as a matter of strategy, with the express hope that the courts would declare it cruel and unusual. Cyanide poisoning is said to be longer and more visibly painful than other methods, but this Arizona inmate lost his gamble when the courts refused to declare it unconstitutional.

Washington and Montana allow a choice of lethal injection or hanging, Idaho and Utah a choice of lethal injection or firing squad. And several states, from Arkansas to Virginia, use either lethal injection or electrocution (which is described at the beginning of this book). In spite of its spectacle, electrocution is thought to be humane by comparison to, say, the gas chamber.

In all, thirty-eight states, as well as the federal government and the U.S. military, provide for capital punishment. The majority, roughly three fourths, use lethal injection, with the same chemicals and the same basic protocol that is described above in the case of Kenneth Brock, although precise details may vary.

There are 3,517 inmates on death rows nationwide at the time of this writing. California has the most, with almost 500; Texas is second, with over 400; and Florida, Pennsylvania, and Illinois are next. Non-hispanic whites account for 43%, African-Americans 39%, hispanics 17%, and other races 1%.

Texas leads in the number of actual executions. In 1997, there were 74 executions nationwide, and half were in Texas. That year's total, however, reflected court decisions that broke a log jam on death row, and the annual average in Texas is much less: approximately twenty executions per year.

This record can be viewed in different ways. The *New York Times* editorial page, for example, is vitriolic about it. "Ordinarily, the death penalty is no big deal in Texas, where liberals are required to carry visas and compassion is virtually illegal," writer Bob Hebert fulminated in the *Times* on January 4, 1998. "It's a state that has shown itself perfectly willing to execute the retarded and railroad the innocent."

But New Yorkers I've talked to, even those who don't agree with capital punishment, aren't normally as prone to exaggeration as this *New York Times* rhetoric. Some are critical of Texas, but at the same time, they tend to recognize that Texas puts its money where its mouth is. Texas carries out the values shared by people of that state, and indeed of most states, including New York.

Another perspective arises from considering that murders, in Texas, usually number between one and two thousand annually. But only a tiny fraction of those qualify as capital murders, and on average, roughly two percent result in actual death sentences. If one avoids the hyperbole of that *New York Times* editorial, whether one agrees with capital punishment or not, one can see that the capital murder statute does do well at selecting only a small percentage of the very worst cases of murder for the possibility of capital punishment.

At the same time, it's important to realize that this is a system operated by human beings, and vigilance is called for lest its imperfections cause terrible miscarriages instead of justice.

*   *   *

What about the victim survivors?[*]

Their reactions are all over the map. A few oppose execution, although that is uncommon. Some, who don't want to think about it, decline to witness the deaths of the killers of their loved ones.

Jim and Linda Kelley are typical of a third group, who achieved closure from an execution. The Kelleys and their daughter, Robin, were featured in a documentary film called *A Kill for a Kill*, which focused upon their witnessing of the death of Leo Jenkins, who murdered their son, Mark, and daughter, Kara, during a robbery in Houston.

"I don't think [the film crew] realized they were therapy for me," said Linda Kelley. "I loved having noise in my house again. I had not had noise and laughter in my house for so long."

She added, "I want people to know you can survive. At one point, I didn't think I could. The pain was so bad, it just outweighed everything."

The Kelleys listened to Jenkins's final statement. They detected no remorse. After that, the execution "[has] taken the pressure from us," Linda Kelley says. "By watching it, I had no questions I had to ask anyone else. I knew what was important for me."

Sometimes, the rhetoric of other survivors is less polite than the Kelleys'. Consider the execution, in California, of William Bonin, the infamous "Freeway Killer" of Los Angeles. Bonin's ghoulish torture-killings left a string of nude and sometimes mutilated bodies along southern California freeways of young teenage boys who had been raped and slowly mur-

---

[*] We have avoided interviewing the actual survivors in the six cases depicted in this book. The reason is simple: All six cases have reached their end. At some point, survivors are entitled to closure, to be free of questions about the event.

dered. Sandra Miller, whose 15-year-old son was one of Bonin's victims, made no bones about her attitude.

"You taught me a few things," she wrote. "How to hate, that I feel I could kill you, little by little, one piece at a time. You'd best get down on your hands and knees and pray to God for forgiveness. I don't know if even he could forgive you. But I hope the Lord can forgive me for how I feel about you.

"P.S. May you burn in hell."

Another survivor hoped that witnessing Bonin's execution would stop his recurring nightmares. "It will make a big difference. He'll be dead in my eyes, in my mental videotape." And another 15-year-old victim's sister recounted her mother's death. "She said on her deathbed her only regret was not witnessing Bonin's death. This is final justice."

These victim statements contrast sharply with the attitudes of people like Brother Bryan McNeill, who called capital punishment "a placebo" when Ronald Clark O'Bryan was executed. NcNeill pontificated, "The death penalty doesn't do anything to help the victims." No matter how you feel about capital punishment, one thing is clear: This kind of remark is arrogant and irresponsible. On the one hand, capital punishment advocates would be wrong to deny the possibility of execution of an innocent. But by the same token, capital punishment opponents act presumptuously when they try to tell victim survivors what will "help" them.

Why do some survivors benefit from the fact of execution? No one can know for sure. But perhaps the reason is simple: Victims and survivors trust in criminal justice. If a horrifying crime remains unredressed, they feel betrayed. The rules turn out not to be what they were taught; mankind and the violence-monopolizing state have ostracized them. This feeling operates at a visceral, almost instinctual level, nurtured in children during toddler years by fairy tales or simple stories in which good vanquishes evil.

On March 22, 1995, a New York judge sentenced Colin Ferguson to life in prison for the murders of six people on the Long Island railroad and the attempted murders of 19 others. "What could be more cowardly," the judge asked, "than entering a train filled with unsuspecting, home-bound commuters and systematically shooting them at point-blank range?" Survivors' frustration at the outcome was obvious, despite the fact that the life sentence was the maximum that New York law allowed. One broke down in tears as she addressed Ferguson in court: "You almost killed me. You continue to cause me pain." Governor Mario Cuomo, who had promised to veto any death penalty bill, had recently lost his last election to Governor George Pataki, who kept his promise to obtain the enactment of one. "Unfortunately," said the judge who sentenced Colin Ferguson, "this new [death penalty] law cannot be applied to you."

And so, one of the arguments supporting capital punishment, perhaps one of the most important, is the solace it brings to some, if not all, victim survivors. It brings back their faith, their hope, their trust. Robin Kelley saw a new vitality in her father after the execution of Leo Jenkins, and she believed her mother could now start the process of healing.

"There's a certain triumph that you feel because the system worked," she says. "Now we can go on with our lives."

And she added, "I'm so excited—I get to be a normal person now."

* * *

And so, what happened to the defendants in this book?

Two of them were executed: Brock and O'Bryan. Two others, Griffin and Sierra, were sentenced to life in prison, and twenty-five years later, both are still in prison, with minimum-inside security levels and parole dates every three years.

The final two, Bodde and Vargas, died on death row of natural causes, while waiting for their petitions, stays and appeals to end.

The cases of Brock and O'Bryan, who were executed after each waited more than a decade, tell us that we have an effective death penalty. But the cases of Bodde and Vargas tell us that because of the built-in delays, we actually may not.

O'Bryan's case reminds us of the important function that capital punishment fulfills in doing justice in our most serious criminal cases. But the other cases show that our system, because of its deliberate bias toward preventing overpunishment, sometimes sentences deserving but less blameworthy defendants more harshly than others whose crimes are worse. And several cases, including Brock's, raise the spectre of the execution of an innocent person, even though all six of these cases were tried with careful procedures, by competent counsel.

Can the death penalty be justified? It all depends upon how you interpret the facts.

Because the problem of capital punishment, no matter how you look at it, will always be filled with paradox.